JAGUAR

HAYNES CLASSIC MAKES SERIES

JAGUAR

SPEED AND STYLE

THIRD EDITION

MARTIN BUCKLEY

First published in November 1998
Second edition published in July 2002
Reprinted February 2003
Third edition published in April 2009

A catalogue record for this book is available from the British Library

ISBN 978 1 84425 587 0

Library of Congress catalog card no 2008943626

Published by Haynes Publishing, Sparkford, Yeovil, Somerset BA22 7JJ, UK
Tel: 01963 442030 Fax: 01963 440001
Int. tel: +44 1963 442030 fax: +44 1963 440001
E-mail: sales@haynes-manuals.co.uk
Website: www.haynes.co.uk

Haynes North America, Inc.
861 Lawrence Drive, Newbury Park,
California 91320, USA

First edition designed and typeset by Drum Enterprises Limited, Ringwood, Hampshire BH24 4DL
Printed and bound in Great Britain

Note on imperial/metric conversions

Unless usually referred to only in metric units (eg engine capacity in cubic centimetres [cc] or litres [l]) or imperial units (eg carburettors in inches [in]), common measurements of length, area, volume, weight and speed in the text and specifications are given in imperial units with metric equivalents in parentheses, except in the following less common instances:

$282 \div$ miles per gallon (mpg) = litres per 100 kilometres (l/100km)
Torque: pounds-force feet (lb ft) x 0.113 = Newton metres (Nm)
Pressure: pounds-force per square inch (psi) x 6.895 = Kilopascals (kPa)

contents

Introduction   6

Part 1 The Saloon Cars

1   The MkV   10

2   The MkVII, MkVIII and MkIX   16

3   The MkX and 420G   24

4   The MkI   36

5   The MkII and 240/340   48

6   The S-Type and 420   62

7   The XJ6 Series I and II   72

8   The XJ6 Series III   84

9   The XJ40   92

10 The X-300 and XJ8   100

11 The X-350   104

12 The S-Type and X-Type   110

13 The XF   124

Part 2 The Sports Cars

14 The XK120   132

15 The XK140   142

16 The XK150   150

17 The E-Type Series I and II   156

18 The E-Type Series III V12   166

19 The XJ-S   172

20 The XK8   184

21 The XK   190

Acknowledgements and Bibliography   198

Index   199

Jaguar *introduction*

The founder of Jaguar, Sir William Lyons, in the mid-1960s with a line-up of MkXs awaiting export. An enigmatic figure, Lyons ruled Browns Lane as a virtual autocracy and kept a tight grip on the purse strings.

To talk about Jaguar before the watershed year of 1948 – the debut of the XK engine – and to put its achievements into context, you have to talk first about William Lyons, although insights into his character are few.

One of the most astute motor industry businessmen of his generation, William Lyons, founder of Jaguar, was an extraordinary figure. For almost 50 years he ran the company as an autocracy, making all the major decisions, and many of the minor ones, on a day-to-day basis. Jaguar Cars had a board of directors but on the rare occasions they met, Lyons, in the 1960s the highest paid executive in the industry, simply told them what was going to happen. As he was the major shareholder there were rarely any voices of dissent.

In contrast to flamboyant leaders like Enzo Ferrari, Lyons was a single-minded man whose discreet clothes and quiet manners hid a steely character and a shrewd business sense. By costing his products carefully, streamlining their production and keeping them current for a long period, he could sell his cars more cheaply than any equivalent on the market – and still make a profit.

In fact, his grip on the purse strings at Jaguar was legendary, and he bought parts for his cars at the lowest prices in the industry. Knighted in 1956 in recognition of his export successes, Lyons combined dynamism and energy with stiff and formal manners that bordered on the Victorian. He

was famous for calling everybody, even close confidants such as his chief engineer (and later Vice Chairman) William Heynes, by their surnames.

It was as a stylist, however, that William Lyons was perhaps at his most brilliant. Although not a stylist in the traditional sense – he rarely put pen to paper – it was his eye for style and line that set him apart from his contemporaries. His flair for what looked right made his SS – and later Jaguar – cars easily among the best-looking on the road, regardless of price. In any roll-call of all-time automotive beauty his SS100 and XK sports cars, not to mention the svelte MkII and XJ6, will go down among the greats.

Lyons made no claims to being an engineer, but once he had assembled the right team around him – led by the brilliant William Heynes – he began to build cars that went as well as they looked. That process began with the SS Jaguars in 1935, and in the post-war years his XK twin-cam engine, inspired by classic pre-war sports car design, would bring exotic high-technology engineering into the realms of the affordable.

But we are jumping ahead of ourselves. The Jaguar story really begins in Blackpool, Lancashire, in 1921 when Lyons met an emigrant from Stockport, Cheshire, called William Walmsley, then quietly earning a modest living building sidecars in his parents' garage. Lyons, just 20 years of age, liked these stylish torpedo-nosed creations built by his new, older neighbour and talked Walmsley into setting up in business with him.

In 1922, bankrolled by both sets of parents, Lyons and Walmsley began working out of premises in Bloomfield Road, Blackpool, under the name The Swallow Sidecar Company. Sales were brisk and soon Swallow had expanded into new premises in Cocker Street; it was here that they built their first Swallow-bodied car, based on an Austin Seven chassis.

Lyons had identified the need for a more fashionable and luxurious version of the little Austin, first as an open tourer and later as a saloon. He was proved right: sales quickly took off, and when Henlys put in a formal weekly order, Lyons and Walmsley decided that they would have to expand yet again, this time by moving to the heart of British motor manufacture, the Midlands.

At Swallow's 40,000sq ft (3,716sq m) factory in Foleshill, Coventry, production leapt from 12 to 50 cars a week, with chassis from Morris, Swift and Standard supplementing the Seven. However, Lyons was not content with his role as a mere coachbuilder, and his association with Standard led to the announcement at the Motor Show in 1931 of Swallow's first 'complete' cars, the SSI and SSII,

using an underslung chassis exclusively designed for them.

SS stood for Swallow Sports (or Standard Swallow according to Standard) and these low-slung and well-equipped machines found immediate favour with buyers who wanted a car that looked expensive but who could not afford the price of a contemporary Alvis or Lea Francis: champagne motoring for the beer-barrel pocket. Some of the bodywork was undeniably pretty – particularly the wonderfully Art Deco Airline saloon, although Lyons did not like it much himself – and if the asthmatic Standard side-valve engines meant that the cars did not go as well as they looked, the buyers did not seem to care.

Lyons bought out the increasingly disenchanted Walmsley in 1934 – the latter's horizons had always been

rather limited compared with the go-getting younger man – and in the same year, with profits and sales rising, the company went public. From this point until his departure in 1972 at the age of 70, Lyons controlled the destiny of Jaguar as the major shareholder.

The first Jaguars did not actually appear until a year later when, at their introduction at the Mayfair Hotel in London, Lyons stunned the industry with his new 2½ litre SS Jaguar saloon. This new car was not just beautifully styled and very fast for its day, being capable of nearly 90mph (145kph), but somehow Lyons had managed to produce it for an amazingly low £385, alongside a side-valve 1½ litre four-cylinder for £90 less.

1929 Austin 7hp Swallow saloon (Neill Bruce).

Here was a car, with its beautiful Lucas P100 headlamps, swooping wing-line and high-class interior, that was fit to be compared with the likes of Alvis and even Bentley, whose own 3½ litre models were certainly no more lively yet cost twice or three times as much. From a company that had only been making complete cars for four years, it was an amazing achievement.

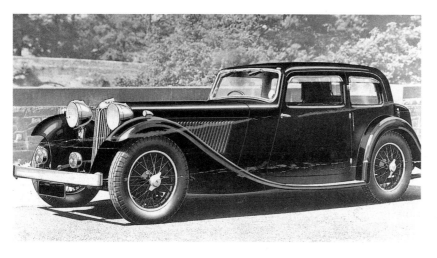

If the Swallows were really just rebodying exercises, the SSI was Lyons's first 'real' car, although it still used mostly bought-in components. This is the re-styled 1934 model.

All SS lacked was the prestige of a proper thoroughbred engine, even if there was nothing essentially wrong with the strong seven-bearing unit used in the 2½ litre. It was smooth, very flexible and, thanks to the attentions of gas-flow expert Harry Weslake, now breathed properly through overhead valves and a pair of SU carbs. Even better, Lyons could buy these engines cheaply from Standard without having to invest in expensive tooling, an arrangement that suited him very well at the time.

With order books bulging, SS could not make enough cars and it was only when the company abandoned time-consuming ash-framing (with steel panelling) in favour of an all-steel shell for 1938 that production rose – after some hair-raising teething troubles – to levels that could begin to satisfy orders and drive down unit costs. A new chassis was laid down for this revised body and at the same time came drophead coupé versions, overhead

valves for the baby 1½ litre and – best of all – a bigger 3½ litre engine to supplement the 2½ litre. Giving 125bhp, 90mph (145kph) and 0–50mph (80kph) in 9 seconds, it made the SS Jaguar exceedingly rapid by the standards of 60 years ago.

There were sports cars too, most famously the glamorous SS100, which was one of the fastest road cars you could buy in the 1930s, although it only sold in small numbers as a glamorous image-builder. The shape was developed from the less well-known SS90, and the 100 could be had with either a 2½ or 3½ litre engine. With the latter unit the beautiful SS100 really would achieve the magic 'ton' and, at £445, it was the performance-per-pound bargain of the decade.

By the beginning of the war SS had built 20,000 cars in eight years and had enough in the bank to emerge from the hostilities in a strong position, having built parts for Stirlings, Mosquitos, Spitfires and Lancasters during the war years. Behind the scenes, Lyons had also developed a twin-cam engine, the XK, that was to be the cornerstone of the company's products for 40 years.

Because of the unsavoury connotations of the original initials, in February 1945 SS became Jaguar Cars and in September of that year went back into production with its pre-war saloon car range. Some 12,000 of these cars were built up to 1948, which is where the post-war history of Jaguar really begins.

Over the decade to come Jaguar would build the world's most desired sports cars, their cars would win at Le Mans five times, and they would fulfil William Lyons's post-war dream of a 100mph (161kph) luxury saloon priced under £1,000. From now on Jaguar would set the standards for the industry, not simply follow them.

The 1935 SS Jaguar was William Lyons's breakthrough car, combining the up-market style for which his earlier machines had been famous with proper up-market performance: the 3½ litre versions could top 90mph (145kph) thanks to a new overhead-valve Standard-based six-cylinder engine. Production continued – as simply Jaguar rather than SS Jaguar – after the Second World War until 1948. This is a 1937 2½ litre model.

The MkV *saloon*

The 1948 MkV was an interesting stop-gap model blending the old-style push rod engine with the new chassis. Independent front suspension brought a new sophistication to the Jaguar saloon, which as a MkV came with a 2½ or 3½ litre engine, while the body had a pre-war flavour but was actually all new.

At Earls Court in 1948, in the shadow of the show-stopping XK120 roadster, was a new Jaguar saloon. In appearance it was conservative, perhaps a little 'safe', yet this car was to be far more crucial to the immediate future of Jaguar than the glamorous XK, which at that point was not viewed as anything other than a publicity-generating low-volume special. The new saloon car – called simply MkV – was to be the mainstay of production at the Foleshill factory while the new twin-cam saloon – the MkVII – was still in preparation.

In many respects the MkV is a forgotten Jaguar, produced for just three years and never regarded as exciting compared with its 100mph successor. Yet it was a good car in its own right, a vast leap forward from the old 'SS' models that had been briefly reinstated after the war, and a car with a subtle charm all of its own.

The MkV was really an old-fashioned British compromise. Jaguar needed breathing space not just to develop the XK engine (in the low-volume XK sports car) but also to get the new MkVII bodyshell into production,

TRE 379

which for the first time would be built outside Jaguar by Pressed Steel. However, it looked as though this was not going to happen for another two years at least, and the current saloons desperately needed to be replaced.

Lyons's answer was to design a car with a traditional body that could be built up piecemeal from small individual parts at the Jaguar works using traditional methods and without heavy tooling costs; power would be provided by the old pushrod six-cylinder engine but in a new chassis with up-to-date independent front suspension designed by William Heynes.

Those few XK engines that were being produced were all being used in the XK120 sports car (which had essentially the same chassis in shortened form) and Jaguar decided that to fit this advanced engine in such an old-fashioned-looking shell would steal thunder from the yet-to-be announced MkVII. (In fact, a few prototype MkVs were fitted with the XK engine by the factory, and some owners fitted them subsequently).

The MkV was the last Jaguar to feature the magnificent bootlid-mounted toolkit. The spare wheel lives behind the numberplate panel, which hinges down.

MkV Saloon & dhc
1948-51

ENGINE:
In-line six-cylinder, cast iron block and head

Bore x stroke	82 x 110mm
Capacity	3,485cc
Valves	Overhead, pushrod
Compression ratio	6.75:1
Carburettors	Two 1.5in SUs
Power	125bhp at 4,250rpm (gross)
Torque	180lb ft at 2,300rpm

TRANSMISSION:
Four-speed manual with synchromesh on second, third and top

Final drive	4.30 or 4.27:1

SUSPENSION:
Wishbones, torsion bars, anti-roll bar
Live rear axle with semi-elliptic springs

Steering	recirculating ball

BRAKES:
12-inch (305mm) drums

WHEELS:
Pressed steel bolt-on 16-inch (406mm) with 5K rim

BODYWORK:
Separate steel body and chassis

LENGTH:	15ft 7in (4.75m)
WIDTH:	5ft 9in (1.75m)
HEIGHT:	5ft 2½in (1.6m)
WEIGHT:	33cwt (1,678kg)
MAX SPEED:	97mph (156kph)
0–50mph (80kph)	10 seconds

PRICE NEW (1949): £1,263 inc PT

2½ litre MkV Saloon & dhc

As 3½ litre except:

Capacity	2,663cc
Bore x stroke	73 x 106mm
Compression ratio	7.3:1
Carburettors	Two 1.375in SUs
Power	102bhp at 4,600rpm

MAX SPEED:	87mph (140kph)
0–50mph (80kph)	11 seconds

PRICE NEW: £1,247 inc PT

PRODUCTION FIGURES:

2½ litre saloon	1,661
2½ litre dhc	29
3½ litre saloon	7,831
3½ litre dhc	972

The interior detailing of the MkV evoked the pre-war cars, but also hinted at the yet-to-be-seen MkVII of 1950. Note the stylised instrument lettering. The position of the ashtray in the bottom of the dash panel means that this is a fairly early car.

To dismiss the MkV as an old-fashioned-looking car is slightly unfair. Lyons supervised the styling of a bodyshell that was an elegant blend of contemporary and traditional – a flowing, dignified saloon that, at a quick glance, could almost have been taken for one of its predecessors. However, they shared not one panel and the MkV had headlamps faired into the wings, modern push-button door handles and half-frame doors that together gave it a contemporary flavour and separated it decisively from its predecessor. The substantial double-decker bumpers hinted at Jaguar's ambitions for the all-important American market, but the car had a flowing elegance that was thoroughly British. Incidentally, the MkV was the last Jaguar to have a hinge-down bootlid (with fitted tools) and a side-opening bonnet.

Under the skin the new chassis was specially designed to accommodate independent front suspension, a first on a Jaguar and in development since before the war. Inspired by the Citroën Light 15, it comprised top and bottom wishbones with ball-jointed stub axles; springing was by elegantly slim longitudinal torsion bars, damping by telescopic shock absorbers. With its box-section side-members and channel-section X-bracing this rigid yet not too heavy chassis was to serve as the basis for Jaguar's big saloons until the beginning of the 1960s.

The live rear axle with its leaf springs and lever-arm dampers looked much as before, but the springs were much softer now, the upswept (rather than underslung) chassis allowing for this. Hydraulic operation for the 12-inch (305mm) drum brakes was a novelty on a Jaguar, and the MkV had smaller wheels and wider rims than its predecessor, wearing the latest Dunlop Super-Comfort tyres.

Both 2½ (102bhp) and 3½ litre (125bhp) versions of the proven Standard-based pushrod six-cylinder engine were available, both with the same Moss gearbox, but there were to be no entry-level 1½ litre four-cylinder versions; weight was up compared with the outgoing model, and the performance of a 1.5 litre MkV would not have been acceptable even by the standards of the late 1940s.

Inside, the MkV used traditional materials and traditional styling, with walnut on the dashboard and door cappings, and stylish instruments – grouped in the centre of the dash – lit beautifully in a violet glow at night. The headlining was mohair, as were the insides of the neat zipped door pockets. Passengers sat on unpleated, piped leather, the front bucket seats being adjustable for height. A heater and demister came as standard, and a little more ventilation could be obtained by sliding back the big steel sunshine roof, another standard fitment.

That the car's handling was sound was proved by its impressive rallying results

For the ultimate in ventilation there was always the MkV drophead coupé, announced at the same time although deliveries did not begin until some time later. Cast in the mould of the old 3½ litre drophead, it utilised much more hand-finishing and timber in its construction. The doors were ash-framed and it continued with the old-style carriage-lock door handles. This was a superbly elegant car with its big chrome pram irons on the hood, and despite the extra work involved in producing it, Jaguar sold the dhc MkV for the same price as the saloon, £1,247 for the 2½ litre and £1,263 for the 3½ litre, both prices inclusive of Purchase Tax.

Compared with the beam-axled cars, the MkV had entered another world of comfort and poise. Bumps or load did not affect its cornering power as had been the case with the old 3½ litre, and William Heynes's independent front suspension damped out road shocks to the occupants perhaps as well as any car

Standard-derived Engines

The MkV was the last Jaguar to use an engine based on a Standard design, and with it ended an association with that company that dated back to the late 1920s and the Swallow-bodied Standards.

The first Lyons-designed car to use a frame specially created for it was the SSI of 1931, and it too used Standard engines. Initially these were six-cylinder side-valve engines of 2 and 2½ litres, used in totally unmodified form in 16 and 20hp guise, their actual non-RAC ratings being 48 and 62bhp. There was a baby four-cylinder version called the SSII, which was also Standard-powered, using at first the 1,006cc Little Nine engine and latterly bigger side-valve units of 1,343 and 1,608cc.

Lyons established a good relationship with Standard's Chairman, R. W. Maudslay, and General Manager John Black. Using this influence, it was arranged that the chassis would be delivered to Standard from Rubery Owen where the engines, transmission and axles would be fitted. They would then be delivered to the Swallow factory at Holbrook Lane, Coventry, where the bodyshells would be fitted. It was a good arrangement for Lyons as it meant that he did not have to invest in any expensive new tooling or factory space.

Later SSI cars had a higher-compression aluminium head and twin carbs, boosting the output to a more exciting 72bhp on the bigger-engined version.

But this was not enough for Lyons, and once his new SS Jaguars were on the stocks he knew that he had to find a way of getting more power. A totally new engine was not an option – SS could not afford it and the deal with Standard was too good to throw away.

What Lyons had to do to fulfil his dream of a new 90mph (145kph) saloon was to find a way of making the existing engine breathe better. He found salvation in a West Country engineer called Harry Weslake. By converting the cylinder head to overhead valves and by the use of clever gas-flowing, Weslake boosted the output to 103bhp. Even better, Lyons then persuaded John Black of Standard to buy the necessary machinery to build the new head and supply complete engines to SS for its new Jaguar saloon, launched in 1935. Later, for 1938, came a 1½ litre four-cylinder ohv engine – effectively two-thirds of a 2½ litre – for the SS Jaguar 1½ litre saloons that had originally retained the old side-valve four-cylinder engine. More exciting was a new longer-stroke 3½ litre unit giving 125bhp and sold alongside the 2½ litre. These bigger engines were also to be found in the SS100 sports car and lived on until the demise of the MkV in 1951.

After the war Standard sold the engine tooling to Jaguar at a generous price, but once Lyons had collected it, Black changed his mind and asked for it back. He proposed that they go back to the old arrangement, or even form a joint company to produce the engines, but Lyons refused, valuing his new-found independence from the unpredictable Captain Black.

on the road. Moreover, it had an engine – in its larger form at any rate – that could make full use of the abilities of the new chassis. What the old pushrod straight-six lacked in outright power it made up for in smoothness and torque, not to mention stamina. Here was a car that could maintain 80mph (129kph) or more for hours on end and top 90 if needs be, when the average family car would have been lucky to manage 70mph (113kph). As a fast, comfortable, long-distance machine the 3½ litre MkV had few peers. The 2½ felt a little underpowered by comparison, but it was sweet, smooth and capable of returning up to 25mpg.

That the car's handling was sound – perhaps even better than that of the car that replaced it – was proved by its impressive rallying results. MkVs came third and ninth in the 1951 Monte Carlo Rally, and third in class in the 1952 RAC Rally.

The MkV is one of those cars that drives newer than it looks (with most 'classics' the reverse is usually the case) – it is a car of basically pre-war appearance with 1950s dynamics. Through corners, its more compact dimensions make it seem more manageable than the big MkVII, yet inside it appears to have much of the space of the later car, particularly in the rear. In fact, the interior is a delight, with a feeling of old-world detail quality not always evident on later saloon Jaguars.

The big 18-inch (457mm) steering wheel (familiar from the later cars) gives relatively accurate control, although its Burman box is lower-geared than that of its predecessor, a concession to the American market.

Silent at tick-over, the long-stroke 'six' has a strong, even pull from as little as 10mph (16kph) in top gear, and has the effortless air of an engine making light of its work. The sporty-looking short floor-mounted lever slices through cleanly if you time your changes properly, and in any case the vintage nature of the Moss 'box does

Buying Hints

1. The MkV bodyshell does not hide rust well, so it should be easy to spot. Check the door bottoms, around the wheel arches and the body rockers, or sills. Feel underneath the running board for evidence of bodging of the important inner sills. The chassis is massively strong, so serious corrosion is rare.

2. On the drophead coupé look for any drop in the heavy ash-framed doors, and make sure that the car is not a left-hand-drive conversion (or even a conversion from a saloon – some were done in the late 1980s when values were very high).

3. The engines are strong, but the 3½ litre, with less coolant capacity and fewer head bolts, can suffer from overheating and subsequent hairline cracks in the block, although the head itself is not prone to cracking. Clogged-up waterways can also cause overheating. Pistons were difficult to find at one stage, but can now be sourced in Australia.

4. The spares situation is not as bad as might be thought since the MkV shares many components with the XK120 and MkVII. Body panels can be difficult, although specialists produce a few repair sections.

5. Look for worn ball joints on the

suspension – greasing points tend to be forgotten. The brakes were never the strong point of the heavy MkV, but should work well enough if everything is in good order.

6. The Moss gearbox has a slow change and parts are becoming difficult to find. Beware of a slipping clutch.

7. Inside, the expensive problems with leather, veneer, carpets and headlining will be obvious, but check that the wonderful bootlid-mounted toolkit is complete – replacement items are very difficult to find.

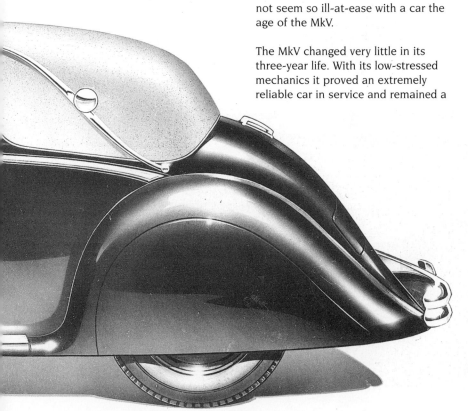

not seem so ill-at-ease with a car the age of the MkV.

The MkV changed very little in its three-year life. With its low-stressed mechanics it proved an extremely reliable car in service and remained a

reasonably common sight until the beginning of the 1970s. Although the new MoT test of the early 1960s killed off many MkVs, it was never such a 'rot-box' as the later cars with their mass-produced Pressed Steel bodywork.

In all 10,493 were built, a respectable figure for a stop-gap model only built for a short period.

The drophead MkV adopted many of the styling touches found on the previous model. The chunky double bumpers gave protection in the American export market to which Jaguar hoped to sell the MkV, paving the way for the success of the MkVII.

The MkVII
MkVIII & MkIX

The MkVII was the realisation of William Lyons's dream of a true 100mph luxury saloon for under £1,000. Jaguar were now able to produce the bodywork in volume thanks to a contract with Pressed Steel, and the car's bulky yet elegant proportions would remain popular for the next 11 years.

Twin-cam, 100mph luxury saloons were pretty thin on the ground in 1950, and still fewer were pitched under the £1,000 barrier (excluding Purchase Tax). No surprise then that Jaguar's new Coventry factory at Browns Lane could hardly keep up with the orders when they announced the flagship MkVII at Earls Court that year. Although the identically engined XK120 sports car tended to grab the limelight, it was the MkVII and its siblings that would fill Jaguar's coffers and position the company for a virtual take-over of the British luxury car market in the decade to come. The ultimate demise of Armstrong-Siddeley, Daimler and Alvis can all be linked to a greater or lesser degree to the stunning sales success of the bargain-priced MkVII, of which 20,000 examples were built up to 1954. Total production of the MkVII and its later derivatives was over 46,000, a figure not matched by the range's successor the MkX/420G.

The MkVII, MkVIII and MkIX differed from later Jaguar saloons in their use of a separate chassis – derived from that of the MkV – with a servo for the big drum brakes and torsion bar front suspension, the live rear end being handled by semi-elliptics. Styling, too, was descended from the pre-war and immediately post-war saloons, but

was more voluminous and well-fed. Classic Lyons, this – a long, bulbous sweeping front wing-line, a smooth taut roof and a harmoniously rounded tail that hid a commodious boot.

British in taste and proportions, American in bulk, was the theme, and if it looked good on the outside, the cabin was even better, with more room than in its predecessors, wide armchair seats and polished walnut veneer on the dash, cantrails and door cappings. There were also nice detail touches such as the toolbox compartments in the doors.

Sheer bulk meant that the MkVII was no sports car but it was more nimble than it looked

In this gentleman's club ambience, the MkVII driver could dominate the road as few others. Third gear alone was enough to dispose of most sports car pretenders, while top could ease the MkVII, no lightweight at 34.5cwt (1,754kg), to 101mph (163kph). More telling was the 3.4 litre XK engine's ability to cruise the MkVII in the 90s in quiet comfort and still return up to 24mpg if good use was made of the (optional) overdrive. Sheer bulk meant that the MkVII was no sports car, but by big saloon standards it was more nimble than it looked – which its success on the track confirmed.

The 1954 MkVIIM brought detail improvements, giving the car a visual affinity with the new XK140 sports car; it can be spotted most easily by its wing-mounted flashing turn indicators and modified rear lights. Horn grilles replaced the fog lamps and the bumpers had a plainer profile with higher-mounted overriders; they wrapped around a bit more at the back, too. The wheels were given rim

Jaguar MkVII
1950–54

ENGINE:
In-line six-cylinder, cast iron block, alloy head, hemispherical combustion chambers

Bore x stroke	81 x 106mm
Capacity	3,442cc
Valves	Twin ohc, one inlet, one exhaust
Compression ratio	7:1 (8:1 optional)
Carburettors	Two 1.75in SUs
Power	160bhp at 5,200rpm (gross)
Torque	195lb ft at 2,500rpm (gross)

TRANSMISSION:
Four-speed manual (optional overdrive) or three-speed automatic

Final drive	hypoid semi-floating Salisbury 4HA

SUSPENSION:
Wishbones, torsion bars, anti-roll bar
Live rear axle with semi-elliptic springs

Steering	Burman recirculating ball

BRAKES:
Girling 12-inch (305mm) drums with servo

WHEELS:
Pressed steel bolt-on 16-inch (406mm) with 5K rim

BODYWORK:
Separate steel body and chassis

LENGTH:	16ft 4½in (5m)
WIDTH:	6ft 1in (1.85m)
HEIGHT:	5ft 3in (1.6m)
WEIGHT:	34.5cwt (1,754kg) (distributed 53% front, 47% rear)

MAX SPEED:	100mph (161kph)
0–60mph (97kph)	13.6 seconds

PRICE NEW (1950):	£1,276 inc PT (1951: £1,694)

Jaguar MkVIIM
1954–57

As MkVII except:

Bore x stroke	83 x 106mm
Capacity	3,442cc
Carburettors	Two HD6 SUs
Power	190bhp at 5,500rpm (gross)
Torque	203lb ft at 3,000rpm (gross)

WEIGHT:	34.75cwt (1,767kg)

MAX SPEED:	105mph (169kph)
0–60mph (97kph)	14.1 seconds

PRICE NEW (1954): £1,616 inc PT	

Jaguar MkVIII
1956–59

As MkVII except:

Bore x stroke	83 x 106mm
Capacity	3,442cc
Carburettors	Two 1.75 HD6 SUs
Power	210bhp at 5,500rpm
Torque	216lb ft at 3,000rpm

WEIGHT:	36cwt (1,8430kg)

MAX SPEED:	106mph (171kph)
0–60mph (97kph)	11.6 seconds

PRICE NEW (1956): £1,830 inc PT	

Jaguar MkIX
1958–61

As MkVII except:

Capacity	3,781cc
Power	220bhp at 5,500rpm (gross)
Torque	240lb ft at 3,000rpm (gross)
Carburettors	Two 1.75in HD6 SUs
Steering	Burman recirculating ball with power assistance

BRAKES	Dunlop discs front and rear

MAX SPEED:	115mph (185kph)
0–60mph (97kph)	11.3 seconds

PRICE NEW (1958): £1,994 inc PT	

PRODUCTION FIGURES:

MkVII	20,939
MkVIIM	9,261
MkVIII	6,332
MkIX	10,005

There are echoes of the XK120 in the sweeping lines of the MkVII, and under the skin it was largely XK with a longer version of that car's chassis and the same twin-cam straight-six engine.

embellishers, and wing mirrors were standard.

There was more power now – 190bhp – thanks to ⅜in (9.5mm) cams and 8:1 pistons. The gear ratios on manual versions were closed up and thicker torsion bars reduced roll.

On the 1956 MkVIII the emphasis was moved towards tycoon luxury and extra chrome glitz, with bigger bumpers and a wider grille. Thin chrome strips on the car's flanks gave it a flashy presence, especially with two-tone paintwork and whitewall tyres (optional in the UK, standard in North America). A one-piece screen, cutaway spats and dual exhausts were further MkVIII identification points, while the revised interior

featured new seats with foldaway writing tables, together with three cigar lighters and two clocks, and an ashtray in every door. On automatics the front seat was now a bench, while the rear seat was restyled as a two-seater, although it could still accommodate three with the armrest up. The seats, cushioned with Dunlopillo rubber, were thicker now, and front-seat passengers sat higher for a better view over the scuttle.

A B-Type cylinder head, a variant on the optional C-Type head with different valve angles and narrower ports, boosted low-speed torque thanks to better gas flow. There was a new inlet manifold with a separate bolt-on water rail and twin SU HD6 carburettors. In fact, acceleration was

The MkVII, VIII and IX in Competition

The MkVII was a more agile car than it looked and managed to return some impressive results in the early 1950s, in both production saloon racing and rallying. However, once the smaller compact Jaguars began to get into their stride, the MkVII disappeared, not to be seen again until Classic Saloon racing became popular in Britain in the mid-1970s.

As far as actual circuit racing is concerned, Silverstone was the only venue that figured in the car's racing history. It made its debut there in May 1952, a factory-prepared example driven by Stirling Moss in the *Daily Express* Production Saloons meeting. In the face of lighter opposition from a Healey Elliott saloon (which was quicker in practice) Moss won, averaging 75.22mph (121kph) and taking the fastest lap. He repeated the trick the following year in a less competitive field.

Seeing the car's potential, Jaguar prepared 200bhp MkVIIs for both Moss and Tony Rolt, as well as providing assistance to the non-factory MkVII of dealer Ian Appleyard. In a

competitive grid that included Tony Crook in a Lancia Aurelia and some surprisingly quick Daimlers, Jaguar took first, second and third, Appleyard winning from Rolt and Moss. Thus Jaguar also took the team prize.

For 1955 the Silverstone factory MkVII team comprised Mike Hawthorn, Jimmy Stewart and Desmond Titterington. So far ahead of the field were the Jaguars that Titterington's spin did not lose him his position and he managed to come in third behind Stewart and winner Mike Hawthorn.

For 1956 the first factory 2.4s began to appear, and the MkVII looked set to be ousted. In the event, mechanical problems blighted the 2.4s of Hawthorn, Hamilton and Coombs, and Bueb won in a MkVII just ahead of Ken Wharton in a highly modified Austin Westminster.

In rallying, the big MkVII showed surprising early promise. The Monte Carlo Rally showed how consistent the cars could be in the hands of redoubtable drivers such as Ian Appleyard, but outright victory did not

come until 1956. Driven by Irishmen Ronald Adams and Frank Bigger, the MkVII completed a trouble-free run that beat Mercedes into second place. The RAC was not so lucky for the big Jaguar, although it returned some respectable placings, a Class win and a 10th overall for Dennis Scott in 1953 (repeated the following year by one J. Ashworth, although he only came second in class).

The compact cars were destined to do well in the tough Tour de France, but here too the big, burly MkVII could hold its head up – in 1953 Novelli and Guido took a best in class.

No discussion about the competition prowess of the MkVII is complete without mentioning the light-alloy-bodied car of Bob Berry. A Jaguar employee, Berry drove this D-Type-engined car to entertaining effect in the late 1950s and early '60s in club racing and it remains the fastest MkVII around Silverstone at a lap speed of 1min 19sec.

MkVII, 1955 Monte Carlo Rally (Rodolfo Mailander/Ludvigsen Library).

Inside, the MkVII was trimmed in restrained good taste. The dashboard was similar to that of the MkV apart from the rounded top rail, but there was more legroom inside and passengers sat on heavier, plusher seats, naturally trimmed in leather on the wearing surfaces.

better than the MkVIIM all through the range, reaching 60mph (97kph) in just 11.6 seconds and chopping a massive 11.9 seconds off the 0–90mph (145kph) time. What was more, the MkVIII could now do 106mph (171kph) while turning in an overall consumption of 17.9mpg, only slightly down on the older car. Certainly 20mpg was within a more moderate driver's grasp.

A 'speed hold' switch on automatic cars was the other important news. A Jaguar patent, the switch operated a solenoid fitted to the rear oil pump so that intermediate gear could be deployed for hills or corners.

More buyers were opting for automatic transmission now, which was well-suited to the torquey XK engine and had first been seen on the MkVII in 1953, and many owners specified this in preference to the difficult-to-handle Moss 'box. The Borg-Warner DG was an American design built in Letchworth and was

common to many British luxury cars of the 1950s and '60s, such as the Rover 3 litre and Humber Super Snipe – probably because there was no alternative. A three-speeder with full-throttle kickdown, it was controlled by a P-R-N-D-L column shifter. 'D' was engaged for day-to-day motoring, while 'L' was intended for slowing the car when descending hills.

Last, and some think best, of the line was the 1958 MkIX, with a 223bhp 3.8 litre engine, power steering and four-wheel Dunlop discs. The 3.8 engine retained the B-Type cylinder head but had a new block with liners; the original block could not be bored out without the risk of fracturing between the bores. Power was up by 30bhp, and torque by 11.5lb ft to 240lb ft. Even with the auto 'box (which most of them had, as manual transmission was now the option) it was a storming performer, good for 117mph (188kph) with restful ton-up cruising. At a shade under £2,000 including Purchase Tax it was also still

MkVIII and MkIX models had extra brightwork, giving the shape a less tall and slab-sided appearance. These were the last separate-chassis Jaguars.

a bargain, especially when it is considered that the up-market Bentley S1 – in many ways a less able car – was three times the price.

Hard-driven examples of the previous models could test the big drum brakes to the limit, so the new Dunlop discs were welcome. They had the quick-change pads and used big 12⅛-inch (309mm) diameter discs at the front [with 12-inchers (305mm) at the back] assisted by a Lockheed suspended vacuum servo with a reservoir. At last the problem of fade was overcome and there was probably no other big saloon on the road that stopped as well as the MkIX.

Some people were less sure about the Burman power-assisted steering. It was higher-geared than before but lacked sensitivity at higher speeds, although it had much more feel than contemporary American systems. Even so, the handling was still excellent for the car's patrician bulk, with surprisingly little roll and decent grip from the crossply tyres, combined with a civilised ride

required of what, for many owners, was first and foremost a quiet luxury car.

There was no way of telling a MkVIII from a MkIX from the outside except by the tiny badge on the bootlid. Inside, too, it was much as before apart from a more powerful heating and ventilation system and a newspaper rack in the rear that was now collapsible and lockable. For a while after the October 1958 launch of the MkIX, the MkVIII continued in production, the last one being made in December 1959.

The MkIX died in 1961 to make way for the unitary, all-independent MkX, and its fortunes hit a nadir in the 1960s and early '70s when thousands succumbed to rot. In addition, as a classic collectable, size and thirst have always cast a shadow over the popularity of these jumbo Jags. Today, rarity value and sheer grandeur are their prime attributes. Compared to other cars of the 1950s, a good example of any of these cars still

This period artwork gives a fairly faithful rendition of the MkVII's sweeping lines without disguising its considerable bulk.

feels lively, as the XK engine was so much better than almost anything else. You sit low in all models, the leather providing little purchase during brisk cornering. Manual steering on everything pre-MkIX can make the cars feel cumbersome around town as the system is both heavy and low-geared; however, an automatic MkIX is still a commanding and brisk point-and-squirt machine, not to mention a thirsty one if you insist on using the performance. Changes will be heavy-handed under full throttle but still a lot quieter than the Moss 'box, which requires technique to drive without noisy embarrassment. Overdrive is always desirable as the car is still capable of quite high cruising speeds – at which it feels directionally very stable.

Above all the MkVII, VIII and IX have presence and gravitas, with old-world charm to go with this surprising ability. A really good car will command as much as £20,000, but few survive in really fine condition and restoration of a sad one does not make sense.

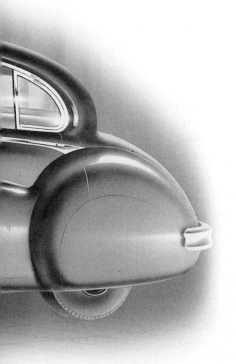

Buying Hints

1. The strong XK engine has a well-known weakness for oil burning (especially in 3.8 litre form) and leaks from the rear main bearing oil seal, the latter requiring engine removal to rectify. An oil pressure of 35–40psi should be maintained at 3,000rpm when hot, 15–20psi at tickover. Low oil pressure can be put down to worn bearings and/or a worn oil pump. More optimistically, it could just be a faulty sender unit or a problem with the oil-pressure relief valve. Timing chain rattle is common; the top chain is adjustable for wear, but the bottom one is again an engine-out job to replace.

2. The Moss gearbox has slow synchromesh and some spares are now difficult to source, but it is mechanically strong. Change quality can vary enormously from car to car. Similarly, spares for the DG automatic gearbox can be difficult, but it is a reliable unit. Regular oil changes and a clean filter are the key to long life. On manuals beware of a slipping clutch, as the engine has to be removed to change it.

3. The torsion bar suspension on these cars has no special problems, but look for the usual worn ball joints – with more than 30 greasing points on the chassis, there is a good chance that some have been forgotten.

4. The steel bodywork, stamped out in quantity by Pressed Steel, is structurally complex and featured only rudimentary rustproofing. The good news is that reproduction repair panels are available. Check the inner and outer sills, especially at the front and the 'D' posts, which you can see by opening the rear doors and removing the rear wheel arch spats. This area is difficult to repair properly.

5. Inner sills should then be inspected carefully. Such is this panel's capacity for rot that even the most immaculate cars tend to have had work done here. Front wings bolt on but are only available second-hand. They rot around the front indicators and it is likely that the sidelight will be beginning to 'lift' underneath the paint. Check the rim of the arch and the front valance between the bumper and the front wings.

6. All four door bottoms are prone to rot due to poor window seals, and the base of the bootlid is also vulnerable. Blocked drain holes also frequently rust the sunroof frames. Inside the boot, check the floor in the corners and where the spare wheel sits, as well as the slam panel where the boot lock is mounted. Petrol tanks rot, so look out for leaks, and check around the filler-cap boxes – one on either side.

7. A sound and presentable interior is absolutely vital to these cars as it provides a large part of their charm. Sections of tatty leather can be replaced, but a full retrim will be mind-blowingly expensive (over five hides were used) and will never look as good as an original with fine patina. Door trims become tatty, but are vinyl-covered so should not be so expensive to deal with. There are over 50 pieces of wood veneer so, again, repolishing will be costly.

The MkX *and* 420G

Packed with the latest high-performance technology borrowed from the show-stopping E-Type sports car, the Jaguar MkX of 1961 was a world-class luxury saloon groomed to compete with the best in the business. Faster and better-handling than the ageing Rolls-Royce Silver Cloud II, more glamorous than the 300SE 'fintail' Mercedes – and vastly cheaper than both – history should view the impressive 120mph (193kph) MkX as the ultimate in 1960s Jaguar saloons and certainly the most sophisticated big car of its day.

Yet buyers never took to this gentle giant of a car in the way that they had to the MkVII, VIII and IX before it; interest had fallen away dramatically even by the time the 4.2 was announced in 1964, and it took a mid-term name change – to 420G – to rejuvenate sales in its twilight run-out years.

Broad in the beam, sumptuously curvaceous, the portly MkX (and its later incarnation the 420G) still holds the title of the widest British production saloon, 6ft 4in (1.93m) across its bulbous hips and 5½ inches (140mm) longer than the big MkIX it replaced. What is more, at a squat 8½ inches (216mm) lower than its predecessor it was also one of the few 1960s cars to live up to the sleek extravagance of its brochure artwork – no need for artistic exaggeration here.

Love it or loathe it, who could deny that the unlucky MkX has a presence and gravitas all of its own and bears the undoubted evidence of Lyons's eye for style? The long elegant sweep of the wing-line carried through from the raked-forward four-light nose to the elongated tail and the hint of MkII in the roof's rounded profile give the car a certain bloated elegance.

Although an impressive car in many ways, the MkX was not the most enthusiastically received of Jaguar's saloon models; many felt that it was too wide and the Americans compared its styling to the 1948 Hudson. Lyons himself was not its greatest fan.

In addition, the sills, which were 7 inches (178mm) deep and 7 inches wide, gave the shell, built by Pressed Steel at Swindon, immense torsional strength, so much so that there had been talk of making the car a pillarless design, as the central pillar contributed very little to the total strength of the monocoque structure. Wind noise sealing is probably the reason why this idea was abandoned, and in the event the MkX featured

The MkX was the ultimate in 1960s Jaguar saloons and the most sophisticated big car of its day

traditional Jaguar plated top door frames. The MkX was the first Jaguar saloon with a forward-hinged bonnet, and the first post-war saloon not to feature spats over the rear wheels.

Launched in 1961 at Earls Court, the MkX was a huge advance on its separate-chassis forefathers, and at £2,500 half the price of its nearest true competitors in the tycoon luxury class. Like all Jaguars, it was carefully costed – hence the bargain price – yet it was perhaps the first post-war car that Jaguar really had to sell; initial North American enthusiasm was tempered by early reliability problems, while British buyers were always resistant to its sheer bulk.

The MkX was originally equipped with the triple-carb 3.8-litre XK engine from the E-Type, and marked the first use of the straight-port cylinder head on a Jaguar saloon. Power went up from the 210bhp of the MkIX to 265bhp with the higher 9:1 compression ratio. As the MkX was slightly heavier than its predecessor, it actually needed that extra urge, but it was no sluggard, topping 120mph

Jaguar MkX 3.8
1961–64

ENGINE:
In-line six-cylinder, cast iron block, alloy head, hemispherical combustion chambers

Bore x stroke	87 x 106mm
Capacity	3,781cc
Valves	Twin ohc
Compression ratio	8:1 (7:1 and 9:1 optional)
Carburettors	Three 2in HD8 SUs
Power	265bhp at 5,500rpm (gross)
Torque	260lb ft at 4,000rpm (gross)

TRANSMISSION:
Four-speed manual with overdrive and automatic optional

Final drive	3.54:1 (manual/auto) or 3.77:1 (overdrive)

SUSPENSION:
Front: independent semi-trailing double wishbones, coil springs, telescopic dampers and anti-roll bar
Rear: independent lower wishbone/upper drive shaft link with radius arms and twin coil springs

Steering	recirculating ball, PAS standard

BRAKES:
Dunlop discs front and rear

WHEELS AND TYRES:
Dunlop RS5 7.50 x 14-inch (356mm) or SP 41 185 x 15-inch (381mm) tyres on bolt-on pressed steel wheels

BODYWORK:
Unitary all-steel construction

LENGTH:	16ft 10in (5.13m)
WIDTH:	6ft 4in (1.93m)
HEIGHT:	4ft 6¾in (1.39m)
WEIGHT:	37cwt (1,881kg)
MAX SPEED:	120mph (193kph)
0–60mph (97kph)	10.8 seconds

PRICE NEW (1961): £2,393 inc PT

Jaguar MkX 4.2 and 420G
1964–70

As MkX 3.8 except:

Bore x stroke	92.07 x 106mm
Capacity	4,235cc
Power	265bhp at 5,400rpm (gross)
Torque	283lb ft at 4,000rpm (gross)
MAX SPEED:	122mph (196kph)
0–60mph (97kph)	10.4 seconds

PRICE NEW (1964/1966):
£2,156/£2,238 (420G) inc PT

PRODUCTION FIGURES:

MkX 3.8	12,977
MkX 4.2	5,680
420G	6,554

NEW 4·2 LITRE MARK TEN SALOON

joins the famous range of Mark Ten, 'S' model, Mark 2 and 'E' Type Jaguars

It is in the brochure artwork that the MkX looks at its best. The 4.2 litre models were a great improvement on the original 3.8s, offering greater torque and much better transmissions.

(193kph) in overdrive top in rare manual Moss-'box form.

Most MkXs were sold with the Borg-Warner DG automatic transmission familiar from the MkIX and fitted with Jaguar's own intermediate hold switch for extra overtaking urge. Worked from a column lever, the automatic knocked just 1mph off the top speed and was actually slightly quicker – by a useful second – to 60mph (97kph). Moreover, a hard-driven MkX would not have been far behind the tearaway MkII 3.8 in a traffic-light burn-up, and all this from a truly lavish five-seater saloon with a boot the size of a coal bunker.

If the performance was impressive for such a giant, the handling and ride were even better thanks to Bob Knight's double-wishbone independent rear suspension. Just as

on the E-Type, the MkX featured a bridge-type subframe to cut road noise, with the limited-slip differential bolted solidly to it in the middle. The driveshaft cleverly doubled up as the top wishbone, while the bottom wishbone was actually more of a forked tubular affair with big alloy hub carriers through which the driveshaft also ran. Damping was by two shock absorbers on either side – each surrounded by a road spring – with 10-inch (254mm) Dunlop disc brakes mounted inboard to reduce unsprung weight. The front end was less remarkable, using MkII-like forged top and bottom wishbones, ball-jointed and with the spring/damper unit top mounting in a hollow pillar. All MkXs had Burman power-assisted steering as standard, a rarity on British cars in the early 1960s.

With the renamed 420G of 1966 came detail improvements to the outer trim (the side finisher being the most obvious) and the interior, although mechanically the car was unchanged.

The dashboard followed the pattern set by the MkII saloons with the main instruments in front of the driver and a bank of smaller gauges in the centre. Power steering was standard on the MkX and most had automatic transmission. This is a 420G with the padded dash top and slightly more shapely seats.

The small 14-inch wheels limited the size of the Dunlop disc brakes to 10.75 inches (273mm) at the front, but even so the MkX had exceptional high-speed braking ability for its day and admirable resistance to fade; sadly, at low speeds, the American-designed Kelsey Hayes 'bellows' servo – which exerted a mechanical pressure on the brake master cylinders rather than a hydraulic line pressure – could give a heart-stopping delayed response.

Inside, the MkX was a bigger and more up-market version of the MkII, and certainly no Jaguar since has been able to match the lavishness of its fittings and furniture or its limousine-like spaciousness. Light burr walnut gave an elegant Edwardian drawing-room feel to this cavernous cabin, not just on the dashboard and doors but framing the windows and on the backs of the

front seats, where picnic tables folded out to reveal full-length mirrors. There was separate heating for the rear passengers – the heating and ventilation was much improved over previous models – with Connolly leather on all the seat facings and a fine wool headlining. Most people forgave the ergonomic shortcomings of the dashboard because the effect as a whole was superb, with its regimented black-on-white Smiths dials and click-clack toggle switches. Starting was still by a push-button, but the MkX had a more curvaceous centre console and a padded shelf under the dash.

In Britain the MkX received a distantly cool reception from the weekly magazines, which were unhappy with the car's sheer size, its overlight power steering and unsupportive seats that made a joke of the car's otherwise exceptional cornering ability. In addition, neither transmission system was highly rated by the pundits: the Moss 'box, with its straight-cut non-synchromesh first gear, was noisy and slow in operation, while the automatic was thought jerky.

In America, where no domestic machine had anything like the MkX's cornering prowess or sporty feel, it made a much better impression with the critics. However, local dealers were soon reporting teething troubles, particularly with the cooling system.

Mindful of these criticisms, Jaguar had been working on a much improved MkX, the 4.2 of October 1964. With this bigger engine came

more torque (283lb ft at 4,000rpm) but an identical power curve (peaking at 265bhp at 3,000rpm), enough to push the 37cwt saloon along at 121mph even in automatic transmission form and improving the acceleration throughout the range: the 4.2 MkX reached the magic 100mph (161kph) as quickly as an automatic 3.8 MkII, and it was no more thirsty than before, turning in just over 14mpg on test.

Although this 4.2 litre unit had the same external block size as the 3.8, it was extensively rearranged inside with altered bore spacings and improved water flow around the cylinders. The crankshaft was substantially beefed up, of course,

The MkX and 420G had the widest rear seat of any British production car, together with plenty of legroom. Electric windows were optional, but picnic tables were standard and featured a vanity mirror.

The Daimler DS420, 1968–92

The Daimler DS420 dates from 1968 and was based on the floorpan of the MkX/420G but with an extra 21 inches (533mm) let into the wheelbase. This successor to the Daimler Majestic Major Limousine and the Vanden Plas Princess, had the driver sitting on a bench seat in front of a glass division while his passengers stretched out in the back in opulent comfort, the rear seat being over 6 feet (1.83m) in width.

The DS420 used a twin-carb version of the XK 4.2 engine and retained the MkX's suspension, Varamatic steering and model 8 Borg Warner gearbox, later supplanted by the model 12 and finally the GM400 unit, as the DS420 kept technical pace with its closest living relative, the XJ6/Daimler Sovereign.

The shape is unmistakable, its sweeping wing-line and noble visage a familiar part of British municipal life for the best part of 30 years. The cars were also bought in large quantities by the funeral trade as mourners' cars or hearses, while with a coat of white paint many did wedding car duty, especially in later life.

But it was not just a car for 'matches and despatches' – countless local

authorities and embassies bought the cars, and in Hong Kong the Regent Hotel still runs a fleet of 22. Even the Queen and Queen Mother have been Daimler Limousine owners, re-establishing the Royal patronage that Daimler lost to Rolls-Royce in the early 1950s.

Originally built at the Vanden Plas works in London, production moved to Jaguar in Coventry in 1979, where it continued until 1992. Trim levels varied from the 'base model' – with wind-up windows – to a mobile boardroom built for Jaguar boss John Egan in 1984 complete with TV, fax, cocktail cabinet and computer.

Always hand-made, the DS420 had a dash like the MkX and 420G, remaining faithful for many years to the old-fashioned column selector for the automatic gearbox, and to the push-button starter and pencil-thin black plastic steering wheel long after production-line Jags had gone rather 1970s-tacky.

Undercutting its nearest rival, the Rolls-Royce Phantom VI, by 50 per cent or more, these big Daimlers

were always fine value; for the plutocrat who wanted to look a million dollars without spending it, the DS420 was a canny buy.

With its race-bred twin-cam Jaguar engine – the last car to use it – the Daimler Limousine was no sluggard either, pulling an easy 110mph (177kph) flat-out, although most never went above a processional 30 or 40mph (48–64kph). The last of the proper carriage-trade limos, the DS420 had to die because, like the Phantom VI, it could no longer keep pace with worldwide legislation and was expensive to make compared with simple 'stretch' jobs on standard saloons.

Apart from hearses, the only special body supplied on the DS420 chassis was the Landaulette, of which two were built.

The MkX lived on as the Daimler DS420 limousine, which used a stretched version of the MkX/420G chassis. Production started in 1968 and lasted until 1992.

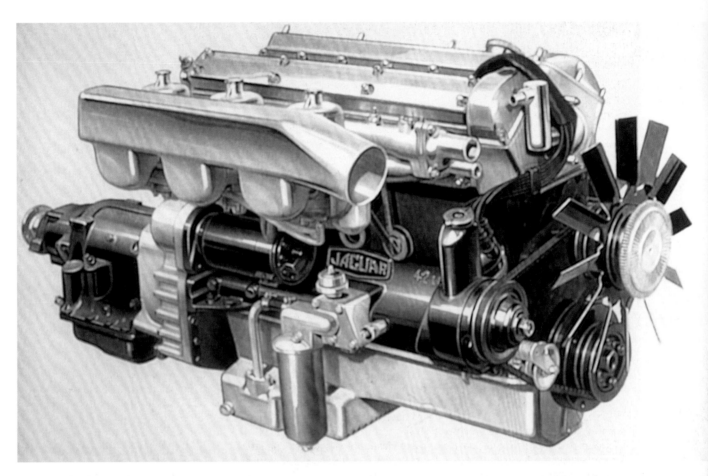

The MkX used the same 265bhp triple-carburettor engine as the E-Type, first in 3.8 litre form then later as a 4.2 with increased torque.

and although the cylinder head remained much as before there was a new inlet manifold. Any potential cooling problems with this new version of the MkX were anticipated with a more efficient radiator and a speeded-up water pump. An alternator replaced the dynamo and the starter motor was the pre-engaged type.

More interesting was the new power steering system, a Marles 'Varamatic' variable ratio set-up: 4.25 turns lock-to-lock around the straight ahead, but only 2.1 turns on half lock, and giving three turns lock-to-lock overall compared with almost four on the 3.8. The brake pedal acted directly on the servo.

Both transmission options were new. The Moss 'box was discarded for a brand new fully synchronised four-

speed unit (with optional overdrive on top), and there was a much improved Model 8 Borg-Warner automatic, much smoother in action and with a 'D2' setting for more economical second-gear starts. Inside little had changed – apart from revised heater controls – and on the outside the only way to tell the new from the old was a small '4.2' script on the bootlid.

In 1965 a 4.2 MkX limousine with a central sound-proof division – but using the standard shell – was offered. Buyers could have cloth or leather upholstery, an intercom, rear window blind and air-conditioning, which was also available on the standard car. Eighteen were built, three of them left-hand drive, and Sir William Lyons himself had one finished in black with West of England cloth.

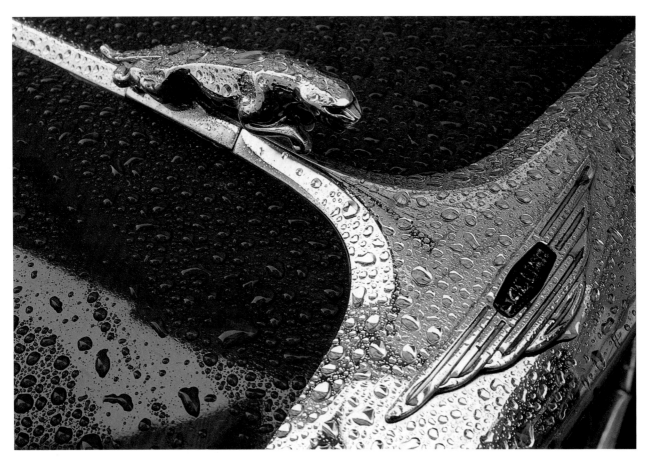

The MkX/420G was one of the last cars to use the leaping jaguar mascot that had been designed by motoring artist Gordon Crosby in the 1930s. It was outlawed by American safety regulations although many owners have fitted them to later Jaguars.

All in all this was a vastly better MkX, and the car it should have been from the start. Smooth, fast and quiet, it was now much more manageable and none of the opposition came anywhere near it as an all-round package. Rolls-Royce and Mercedes competition was double or nearly treble the price, while cheaper options like the Vanden Plas 4 litre R could not match the Jaguar in any department except interior appointments. The low-volume Lancia Flaminia saloon was an undoubted thoroughbred in handling and build quality, but had nothing like the power. In fact, it took a supercar like the 135mph (217kph) Maserati Quattroporte to substantially outrun the MkX in the saloon car class.

Two years later, at Earls Court in 1966, the MkX became the 420G, causing instant confusion with its slimmer sibling – the new S-Type-

based 420 – that continues to this day.

Nobody really knows what the 'G' stands for – there was no 'official' line – but the general consensus seems to be 'Grand'. The shape remained unchanged, but a new bright metal beading to break up the massive flanks was the most instant visual give-away. The front grille was also changed – with a thick central strip – as were the wheel trims with their new black centre badges. Inside the 'G' the skull-threatening timber dash rail was now padded (and equipped with a transistorised clock), while the seats were reshaped slightly to give more lateral support, a consistent road tester's gripe. Mechanically nothing changed and the car could still be ordered as a limousine, in which form 24 were built.

The MkX Variants

The MkX had close in-house competition from the big Daimler Majestic Major, Jaguar having bought the company in 1960. Although a patrician and old-fashioned-looking machine next to the sleek MkX, the Majestic had an impressive 4.5 litre V8, which, embarrassingly, made it marginally faster than the Jaguar. Thus it was not long before Jaguar engineers had a Daimler-engined MkX hack running at MIRA, clocking top speeds of up to 134mph (216kph) and knocking as much as 6 seconds off the 0–100mph (161kph) time. For a while there was talk of a Daimler version of the car, but a combination of company pride, and the fact that the big V8 designed by Edward Turner was not really tooled up for quantity production, meant that the project went no further.

Jaguar also tested its V12 engine in the MkX, both in four-cam and two-cam versions; the latter had more torque and bottom-end urge, whereas the four-cam was savagely quick beyond 3,500rpm and could approach 150mph (241kph), but was sluggish low down.

Such was the strength of the MkX shell that it was inevitable that a convertible would appear. Hinckley-based Jaguar specialist Graig Hinton developed a surprisingly elegant two-door conversion with an electric hood, the mechanism for which came from the Rolls-Royce Corniche. It was totally pillarless and could be ordered with electric front windows. As many as 12 were produced, mostly for export. Hinton also built the MkX-based Mercedes staff car for the film *Raiders of the Lost Ark* in the early 1980s.

The Majestic Major was an in-house rival for the MkX and many considered its 4.5 litre V8 superior to the engine of the Jaguar. A 'Daimlerised' MkX with this power unit was briefly considered, but when the prototype was found to be faster than the Jaguar the project was dropped.

Production of the 420G ended in 1970 when this, still the biggest ever Jaguar, finally deferred to the standard-setting XJ6.

Of the 25,000 MkXs and 420Gs produced, many have succumbed to rust or banger racing, and today the MkX is only just beginning to find its feet as a classic Jaguar saloon worth preserving.

There is much that is portentous of the XJ6 in the way the MkX conducts itself. Do not be fooled by its bulk – this car can be really hustled, and is quicker than a 4.2 XJ automatic all the way up to 100mph (161kph) despite an elderly automatic gearbox that lacks sensitivity. The old Borg-Warner 'D1/D2' set-up has a low-gear hold and lazy change-up points set in the interests of seamless progress rather than ultimate poke. In 'D1' it will go through all the gears from rest,

while 'D2' gives just intermediate and top for economy and smoothness. In 'D1' bottom can be engaged below 30mph (48kph) – or second up to around 60mph (97kph) – by stabbing the heavily sprung throttle. It is better, however, to take matters into your own hands – grab 'Low', listen to the three carbs suck mightily and feel the car leap forward with surprising urgency. Keep your foot in the Wilton and you'll soon be clocking 90mph (145kph) with plenty to come, only wind rustle around the quarter-window rubbers disturbing the drawing-room calm.

The gearing on this stable motorway mile-eater could usefully be higher than the slightly fussy 21mph (34kph) per 1,000rpm, but the rare manual overdrive version is necessary for genuine long-striding cruising ability. Four-fifths of MkX/420Gs were autos, and the manual, although slick

The MkX engine was largely the same as that fitted to the E-type with triple SU carburettors and an output of 265bhp. This is a 420G identifiable by its ribbed cam covers.

enough in later all-synchromesh form on the 4.2s, somehow does not suit the car.

One soon gets used to the width of the MkX or 420G, and it has the torque to haul itself out of any situation, while a fairly high driving position lends further confidence, with only the rear extremities out of view. It is also swervable and tolerant of clumsy inputs in a way that no equivalent American car would be – and it is American cars that are inevitably compared with this massive Jaguar.

The all-disc brake system is sensitive enough for checking the car quickly in traffic without the dramatic over-servoed lock-up usually found in contemporary drum-braked American cars. Hauling it down from speed on the broad, firm pedal, the brakes feel strong and balanced, and every bit as good as those of an early XJ. The earlier bellows-servo 3.8 MkX is less impressive, particularly at low speed.

Strapped tightly into the broad seats, comfortable despite a lack of rake adjustment or meaningful side support, the MkX will whisk you quickly through roundabouts with modest understeer and well-checked roll, although anyone unrestrained on the massive rear bench could find themselves bouncing off the walnut door cappings as the car swings between locks. Rack steering did not arrive until the XJ, but the Varamatic set-up on the 4.2 versions is excellent by 1960s standards.

All the MkX lacks is true steering feel, a quality denied Jaguar saloon drivers until the current XJ line. Cornering agility was only ever a side issue to ride and refinement with the MkX/420G. Supple and absorbent, the ride almost attains XJ excellence, which should come as no surprise as the cars share many components, principally Bob Knight's superb wishbone rear end. The MkX does not ride quite so serenely as an XJ – or

Buying Hints

1. Engines will do 150,000 miles if well maintained, but the 3.8 was always an oil-burner – as little as 200 miles to a pint. Look for a minimum 40lb oil pressure when hot at 3,000rpm.

2. All manual gearboxes are strong, but be warned that clutch replacement requires removal of the engine. Parts for the early Moss gearbox are difficult to find, and while automatics are also robust, there are some spares problems on the DG unit.

3. Look for perished radius arm mountings and check the condition of all rubber bushes on the independent rear suspension. Four dampers and four springs mean that refurbishment of the suspension is expensive.

4. Inboard rear brakes can give trouble when they pick up oil from a leaking differential. Also the Kelsey Hayes servo on the 3.8 is troublesome; conversion to a later type is advised.

5. The unusual 14-inch (356mm) rims meant that tyres were once difficult to find for the MkX, and for many owners the only option was van tyres, which had the wrong speed rating. Now this size is being remade, or an unobtrusive modification is to fit XJ6 15-inch (381mm) wheels.

6. The MkX and 420G have fared better than many Jaguars in terms of corrosion. However, inner and outer arches front and rear should be checked, as well as the rear edges of the front wings, the rear wings under the bumpers and, of course, the inner and outer sills. Doors can rot along the bottom, and on bad cars problems may be encountered at the bottom of the front screen pillars.

7. Much of the brightwork is easy to find as it was shared with the MkII, a model much better served by specialists.

8. The interior should be good to excellent on any car considered; refurbishment of torn leather, peeling veneers and rotting Wilton carpet does not make sense on a car of such relatively low value.

filter out engine and road noise quite so efficiently – but there can be little doubt that it was the best-riding steel-sprung car in the world before 1968.

The MkI *saloon*

Collectors and fashion followers have often overlooked these first-of-the-line compact 2.4 and 3.4 Jaguars, while historians casually dismiss them as the warm-up act for the much better MkII. But there is a purity about the Jaguar 2.4 that gives it a unique appeal, and if a good one can be found (many succumbed to the British 10-year MoT test in the 1960s) it is surprising how capable Jaguar's first compact unitary saloon still feels.

The suspension is well isolated, the ride supple, and the car has an assured cornering poise that sets it leagues apart from its fumbling contemporaries. Alvis, Bristol and even Armstrong-Siddeley may have produced cars that were the equal of the 2.4, but at prices that put them out of contention.

In rare 3.4 form it is something of a hot-rod – not far behind a 3.8 MkII – but even with the 2.4 litre engine it is a sweet and brisk car well able to keep up with modern traffic. Embarrassingly for Jaguar, it was always faster than the heavier 2.4 MkII that replaced it. This free-revving short-stroke version of the XK is not prodigiously torquey, but it is certainly flexible and good for a top speed of over 100mph (161kph), although it is happier at 80 (129).

The smooth lines of the new compact Jaguar were inspired by the MkVIII, but small windows reflected uncertainty about the strength of the new monocoque construction; visibility through the slot-like rear window was limited, but its engine was sweet and free-revving.

Only the claustrophobic feel of the interior dates it significantly compared to the MkII, but in fittings and appointments the baby Jaguar could be compared with the best.

So if the humble 2.4 MkI still feels so capable today, how must it have seemed 40 years ago? Introduced in October 1955, the 2.4 (it was known only retrospectively as the MkI) was an important car for the company and

Such was its impact and sheer value for money that it wiped out Jaguar's British opposition in one fell swoop

a completely new concept in saloon Jaguars. All the four-door cars that Jaguar had built before it had been large by European standards, but now they had a contender in the medium-sized sports category for buyers who did not want anything as massive as the MkVII, but certainly would not consider something as short on practicality as the XK140 fixed-head.

The 2.4 brought the company into a whole new price class (there had been no small Jaguar since the demise of the 1½ litre) and introduced it to a new set of potential buyers, and it was to sell in the kind of numbers with which Jaguar had not had to deal before. Such was its impact – and its sheer value for money – that it wiped out Jaguar's British opposition in one fell swoop.

The big news was that the 2.4 had unitary construction, a first on a Jaguar. In those days, stress engineering was still something of a mystical art, which meant that Jaguar (like everyone else) took a belt and

Jaguar MkI 2.4 1955–59

ENGINE:
In-line six-cylinder, cast iron block, alloy head, hemispherical combustion chambers

Bore x stroke	83 x 76.5mm
Capacity	2,483cc
Valves	Twin ohc, one inlet, one exhaust
Compression ratio	8:1 (7:1 and 9:1 optional)
Carburettors	Two 24mm Solex downdraught
Power	112bhp at 5,750rpm (gross)
Torque	144lb ft at 2,000rpm (gross)

TRANSMISSION:
Four-speed manual with synchromesh on second, third and top
Laycock de Normanville overdrive optional
Optional Borg–Warner DG speed automatic

Final drive	hypoid semi-floating Salisbury 4HA
Ratios	4.27 (standard),

4.55 (overdrive), 4.09, 4.55, 3.27, 2.93 available to special order

SUSPENSION:
Front: independent semi-trailing double wishbones, coil springs, telescopic dampers and anti-roll bar
Rear: live axle with cantilever semi-elliptic springs with twin parallel radius arms, Panhard rod, telescopic dampers

Steering	recirculating ball, 4.8 turns lock-to-lock

BRAKES:
Lockheed drums front and rear.
Discs from 1958

WHEELS:
Pressed steel bolt-on 15-inch (381mm) 4.5K (later 5K) wheel, or optional 15-inch 5K knock-off wire wheel with Dunlop Road Speed 6.40 x 15 tyres

BODYWORK:
Unitary all-steel construction

LENGTH:	15ft ¾in (4.59m)
WIDTH:	5ft 6¾in (1.7m)
HEIGHT:	4ft 9½in (1.46m)
WEIGHT:	28.5cwt (1,449kg)
MAX SPEED:	101mph (163kph)
0–60mph (97kph)	14.4 seconds

PRICE NEW (1955): £1,269 inc PT

Jaguar MkI 3.4 1957–59

As MkI 2.4 Saloon except:

Bore x stroke	83 x 106mm
Capacity	3,442cc
Carburettors	Two 1.75in HD6 SUs
Power	210bhp at 5,500rpm (gross)
Torque	216lb ft at 3,000rpm (gross)
WEIGHT:	29.5cwt (1,500kg)
MAX SPEED:	120mph (193kph)
0–60mph (97kph)	9.1 seconds

PRICE NEW (1957): £1,672 inc PT

PRODUCTION FIGURES:

2.4	19,992
3.4	17,405

Rust and the introduction of the MoT test in the 1960s have made sure that the 2.4 and 3.4 MkI Jaguars are now rare cars.

braces approach to building a unitary body – in other words, making anything they were not sure about bigger and stronger just to be on the safe side. So although the 2.4 was, at 27cwt (1,373kg), a useful 7cwt (356kg) lighter than the bulky MkVII, it was still quite a bit heavier than it needed to be – just look at the thick screen pillars.

Developed over three years in close co-operation with Pressed Steel of Oxford, the body undoubtedly contributed most to the £100,000 development bill with which Jaguar were saddled, making the 2.4 the most expensive project the company had ever undertaken.

The body was based around two straight longitudinal members welded to the ribbed steel floor to form box sections, and running from the front

suspension mountings to the rear wheel arches and spring anchorages. There were further transverse sections under the radiator mounting and beneath the front seats, while behind the rear seats everything was kept together by the wheel arch and seat pan pressings. Two more box members running along each side of the engine bay transferred front-end stresses to the bulkhead and scuttle, while outer body sills provided another front-to-rear-end box section. The inner and outer wings were welded on for strength.

William Lyons had a rare eye for styling and, like every Jaguar and SS before, the 2.4 was witness to his unerring eye for a good line. The most noticeable thing about the car was that it was not very big – at 15ft 0¾in (4.59m) long, 5ft 6¾in (1.7m) wide and 4ft 9½in (1.46m) high, there was considerably less of it in every direction than the barge-like MkVII. The overall style was best described as a mixture of XK140 up front, with the same bulbous wing-line and cast alloy oval grille, and a tail not unlike a downsized MkVII, with a smoothly rounded bootlid falling down to bumper level, and pimple-like rear light units on either side. However, the thick, full-frame doors, slot-like rear window and bulky screen pillars gave the 2.4 a look of its own. Lyons called it the 'rotund' style, which perfectly describes the look of the chunky little 2.4.

Rear wheel spats were another 2.4 feature, and there was little chrome tinsel to spoil the basically clean lines. Only the big, aggressive bumpers – which seemed to be looking for an accident – caught the eye. The leaping Jaguar mascot was only fitted to the special-equipment cars.

In fact, most of the 2.4s built were SEs. The standard 2.4, lacking heater, tachometer, armrest, screen washer, twin fog lamps, cigar lighter, courtesy switches for the rear interior lights, and the customary vitreous enamel finish on the exhaust manifolds, could be bought for £29 less, but few thought the saving worthwhile.

Inside, the 2.4 was a great package, with all the refinements of the big MkVII and almost equal accommodation (perhaps with the exception of rear legroom). There was only an inch less in the distance between the front of the dash and rear seat squab compared with the less efficient MkVII.

Once inside, you would not have guessed that you were riding in the cheapest model in the range. All the seats were leather-faced, there was

full carpeting, and the dashboard, door cappings and cantrails all had

The brochure artwork emphasises the smooth, modern profile of the 2.4. As an all-rounder it had no rivals at its price.

the usual walnut veneer finish. The driver had a full set of instruments, with a 120mph speedo and rev-counter in the middle, flanked by fuel and combined oil pressure/water temperature information, together with an ammeter and an electronic clock, all mounted on a central veneered panel. Twin gloveboxes were mounted at either end of the dash, there were map pockets in the doors, and two-speed wipers with vacuum-operated washers on the special-equipment version.

The floor change, at first with a strange cranked lever, later with a straight, stubby affair, controlled the usual Moss four-speed transmission with its crash first gear. One of the major 2.4 options was a Laycock overdrive unit, operating on top gear only. This that gave a long-legged 3.54:1 overall gearing, and was hitched up to a lower 4.55 axle rather than the standard 4.27, which meant an easygoing 21.8mph (35kph) per 1,000rpm.

The boot was a decent size, with the wheel mounted under the floor and a complete toolkit stowed within the wheel. However, access to the tight-fitting twin-cam engine was poor, the dynamo and starter motor being especially hard to reach.

This styling mock-up shows how Lyons liked to work with full-sized representations rather than small-scale models. The shape was a mixture of MkVII and XK.

Inside, good packaging meant that the 2.4 was hardly any less roomy than the big MkVII, but passengers had to climb over the high, strength-giving sills. This modified car has a wooden three-spoke sports steering wheel which was a popular period accessory.

Technically there was much of interest. In particular, the suspension systems, designed by William Heynes, were new. At the front, out went the MkVII/XK120-style torsion bars and in came coil springs, unequal-length wishbones, and Girling telescopic dampers, on a pressed steel subframe. The upper of the rear-inclined wishbones was a pressing, the lower a forging with the coil spring attached and retained by a hollow steel pillar on which the top wishbone was pivoted. There were upper and lower ball joints for wheel movement and steering.

The most remarkable thing about the front suspension was that subframe, which was detachable and insulated from the body by rubber mountings –

there was no metal-to-metal contact anywhere between the body and the subframe. In terms of noise suppression it was a major advance because early unitary bodies could end up as sound boxes without the added insulation from the mechanical components provided by a separate chassis. About the only real disadvantage of the system was that the whole thing had to be removed to take the sump off the engine.

Bob Knight, Jaguar's chassis engineer of the 1950s, '60s and '70s, is still proud of the company's achievements with this suspension, although the period of the 2.4's development is not remembered with affection by Browns Lane veterans. It pressed the still small company's financial and manpower resources to their limit at a time when the racing programme was also taking up a lot of time, money and energy.

Burman recirculating ball steering, also subframe-mounted, was used and again substantially insulated from the steering wheel by twin universal joints and further rubber bushes on the inner wishbone and anti-roll bar mountings. The big 17-inch Bluemels wheel was adjustable for fore and after movement by a knurled ring on the column.

Bob Knight, who joined Jaguar just after the war, was a chassis expert responsible for the exceptional refinement of the MkI.

The rear suspension was novel. Long cantilevered five-leaf springs, semi-elliptics turned upside-down, were used, attached to the live axle by rubber-bonded bushes fixed to extensions on the axle casing. They were anchored to the car's structure at the other end inside the longitudinal chassis rails and were bolted together in the middle between two rubber blocks. Two trailing arms from the seat pan to brackets above the axle gave further location, and there was also a Panhard rod (adjustable) to stop excessive

The MkI in Competition

The fact that the compact MkI had enormous potential in competition – both as a saloon racer and in the classic road rallying events like the Tour de France – was not lost on the leading protagonists of its day, although Jaguar's withdrawal from competition in 1956 meant that factory involvement would be limited to preparing cars for private owners.

The baby 2.4 was rapid enough in the right hands – Paul Frère gave the car its first victory at Spa in a production car race in 1956, and in the UK drivers like Peter Blond proved tenacious class winners in the car.

But the 3.4 was the real sensation. Nothing could touch it – especially once disc brakes had been homologated and the suspension had been beefed up with heavy-duty anti-roll bars, stiffer leaf springs and a limited-slip differential. Under the bonnet, the engines were equipped with C-Type cylinder heads, high-lift camshafts, twin 2-inch SU carburettors, 9:1 compression pistons and lead-bronze bearings. A racing clutch would be fitted together with a close-ratio gearbox, sometimes with overdrive locked out. The rear axle ratio was uprated to 3.5:1 and the battery was transferred to the boot for better weight distribution. Racing tyres were, of course used, and a straight-through exhaust system.

The teams of Tommy Sopwith and John Coombs are perhaps most closely associated with the car's success, using star drivers such as Mike Hawthorn (who was to lose his life in a 3.4 on the road), Duncan Hamilton, Roy Salvadori and Ivor Bueb to wring every ounce of performance out of the cars. Walt Hansgen – who drove Jaguars for

Briggs Cunningham in the USA – won in a 3.4 in a special saloon race at Silverstone on Grand Prix day in 1958 after the redoubtable Sopwith lost a wheel.

Wherever it went, the 3.4 had the edge in power if not always in handling: at the Christmas Brands Hatch Touring Car Race held on Boxing Day 1957, Tommy Sopwith got out in front from the start in a 3.4, while Sir Gawaine Baillie in another 3.4 duelled with an unlikely Ford Anglia – which was much slower on the straights, but faster through the corners – for second position. The race was won by Sopwith, who also took the fastest lap, at 63.77mph (102.6kph), a new saloon car record.

But it was Silverstone and the production saloon event that was the scene of the 3.4's greatest successes. Cornering on their door handles, their rear wheels smoking, MkIs could usually be seen battling it out for the top four or five places. The beginning of the 3.4's dominance at the Northamptonshire circuit was in 1957, when cars were prepared by the factory for Hamilton, Hawthorn and Bueb. For five laps Mike Hawthorn – still only 27 – was followed by Archie Scott-Brown in another 3.4, with Duncan Hamilton and Ivor Bueb fighting wheel-to-wheel for third and fourth. It was not long before Scott-Brown's car had highlighted the model's one serious failing – brake fade – and that left Mike Hawthorn with an unassailable lead. He went on to win the race at an average speed of 82.19mph (132.24kph), breaking the previous year's lap record of 81.68mph (131.42kph) – held by a Mark VII. Second place went to Duncan Hamilton at an average of 81.73mph (131.5kph) and third-place man was

Ivor Bueb at an average of 80.11mph (128.89kph). The team prize also went to Jaguar – and the dominance of the 3.4 in saloon car competition had begun.

The supremacy of the 3.4 at Silverstone continued until 1959, completing an unbroken record of 11 consecutive annual wins at the event for Jaguar. Only the introduction of the faster, more manageable MkII 3.8 broke the MkI's run of success on the track, although the last ones were still winning in 1961.

However, it did not quite end there. In the 1970s, Pre-'57 Historic Saloon racing gave the model a new lease of life as a popular and successful choice.

In rallying, too, the car proved popular – on the 1958 Monte Carlo Rally no fewer than 30 Jaguars were entered, most of which were 3.4s. Suffolk farmers Don and Erle Morley were one of the most effective pairings in the MkI and took their brand-new 3.4 to an overall win in

the tough Tulip Rally in 1959. The same year Bobby Parkes and George Howarth won their class in the Monte Carlo Rally and took eighth overall, with Philip Walton and Michael Martin ninth and Eric Brinkman and John Cuff 37th in 3.4s. This was enough to earn Jaguar the Charles Faroux team award that year.

In Britain the MkI's best RAC showing was 1958. On the first test stage at Prescott, Sopwith was fastest in his class with a 3.4, and at the end of the rally Waddilove won his class in a 2.4, with Brinkman first in his class with a 3.4, followed by Sopwith in second place.

Although Spanish driver Hermanos da Silva Ramos won the Tour de France in a 3.4 in 1959, the event had been less lucky for British entrants, particularly in 1958. Jaguar had the Whitehead brothers, Tommy Sopwith and Sir Gawaine Baillie with Peter Jopp, all driving 3.4s. Sopwith drove magnificently and soon took the lead in his class with the Whitehead brothers close behind.

Unfortunately, when entering Le Touquet Sopwith's car collided with a taxi and the delay put him out of the rally. Peter Whitehead then took the lead but had a fatal accident when the car ran off the road and fell 30 feet. Graham Whitehead was driving at the time and was only slightly hurt, but his brother Peter died from his injuries. The one remaining MkI, driven by Sir Gawaine Baillie and Peter Jopp, finished third in class.

As the MkII began to take over in 1960, MkIs continued to turn up in minor rallies throughout that and the following year, the last notable result being first in class in the 1961 Circuit of Ireland, the car a 3.4 driven by H. J. O'Connor-Rorke and J. Cuff.

A 3.4 saloon dices with a MkVII at Silverstone. The compact Jaguars were unbeatable in the saloon class at that circuit for many years.

Lyons stands beside his first monocoque model, the 2.4. In less than four years 37,000 examples were sold.

76.5mm stroke. The shorter stroke also meant a short block, so the weight of the engine was reduced by 50lb (23kg) – useful on a car that even so ended up with 55 per cent of its weight over the front wheels.

For economy's sake the unit was de-tuned slightly; for the first time since the 1930s Jaguar forsook SU carbs and fitted a pair of Solex B32s with the mildest 5/16th (8mm) lift cam. It was rated at 112bhp at 5,750rpm, and put its power through the usual Moss gearbox via a single-plate Borg & Beck clutch.

The 2.4 was a fast car for the 1950s: top speed was just over the 'ton', with 0–60mph (97kph) in around 14 seconds – in other words the kind of performance that normally required an extra litre. The little XK engine had a willing sweetness denied the longer-stroke variants, but because it had to be worked that bit harder, fuel consumption was disappointing. Generally only a gently driven 2.4 bettered 20mpg, making it almost as thirsty as the bigger, faster MkVII.

Even in the mid-1950s the weekly magazines – very restrained in their criticism – were complaining about the laborious change quality of the 2.4's Moss gearbox, and buyers would have to wait until 1958 for an automatic alternative, although the optional overdrive was much appreciated. It would be another ten years before Jaguar would offer a proper all-synchro 'box of their own design to match the excellence of the XK engine.

The 2.4 was perhaps most admired for its suspension, which combined good handling with a supple, quiet ride. Thrown into a turn, the 2.4 rolled a good deal and displayed strong understeer, but gripped well and, unlike many live-axled cars of the day, its roadholding was little affected by bad surfaces. The sound insulation measures had also been successful, with road noise

sideways movement of the axle. The axle was a Salisbury 3HA unit with a notably narrow track – only 4ft 2¼in (1.28m) compared with 4ft 6⅜in (1.39m) at the front. This was to prove one of the car's failings, and was an area where the MkII would be a major improvement. Inside the 15-inch-diameter (381mm) pressed steel wheels were Lockheed 11⅛-inch (295mm) drum brakes with servo.

The engine was the now familiar XK in-line 'six', with its chrome-iron block, alloy head, chain-driven overhead camshafts and seven-bearing crankshaft. For a time, Jaguar was thinking of going ahead with production of the four-cylinder XK engine for the 2.4, this being a unit that had first been seen alongside the 'six' in 1948. However, lack of smoothness, the benefits of parts rationalisation with the bigger six-cylinder unit, and pure snob appeal killed the idea stone dead.

The new capacity for the engine was 2,483cc, and it was essentially a shorter-stroke version of the 3.4 with the same 83mm bore but a shorter

Mike Hawthorn and his MkI

Not yet 30 years old, the retiring World Champion driver Mike Hawthorn lost his life in a 3.4 Jaguar, VDU 881, in 1959. On a wet and very windy 22 January, driving to London to meet the widow of his great friend Peter Collins (who had died the previous year driving for Ferrari), he crashed the green 3.4 in a horrific accident, the cause of which has never been entirely established.

Although Jaguar claimed that the car, which had raced in the Silverstone Tourist Trophy meetings in 1957 and '58, was 'virtually standard', this was not quite the case. It had high-compression pistons, 2-inch SUs, firmer springs and competition shock absorbers all round. Special rear wheels increased the track and, naturally, it was fitted with disc brakes all round, by Dunlop.

It was undoubtedly very quick and Hawthorn always drove it very quickly, often indulging in hair-raising dices on the road in the those pre-speed-limit days, especially if he spotted one of his racing colleagues. Chris Nixon's book on the lives of Mike Hawthorn and Peter Collins, Mon Ami Mate, gives the most complete account, condensed here, of Hawthorn's fateful last drive.

Driving along the A3 that day, Hawthorn encountered Rob Walker, driving his Mercedes 300SL to his garage in Dorking. Hawthorn had a particular hatred for all things German so at the sight of the white Gullwing he would have been particularly fired up. He caught up with the Mercedes, registered ROB 2, on the Hog's Back and gave Walker a friendly wave. They accelerated down the rain-soaked hill together, probably doing more than 100mph (161kph). The Jaguar overtook the Mercedes in the left hand curve as they passed John

Coombs's garage, then, going into the a mild right-hander that followed, the Jaguar started to slide and suddenly spun, careering backwards across the road and disappearing from Walker's view. It clipped a traffic island in the centre of the road and continued across the carriageway, clipping the tail of a lorry then disappearing in a cloud of mud and water.

Its final resting place was wrapped around a tree, almost split in two. Hawthorn ended up in the back seat of the car, and by the time Walker arrived on the scene just moments later it was too late; as Walker was looking at him Hawthorn breathed twice, then his eyes glazed over. The coroner's report said that he had died as a result of a fractured skull, fragments of bone being driven into the brain.

There was much speculation as to the cause of the accident. Some said Hawthorn could have had a blackout (he had kidney problems). Others maintained that the limited slip diff

had seized, or a disc brake had locked on, or that the experimental Dunlop tyres had somehow failed to cope. However, when Jaguar dismantled and inspected the remains they could find nothing wrong.

We will probably never know the exact cause, but Chris Nixon offers perhaps the most plausible explanation in Mon Ami Mate. He reveals that Hawthorn's Jaguar had been fitted with a hand throttle the week before, which fits in with Rob Walker's comment that the engine was still running flat-out when the car was travelling backwards. It seems probable that some part of the device failed or that, in the heat of the moment and in an attempt to disengage it, Hawthorn had increased the speed of the engine.

Mike Hawthorn, driving a Jaguar D Type, battles it out with Juan Manuel Fangio in a Mercedes Benz 300SLR at Le Mans, 1955 (Rodolfo Mailander/Ludvigsen Library).

transmission well suppressed by Bob Knight's rubber insulation.

Driver appeal of the comparatively low-slung, sleekly styled 2.4 eclipsed most British rivals – the Daimler Conquest and Riley Pathfinder looked and felt decidedly ponderous by comparison – although perhaps Armstrong-Siddeley's largely unsung 234/236 range was fit to be spoken of in the same breath, and the Alvis Grey Lady was certainly a much nimbler car than its matronly looks suggested. Both were far more expensive, of course, and the 2.4 was yet another Jaguar-engineered nail in their respective coffins.

In America, where it was hoped that the 2.4 would sell in huge numbers,

Jaguars were expensive compared with homegrown cars and the new compact's economy tag did not really cut any ice with enthusiasts there who simply wanted more performance for their money. Virtually any big American V8 saloon could touch 100mph and match the 2.4's acceleration, even with their habitual automatic transmission.

The Americans got the compact Jaguar they had been waiting for in 1957 when the 3.4 saloon was announced, using the bigger 210bhp engine with the new option of a Borg-Warner automatic transmission. Outwardly it could be spotted by its XK150-style grille with thin slats and its cutaway rear spats.

The 3.4 litre engine made the compact Jaguar into a 120mph (193kph) car, (probably the first production saloon to achieve that speed in standard form), but brought sharply into focus the shortcomings of the drum brakes. They were just not up to the job of stopping the car repeatedly from the sort of speeds it was capable of attaining so quickly, and before long – and after comments in a weekly magazine road test that were very close to the bone for the time – a Dunlop four-wheel disc brake option was introduced; most people very wisely took this up. There was also a question mark over the 3.4's ultimate handling. The narrow rear track certainly had something to do with the feeling of high-speed instability, and in the wet a less than carefully driven 3.4 could be an unruly handful.

But it was a sensational performance saloon for its day and, for all its failings, it was much appreciated by the Americans, who lapped up a large proportion of 3.4 production between March 1957 and September 1959.

The 3.4s were replaced by the MkII range in October 1959, these revised cars being better in every way and going on to be the most successful and best-loved Jaguar saloons of their era. Almost at once the MkI was rendered something of an orphan, and although it has been carried along on the coat tails of the MkII as a classic, its following is much smaller; today not many more than 500 survive on UK roads.

This 3.4 MkI was modified to resemble Mike Hawthorn's famous racing saloon, with painted wire wheels rather than chrome or enamel.

Buying Hints

1. The condition of the bodywork is particularly crucial with the MkI as spares are scarce and nobody is making repair panels. MkII body parts can sometimes be made to fit, however, and bonnet, boot, inner wings, front crossmember, petrol filler door, inner and outer sills, splash panels, floors and rear wheel spats are interchangeable with the MkII.

2. The bumpers are also common with the MkII, but many smaller brightwork and lighting items such as door handles are not, and may require expensive replating. Care is therefore needed.

3. As usual, restoration of the fine-figured veneers and leather is pricey and little is interchangeable with the better-served MkII.

4. Check for rot under the rear seat (if all is well the vendor will not mind the cushion being removed). Remember that this is a critical area of strength on which the spring hangers – and thus the axle itself – rely for location.

5. Inside the boot look at the damper mounting points; by removing the hardboard trim at the sides, a view of the boot floor edges and wheel arches can be obtained.

6. Underneath, look at the spring hanger box sections that locate the leaf springs; these collapse to leave the spring resting directly on the bodywork. The Panhard rod mountings are also worth checking. You might find rust in the spare wheel well, and also under the boot floor.

7. Look at the sills; not only the outers – rust here will be obvious unless oversills have been fitted – but more importantly the inners (the flat vertical wall section that runs along adjacent to the floorpan). Any rot here will certainly lead to structural problems. Look, too, at the jacking points, which give an indication of the sills' condition – although testing them is probably not a good idea. Looking at the floor, damp carpets probably mean that there is a hole somewhere.

8. At the front, look for rust on the front valance under the bumper – not too much of a problem – and the 'crows feet' that support the front of the wings. The outer wings – virtually unobtainable for the MkI – corrode around the sidelight housings (look for bubbles) and the edges of the wheel arches.

9. At the rear, look for problems at the top near the closing panel behind the wheel, sealed against the outer wing by a rubber strip. Water gets past this fairly easily with subsequent corrosion of the bottom edge of the wing and the sills.

10. Under the bonnet, look for problems around the hinges for the bonnet and the battery box, although the bonnet itself rarely suffers.

11. Door bottoms are rust-prone, especially when the drain holes become blocked, although the frames themselves are usually saveable.

12. The double-skinned rear valance is a custom-made mud trap, with road dirt forced up from the rear wheels. On the bootlid, rust comes through along the bottom edge where the sealing rubber collects water.

13. On the move look for 40psi oil pressure at 3,000rpm with a warm engine (ideally not less than 15psi at tickover) and not too much blue smoke at the back when you accelerate – a slight blue haze is nothing to worry about. The XK is a fairly leaky engine by nature, but steer clear of one that drips oil from the rear main bearing oil seal: that is an engine-out job to rectify. Rev the engine between 1,500 and 2,000rpm and listen for timing chain rattle.

14. Gearboxes are strong but parts for both manuals and automatics are becoming scarce. Overdrive trouble is often nothing more serious than a faulty solenoid. Clutches are long-lived but replacement is again an engine-out job.

13. A drooping nose betrays tired front coil springs, while the Metalastik bushes on the front subframe perish and split in time, giving a sloppy feel to the ride and handling. The rear springs settle and the top leaves can break – is the car low or lopsided at the back?

14. The drum brakes are adequate for the 2.4's performance, but you are better off with a later disc-braked car; the early-type disc brakes are awkward to maintain. Lack of servo effect in the brakes could be down to the rust-prone vacuum tank located in the offside wing.

The MkII
and 240/340

For a luxurious four-seat family saloon the 3.8 MkII was uniquely quick in 1959, and uniquely cheap. That year marked the dawn of Britain's motorway age, with the new M1 stretching from London almost into Leicestershire, and about the only cars the driver of the new Jaguar 3.8 MkII had to move over for were Astons – the recently introduced DB4s – Maseratis, Ferraris or, maybe, big Mercedes 300SLs, but such exotica were a rare sight in those days and three times as expensive as the Jaguar.

Foreign saloons? Nothing even came close to the 3.8 MkII's performance for the price, and none had its clean good looks and that sumptuous gentleman's club interior. Here was a £1,800 saloon that would cruise at 100mph (161kph) all day long, top 125mph (201kph), and still have discernible acceleration in hand when you flicked into overdrive top at 110 (177).

Few cars have been hailed as such radical improvements over their predecessors as the Jaguar MkII when it was introduced at the 1959 Earls Court Motor Show. It looked better, went better, and was a safer car than the MkI. Until the advent nine years later of the standard-setting XJ6, it was the best-selling Jaguar saloon car ever, with sales figures totalling almost 100,000 by the time production finally ended in 1969.

With an eye to retaining the existing tooling – and thus keeping the costs down – Lyons had nonetheless succeeded in dramatically changing the compact Jaguar's looks. Although the sills, bonnet and boot lid were as before, every other aspect was radically altered. The claustrophobic feel of the earlier car's interior was gone, thanks to no less than 9½ inches (241mm) of extra glass on each side of the car. The heavy, full-frame doors were replaced by new half-frame affairs that used separate, slim chrome frames at the top bolted to the main door frames, a clever device first seen on the MkV.

Although the outline remained the same, Jaguar slimmed down the look of the MkII by incorporating a much larger glass area. Window frames were now chromed and the rear side windows extended behind the doors. The rear window was much bigger and wrapped around, and the rear light units were larger.

Jaguar MkII 2.4
1959–67

ENGINE:
In-line six-cylinder, cast iron block, alloy head, hemispherical combustion chambers

Bore x stroke	81 x 76.5mm (151.5cu in)
Capacity	2,483cc
Valves	Twin ohc, one inlet, one exhaust
Compression ratio	8:1 (7:1 and 9:1 optional)
Carburettors	Two 24mm Solex downdraught
Power	120bhp at 5,750 rpm (gross)
Torque	144lb ft at 2,000rpm (gross)

TRANSMISSION:
Four-speed manual with synchromesh on second, third and top (all-synchro 'box from October 1965), overdrive optional
Optional three-speed automatic

Final drive ratios	4.27 (standard), 4.55 (overdrive),

4.09, 4.55, 3.27, 2.93 available to special order.

SUSPENSION:
Front: independent semi-trailing, double wishbones, coil springs, telescopic dampers and anti-roll bar
Rear: live axle with cantilever semi-elliptic springs with twin parallel radius arms, Panhard rod and telescopic dampers

Steering	recirculating ball. Power steering optional

BRAKES:
Dunlop discs front and rear

WHEELS:
Pressed steel bolt-on 15-inch (381mm) 4.5K (later 5K) wheel, or optional 15-inch 5K knock-off wire wheel with Dunlop Road Speed 6.40 x 15 tyres

BODYWORK:
Unitary all-steel construction

LENGTH:	15ft ¾in (4.59m)
WIDTH:	5ft 6¾in (1.7m)
HEIGHT:	4ft 9¼in (1.47m)
WEIGHT:	28.5cwt (1,449kg)
MAX SPEED:	96mph (154kph)
0–60mph (97kph)	17.3 seconds

PRICE NEW (1959): £1,534 inc PT

Jaguar MkII 3.4
1959–67

As MkII 2.4 Saloon except:

Bore x stroke	83 x 106mm
Capacity	3,442cc
Carburettors	Two 1.75in HD6 SUs
Power	210bhp at 5,500rpm (gross)
Torque	216lb ft at 3,000rpm (gross)

WEIGHT:	29.5cwt (1,500kg)

(distributed 59% front, 41% rear)

MAX SPEED:	120mph (193kph)
0–60mph (97kph)	11.9 seconds (auto)

PRICE NEW (1959): £1,669 inc PT

Jaguar MkII 3.8
1959–67

As MkII 2.4 Saloon except:

Bore x stroke	87 x 106mm
Capacity	3,781cc
Carburettors	Two 1.75in HD6 SUs
Power	220bhp at 5,500rpm
Torque	240lb ft at 3,000rpm

WEIGHT:	30cwt (1,525kg)

(distributed 56.5% front, 43.5% rear)

MAX SPEED:	125mph (201kph)
0–60mph (97kph)	8.5 seconds

PRICE NEW (1959): £1,779 inc PT

Jaguar 240
1967–69

As MkII 2.4 Saloon except:

Power	133bhp at 5,500rpm (gross)
Torque	146lb ft at 3,700rpm (gross)
Carburettors	Two 1.75in HS6 SUs
Tyres	Dunlop RS5 6.40 x 15 or SP 185 x 15 on 5K
LENGTH:	14ft 11in (4.55m)

PRICE NEW (1967): £1,365 inc PT

Jaguar 340
1967–68

As MkII 2.4 Saloon except:

Bore x stroke	83 x 106mm
Capacity	3,442cc
Carburettors	Two 1.75in HD6 SUs
Power	210bhp at 5,500rpm (gross)
Torque	216lb ft at 3,000rpm (gross)
WEIGHT:	30cwt (1,525kg)

(distributed 59% front, 41% rear)

WHEELS: 15-inch (381mm) pressed steel with Dunlop RS5 6.40 x 15 tyres or SP185 x 15 on 5K

LENGTH:	14ft 11in (4.55m)

PRICE NEW (1967): £1,442 inc PT

Daimler 2.5 V8 and 250 V8
1962–69

As MkII 2.4 Saloon except:
ENGINE:
90 degree V8, cast iron block, alloy head, hemispherical combustion chambers

Bore x stroke	76.2 x 69.85mm
Capacity	2,548cc
Valves	Pushrod ohv
Compression ratio	8.2:1
Carburettors	Two HD6 SUs
Power	140bhp at 5,800rpm (gross)
Torque	155lb ft at 3,600rpm (gross)

TRANSMISSION:
Three-speed Borg–Warner Type 35 automatic or (later) four-speed with optional overdrive

Final drive	Hypoid semi-floating Salisbury 4HA, 4.27:1
WEIGHT:	29cwt (1,475kg)

(distributed 56.4% front, 43.6% rear)

MAX SPEED:	112mph (180kph)
0–60 mph (97kph)	13.8 seconds

PRICE NEW (1963): £1,569 inc PT

PRODUCTION FIGURES:

2.4	25,173
3.4	28,666
3.8	30,141

Vision was further improved by a new semi-wraparound rear window, 3 inches (76mm) deeper and 7 inches (178mm) wider than before. A MkII could also be identified by its new chrome rain gutters and by slimline door handles designed to keep the locks clean.

At the front the grille had a central chrome rib to set it apart from the old car and, to bring the compact Jaguar in line with XK150 and MkIX styling, the sidelights moved to new housings on the tops of the wings, with flashing indicators below where the lights had been. The big bumpers stayed, but the overriders were further apart at the front and the rear bumper was deeper, with a 'Disc Brakes' badge in the centre. Bigger

rear light clusters now housed separate lenses for the indicators. The rear skirt was deeper to hide the fuel tank, and the sides of the rear wings were altered to house the wider rear axle and had narrower wheel spats with a less obvious lipped edge.

The inside of the car was all new apart from the rear seat cushion and the door and window handles. The main instruments – white-on-black Smiths speedo and rev counter – were now mounted in front of the driver behind a new 17-inch (432mm) two-spoke steering wheel with half horn ring. An impressive array of toggle switches – fully labelled and illuminated – shared the centre of the dash with a push-button starter, the ignition switch and the cigar lighter.

The front of the car now featured flashing indicators and side lights on the tops of the wings. The front grille was also new, and there were spotlights where the air intakes had been.

The front seats, much more generous than before especially in the thickness of the backrest, now had picnic trays set into their backs. There was best-quality Wilton carpet underfoot and, as before, all the doors had timber cappings, finishing off an interior that was difficult to improve on at any price, never mind at over £1,500 (tax included) for the basic non-overdrive 2.4.

However, it was what could not be seen that made the MkII such an improvement over the MkI. The rear track was wider to allay fears about high-speed instability, and the roll centre was raised to curb body roll.

There was still strong understeer, not helped by the five-turns lock-to-lock unassisted steering on early cars that made correction of oversteer an imprecise art, but there was far less puddingy roll. What is more, the ride was an excellent compromise between high-speed firmness with good damping and low-speed absorption of bumps. Only rough surfaces taken at speed ruffled the live rear axle's composure.

The four-wheel Dunlop discs were well up to the job of stopping the car time and time again from three-figure speeds, and with the accelerative powers of the biggest engine they

Inside, the dash now had main instruments in front of the driver with minor gauges and toggle switches on a fold-down centre panel. The steering wheel was new and the whole interior was lighter and more airy.

avec plus de 30 innovations pour votre confort et votre sécurité

Placés sous le signe de la perfection dans l'aménagement, les nouveaux modèles de la série « Mark 2 » présentent des traits de confort exclusifs et un luxe de commodités nouvelles qui, ajoutés à la puissance, à la robustesse bien connues des Jaguar, à leur merveilleux silence, en font les voitures à hautes performances les plus luxueusement équipées de l'année. C'est, à un degré jamais atteint auparavant, l'alliance de la perfection technique et de la distinction... C'est le superbe aboutissement d'efforts guidés par les hautes exigences de qualité dont Jaguar s'est toujours inspiré.

JAGUAR

Avec freins à disque aux 4 roues

Importateurs exclusifs

pour la Suisse romande et le Tessin: **GARAGE CLAPARÈDE S.A. Genève, M. Fleury, administrateur**
pour la Suisse allemande: **EMIL FREY AG, MOTORFAHRZEUGE, ZÜRICH**

Big bumpers, bootlid and bonnet were among the few carry-over outer parts from the MkI models, but the MkII had a wider rear track thanks to a wider axle casing – so handling was improved.

needed to be. The 3.8 was a 110mph (177kph) cruiser in the days when most cars were struggling to do 80 (129), and with either the manual or the automatic 'box it had the kind of pick-up that the average driver was just not used to: 0–100mph (161kph) took only 25 seconds, and a quick change to third at 60 (97) to get past a dawdler on a fast A road would have the 29.9cwt (1,520kg) Jag touching 80 in only 5.3 seconds. With overdrive – which virtually every manual 3.8 had – the engine was only turning over at 3,800rpm at 100mph.

This new big-engined car used the 3,781cc 220bhp version of the XK, lifted directly from the big MkIX, and was really aimed at the North American market where it would be most appreciated. It came with the Thornton Powr-Lok limited slip diff as standard and was priced at £1,779

(including tax) on its introduction in the UK, with the standard non-overdrive Moss gearbox, with or without Laycock overdrive, or the optional Borg-Warner three-speed automatic.

The 210bhp 3,442cc engine with the B-Type head used in the 120mph (193kph) 3.4 MkII was fitted unchanged, although performance was down compared with the MkI 3.4 because of the new car's increased weight.

At the bottom of the MkII range was the meek and mild 2.4, indiscernible from its more powerful brothers unless you got near enough to see the badge on the front grille. The 2.4 litre engine was given a new B-Type cylinder head for freer breathing and more torque. It could put out a respectable 120bhp at 5,750rpm, compared with the old unit's 112bhp at the same engine speed. The Solex carbs remained, however, and with the extra 1cwt (51kg) of weight to pull the MkII 2.4 couldn't do the 'ton', and had scarcely any economy advantage either, 16–18mpg being the norm.

The Moss gearbox with its weak synchromesh and heavy clutch was hard work and many buyers were opting for the Borg-Warner three-speed automatic – just stick the column lever in Drive, floor the

throttle and let the self-shifter rocket the 3.8 up to 60mph (97kph) in 9.8 seconds [the middle gear was good for 80mph (129kph)], and the 'ton' in a further 19 seconds.

Detail improvements were made to the MkII every few months during its eight-year run, but the only truly major improvement (apart from changes to the piston rings to improve oil consumption) was the option of power steering from September 1960. This made low-

In 3.4 and especially 3.8 form the MkII was an extremely quick saloon. In fact, with the bigger engine and manual gearbox it was quicker than 80 per cent of contemporary two-seater sports cars. Top speed was 125mph (201kph) with 0–60mph (97kph) attainable in 8.5 seconds.

Daimler V8: The Crinkle-cut Jag

The Browns Lane engineers saw little future for the crude, ugly and badly made SP250 sports car when Jaguar acquired Daimler in 1960 (it died in 1964), but they had a lot of time for Edward Turner's V8 engine. For its power (140bhp gross at 5,800rpm) it was a compact unit, although oversquare in its dimensions (76.2 by 69.85mm giving 2,548cc) with its cylinder banks arranged in a 90-degree vee formation. The block was iron for rigidity, the interchangeable heads in alloy for lightness. Hemispherical combustion chambers meant efficiency and high revving ability, especially as the pushrods were short, Duralumin-centred designs, operated by a single high-mounted camshaft. The crankshaft was short and strong with five 2-inch-diameter (51mm) main bearings. The engine breathed through a pair of SU HD6 carbs.

To install the unit in the MkII shell to create the so-called Daimler 2½ litre V8 saloon, a number of minor alterations were needed. The water pump, now mounted centrally on the front face of the cylinder block, was

The V8 engine was originally designed for the bizarre Daimler SP250 sports car, a car William Lyons always hated.

integrated with a double-grooved pulley carrying the cooling fan. One belt took drive from the crankshaft – via a spring-loaded jockey wheel – for the water pump, while the belt in the other groove drove the dynamo. There was yet another double pulley where the fan used to be on the end of the crankshaft damper, driving the optional Burman power steering pump. Other minor changes included changing the angle of the oil filter and a new paper-element air filter.

The Daimler V8 and Borg-Warner Model 35 automatic gearbox weighed 592lb (269kg), 140lb (64kg) less than the 2.4 engine and auto 'box, so that meant revised spring rates and softer damper settings to compensate. The Daimler only came with automatic transmission in its original incarnation, using the Model 35 unit without the speed-hold facility of the MkII's DG 'box. Jaguar assumed, probably quite rightly, that few Daimler buyers would want to change gear themselves when an obedient auto-shifter could do it for them. The Daimler was the most powerful car to use the Model 35 at the time, so there was a heat exchanger built into the bottom of the engine's radiator to cool the oil. From the outside the Daimler could be identified by its new fluted

radiator with a 'D' motif where the leaping jaguar normally sat. At the back, on the bootlid, the mazak-plated numberplate/reversing light nacelle was now fluted, and there were 'Daimler' and 'V8' scripts as well as the usual Jaguar 'automatic' badge. There was yet another 'D' motif where the 'Disc Brakes' badge normally sat on the MkII, and of course the hub caps now had a 'D' in their centre raised sections.

It was inside that the Daimler, launched in October 1962, differed most noticeably from the Jaguar. There was no longer a centre console, just a carpeted bulge, with the heater controls, radio speaker and a new type of ashtray fixed to a separate veneered walnut panel bolted to the underneath of the dash, which meant that a new type of split bench seat could be used with twin armrests. It was still leather-trimmed and still did not recline as standard, and for some reason Jaguar did not see fit to supply Daimler buyers with picnic trays. They did get an identical dashboard, however, with the 2.4's speedo and manual choke slide control, although the rev-counter was red-lined at 6,000rpm. The V8 had three interior lights to the Jaguar's four and a new type of solid-backed foam headlining in an attempt to give a tad more headroom.

Compared with the bigger-engined MkIIs, with which it competed on price if not appeal, the Daimler was a far more genteel machine. The engine was turbine-like in its smoothness up to – and beyond – the 6,500rpm red line, but it needed to be because with the low 4.55:1 rear axle giving only 16.6mph (26.7kph) per 1,000rpm, it was pulling maximum revs at its

respectable 110mph (177kph) top speed. This was not very relaxing and certainly not conducive to good fuel consumption, which worked out at a thirsty average 16mpg. Still, there was plenty of acceleration in hand – 0–60mph (97kph) in 13 seconds, 0–100mph (161kph) in 42 seconds – even if the Borg-Warner automatic did get a little jerky in its changes
at anything but gentle speeds. If anything, the Daimler handled in a rather more nimble fashion than the MkII, with less weight over the front wheels meaning less understeer and generally lighter control, although the steering was still too slow-geared to be truly sporting and lacked feel when the optional power assistance was specified.

Over the years the Daimler V8 changed little. Jaguar soon caught on to the under-gearing problem and in April 1964 a higher 4.27:1 final drive was used, adding 4mph (6.5kph) to the top speed and very little to the acceleration times, although the relatively poor low-speed torque of the V8 was rather more obvious now. A new type of Borg-Warner Model 35 auto 'box was fitted from June of the same year, with 'D1' and 'D2' settings on the column selector. In 'D1' the car set off from rest in first, while in 'D2' first was locked out and the car would pull away more slowly but more smoothly and economically. From February 1967 you could order your Daimler V8 with the Jaguar all-synchromesh manual gearbox, with or without overdrive; this had little effect on the top speed but improved acceleration considerably. Even so, manual transmission was a little-seen option.

The biggest changes in the small Daimler's career came in September 1967 when, in line with the 240/340

Jaguars introduced at the same time, it became the 250 V8. As with the bargain-basement Jags, the 250 was given slimline bumpers, the same modified front and rear valances, and new-style hub caps, while inside there was a 420/Sovereign-style padded dash top and door cappings (with veneer only on the top edge of the window sills) and a new-style perforated hide for the seats. The front bench now at last had reclining backrests as standard and the Daimler retained its fog lights, unlike the 240/340 with their standard equipment cut down to the bone. Marles Varamatic assistance for the steering was now available as an option in place of the more orthodox Burman system previously offered, and among the other mechanical changes were new pistons and the fitting of an alternator instead of the dynamo used until then.

The 250 V8 was priced at £1,697 for the automatic car, putting it on an exactly equal price footing to the overdrive-equipped S-Type 3.4, and it stayed in production until August

The Daimler V8 showed only minimal differences from the MkII, mainly the 'crinkle-cut' grille. The car appealed to older, more sedate drivers who did not like the 'flash' image of the Jaguar.

1969, the last right-hand drive car of the series coming off the lines on the 5th of that month, so it actually outlived the 240 by three months. Most Daimler V8s stayed in Britain and none were officially exported to North America.

What is now thought of as a kind of second-best alternative to a MkII was actually a much-sought-after car in its day, appreciated by more mature drivers who did not want the aggression of the MkII or the sheer bulk of the MkX or Daimler's massive (but very fast) Majestic Major.

MkIIs on the track

The MkII, in 3.8 litre form, started its racing career in 1960, following in the successful footsteps of the MkI 3.4. It was to dominate the saloon car racing scene for three years, always in private hands as Jaguar had officially pulled out of competition in 1956. They were capable hands, however, and those three years provided some of the most exciting moments in saloon racing history.

Tommy Sopwith's Equipe Endeavour and John Coombs were the major players, and with big names such as Roy Salvadori, Jack Sears, Bruce McLaren, John Surtees, Mike Parkes, Sir Gawaine Baillie and, later, Graham Hill, there was intense rivalry between teams, so much so that no individual Jaguar driver would become British Saloon Car Champion.

Right from the beginning the big American saloons were showing their mettle, albeit not too reliably at first. At Silverstone in May 1961 the power of Dan Gurney's Chevy Impala looked set to trounce the MkIIs until his nearside rear wheel came off, leaving the way wide open for Graham Hill in the Coombs MkII. In 1962 Hill took the MkII to victory at Oulton Park, Silverstone, Mallory Park and Snetterton, and really became the man to beat in the compact Jaguars.

The American challenge reared its head again at Brands Hatch in 1962, when a pair of Chevy IIs driven by Peter Sachs and Charles Kelsey successfully took on Roy Salvadori's Coombs car. Even the faithful XK engine could not match the straight-line wallop of the big V8s, especially as the Yanks' suspension was thoroughly sorted by British tuning specialist Alexander Engineering.

Salvadori regained Jaguar prestige against the Chevys at Crystal Palace, but the writing was on the wall for the big cats.

The following year started well for the MkIIs with a win for Graham Hill at Oulton Park in April, while at the Goodwood Easter meeting MkIIs took the first five places, with Hill the victor again. However, it was not long before the Yanks were on the scene again, with Jack Sears behind the wheel of the 7 litre Galaxie, which easily trounced Salvadori into second place at Silverstone in May. Sears took first comfortably at Crystal Palace, followed by the Jaguars of Salvadori and Hill, Baillie's Ford taking fourth. Sears went on to beat the Jaguars at Snetterton and Silverstone, and at the August Bank Holiday meeting at Brands Hatch Jim Clark took a Galaxie to a win over Hill's MkII, Salvadori taking third.

One of the last great MkII outings was at the Brands Hatch six-hour race in 1963. It was a star-studded event with Brabham, Gurney, Baillie and Jopp out in the Galaxies, and Mike Salmon, Roy Salvadori and Denny Hulme fielding the big cats. The weather was against the Fords on this occasion, with Gurney spinning off in the heavy rain. The Hulme and Salvadori partnership was victorious after the Salmon/Sutcliffe MkII was disqualified for having oversize inlet valves.

It was the Lotus Cortina that finally finished off the MkII on the track in Britain, and from 1964 onwards Jaguars were rarely seen in the thick of the action.

As for rallying, by the time the MkII came on to the scene in 1959/60 the sport was changing in Europe, with

more special, rough stages that were hardly ideal for a car of the MkII's size and weight. Still, for a brief period it did find a little success. In 1960 a pair of MkIIs driven by Frenchmen José Behra/René Richard and Englishmen Bobby Parkes/Geoff Howarth each won a Coupe des Alpes in the tough Alpine Rally and came third and fifth overall. Only six other cars got a Coupe that year. In 1961 Sir Gawaine Baillie and Peter Jopp won their class, but Bobby Parkes and his two-man crew of George Humble and Roy Dixon had less luck the following year, their 3.8 holing its sump and, later, a piston during the Monza high-speed tests. In 1963 Dan Margulies, navigated by John Brown, did well early on the Mont Ventoux stage, but later lost the bonnet at speed and was finally finished off by braking problems.

The MkII made its first appearance in the Monte Carlo Rally in 1961, when Philip Walton's car came in a lowly 130th, although he at least had the satisfaction of a win in the optional Mont Agel hillclimb stage. One of the last appearances of a MkII in the Monte was John Cuff's 3.8 in 1966, which along with nine other British contenders was disqualified for infringing headlamp dipped beam regulations.

The MkII had little involvement in the RAC Rally, although Jack Sears's excellent performance against the more suitable Saabs and Austin-Healeys in the 1960 event resulted in a creditable fourth overall.

The Tour de France was an ideal event for a car of the MkII's capabilities, mixing road sections with circuit racing and hillclimbs. As far as Jaguars are concerned, the event will always be associated with

Frenchman Bernard Costen whose white cars won the touring car category every year from 1960 to 1963. Just as in saloon car racing, it was the Americans who challenged the Jaguars first in 1963, where the greater power of the 7 litre Galaxies could overhaul the Coventry machines on the straights. Even then, luck was on the quick Frenchman's side and he gave the MkII its fourth Tour win after the Galaxie lost its sump plug on a level crossing. It was the Mustang that finally banished the MkII in 1964, and Costen had to make do with a third.

A quartet of 3.8s at the 1962 Aintree 200 meeting, led by Jack Sears in the Equipe Endeavour entry (Neill Bruce).

speed manoeuvres much less muscle-building (the car was always praised for its 38-foot (11.58m) turning circle), but the combination of extreme lightness and low gearing was not a happy one for keen drivers. With manual steering there was always the option of a quicker box offering 1.2 fewer turns, but with – for most drivers – intolerable low-speed heaviness.

The heating and ventilation were never any good. Jaguar tried to improve the matter with a water valve hitched up to the temperature control flap and operated by a hot/cold lever, but many American owners resorted to bulky air-conditioning units, either mounted in the boot or under the dash.

The other significant change came in 1965, when the all-synchro gearbox finally found its way into the compact Jaguar, giving a far lighter, quicker and shorter-travel change with strong synchromesh on all four gears. There was also a new Borg-Warner Type 35 gearbox to replace the DG unit, with P-R-N-D1-D2-L positions on the selector, the 'D2' position locking out bottom gear altogether for smoother about-town driving.

Less welcome, in September 1966, was the introduction of plastic Ambla upholstery, banishing leather seat facings to the options list for the first time on a Jaguar.

With S-Type (and soon 420) production in full swing, Jaguar were keen to give the MkII real value-for-money appeal, and to keep costs down it was necessary to cheapen the car's equipment levels. You can spot a late MkII by its dummy horn grilles, replacing the Lucas fog lamps. The last MkIIs were built in September 1967, but that was not quite the end of the line for compact Jaguars. Enter, with little fanfare, the 240 and 340.

Taking the simplification of the MkII range a stage further, the most noticeable thing about the new entry-level Jaguars were the slimline S-Type-style bumpers front and rear; the now more exposed valances were reshaped in sympathy. There were new 420-style hubcaps, while the Ambla seats and dummy grilles were as they had been on the later MkIIs. The woodwork inside was lighter and had less figuring in the veneer, while the carpets were now cheaper nylon affairs, replacing the Wilton. Finally, there was a new plastic toolkit holder in the boot, instead of the old wood and metal case.

The 240 had a new straight-port E-Type cylinder head, which with the twin SU carbs meant that power was boosted from 120bhp at 5,750rpm to 133bhp at 5,500rpm, while torque was up from 138lb ft at 3,000rpm to 146lb ft at 3,700rpm. The 240 kept the dashboard choke control but there was improved water circulation with a full-flow system and a water-heated induction manifold with a built-in water rail. Other changes included a wax thermostat, side entry cables on the distributor cap and a paper element oil filter. These later XK engines also had ribbed cam-covers.

The 240/340 models of 1967 were slightly cheapened entry-level cars with Ambla plastic trim. With its improved breathing, the cheapest Jaguar could now achieve 100mph (161kph) easily. Slimline bumpers are an instant recognition point.

Amazingly, there was a price increase of only £23 over the previous 2.4 manual and manual overdrive models, while the 340 manual-change cars were exactly the same price as before and the automatic versions of the 240 and 340 were actually £16 and £39 cheaper respectively.

The 240's extra power meant that it could now beat 100mph easily (top speed was around 105) with much better acceleration than the old 2.4: with the all-synchromesh 'box 60mph (97kph) was attainable in 11.5 seconds, and 30–50mph (48–80kph) in top in 9.1 seconds. Moreover, the 240 was smoother and quieter yet retained excellent flexibility, with the ability to pull away smoothly in top from as little as 10mph (16kph).

The 340, unchanged mechanically, drove more or less like the old 3.4, although if John Bolster's *Autosport* road test of a manual overdrive car in 1968 was anything to go by, it was a touch faster. With its 124mph (200kph) top speed and 8.8-second 0–60mph (97kph) time, it was almost as fast as the discontinued 3.8. Then again, Bolster's figures were usually on the optimistic side!

The 340 lasted only 12 months, until September 1968, and is the rarest of the MkII-based cars with only 2,265 right-hand-drive and 535 left-hand-drive examples being built. The 240 was much more popular and lasted until April 1969, by which time 3,716 rhd and 730 lhd cars had been built.

Although officially the 3.8 engine was never fitted to a 240/340 shell, Jaguar did build nine 380s between December and May 1968 to special order for customers who had

previously run MkII 3.8s. All had 3.8 grille badges and some even had '380' badges on the bootlid. All are said to have had leather upholstery and most manual transmission. Only one 380 is known to survive.

Powerful and high-geared, the MkII is still a consummate outside-lane machine with the legs, and the heart, to run with the fit young moderns. A healthy manual example with overdrive is still at its best reeling in those long grey strips of road at three-figure velocities, wind noise and

The 240 was smoother and quieter, yet retained excellent flexibility, able to pull away smoothly in top from 10mph

a certain instability in side winds the only deterrent to really pressing on; 100mph (161kph) represents a cantering 3,800rpm in overdrive, so at 70 or 80 (113 or 129) the twin-cam XK lump is barely ticking over. Such is its abundant torque that it will storm hills in overdrive that would leave multi-valve youngsters looking breathlessly for a lower cog. Flick up the overdrive switch on the column and you get really vigorous direct-drive pick-up – watch the needles sweep rapidly, in unison, around the handsome Smiths dials to 110mph (177kph) and 5,500rpm as lesser cars recede in the mirror.

Around town the clutch pumps up thigh muscles and the unassisted steering requires enormous effort at anything below 20mph (32kph). The Moss 'box can be mastered once you remember to use all the clutch travel and blip coming down into second. Third and top snick in nicely, but

The MkII 3.8 was favoured road transport of many in the racing world, including Graham Hill and Colin Chapman. Here Chapman takes delivery from 'Lofty' England.

you are into the realms of roughness as the XK betrays its age and its long stroke. Better to exploit the torque, with smooth seamless pulling from 15 or 20mph (24 or 32kph) even in overdrive top – using the gears becomes optional.

The nose-heavy weight distribution equals determined understeer in the MkII. Combine that with low gearing – nearly five turns, lock-to-lock – and a sloppy, dead sector around the straight-ahead and you have a car that likes to take bends early and be held tight into them if you do not want to swing out wider than you intended. The limited-slip diff puts the power down pretty well in the dry so you can tramp quite hard on the throttle when pulling out of a corner.

In the wet the tail will skip out on even a fairly light throttle, and that means lots of wheel twirling to set the car straight again. The heavy leaf-sprung Panhard-rod-located rear axle does not like bumps, and it will hop and bounce a bit when asked to perform on tight, poorly-surfaced corners under a heavy foot.

Chasing after even a modest modern will be quite hard work in the roly-poly MkII, your confidence hardly boosted by slippery seats that contribute little in terms of location in bends: tighten your seat belt and grip the wheel harder is the only answer.

You make up the time between the bends and, once again, the hard-charging executives – or even off-duty racing drivers like Graham Hill – who bought 3.8s in their thousands reckoned that it was worth putting up with less than pin-sharp handling at the bargain-basement price.

The demise of the MkII left the door wide open for a new generation of compact, quality performance saloons in the mould of BMW's 5 Series. Jaguar's retirement from this sector of the market was an almost

bottom, with its exaggerated lever movement, is a straight-cut 'crash' and shrieks like a siren, an exciting, evocative noise familiar from many a film soundtrack. Going back into second you have to feel it through gently until the lever hits home with a snick.

Along not-too-demanding B roads the MkII reels in the straights with full-blooded gusto, its classic double-barrelled cam whine dominating all other sounds as you wind the engine out to 4,000rpm in the intermediates. Much more than that, however, and

Duncan Hamilton and Mike Hawthorn had planned to produce an estate version of the compact Jaguar. In the end just one was built and used by the factory as a rally service barge. This is stylist Roy Nockolds' clay model of the car.

fatal mistake, and it is no accident that, as I write, a 'new' MkII is being readied for production.

Today, the charisma of the MkII transcends mere nuts and bolts. It broke no new technical ground and did nothing much better than most other upper-middle-market luxury cars (except go very fast in a straight line), yet somehow it had a blend of good qualities that ingratiated itself with the car-buying public in a way that few saloons ever have.

Buying Hints

1. Structurally the MkI and MkII are identical, so all the points raised in Chapter 4 are also relevant here – the sills, rear seat pan and spring hangers are all crucial areas. The good news is that the MkII is much better served by specialists than the MkI.

2. Poor window sealing around the glasses means that the door bottoms are rust-prone, especially when the drain holes become blocked, although the frames themselves are usually saveable.

3. The double-skinned rear valance is a custom-made mud trap with road dirt being forced up from the rear wheels. On the bootlid, rust comes through along the bottom edge where the sealing rubber collects water.

4. Again, all engine and mechanical comments for the MkI

apply. There should be 40psi of oil pressure on the move, and not too much blue smoke; beware of rear main bearing oil seal leaks. Also, check that the engine and chassis numbers match – 2.4s have been converted to 3.8s before now.

5. Look out for 240s/340s that have been converted to MkIIs; 240/340 chassis numbers begin with IJ.

6. Daimler V8s tend to command about the same price as the 2.4 Jaguar MkII, or 20–25 per cent less than the comparable 3.4 and 3.8. The Daimler engine is a well-known oil burner even when in sound condition, so a little blue smoke should not be a worry. Look for 35–40psi of oil pressure on the move, and 15psi at tick-over. Carbon build-up can cause the valves to stick open, and the aluminium heads are subject to corrosion.

The S-Type
and 420

With neither the MkII's performance nor the all-round refinement of the XJ6, it is fashionable to dismiss the S-Type as a poor relation among 1960s Jaguars. It is easy to forget, however, that until the advent of the XJ6 in 1968 the S-Type was regarded by many as the best all-round saloon car that Jaguar had yet built.

As a package it was a fine compromise, with MkX comfort and roadholding thanks to the best independent rear suspension in the business, grafted on to a compact MkII-based shell. With its long-tailed MkX-like rear end, it had more prestige appeal than the MkII, but managed to keep costs down by using as many of the existing components as possible, although only the bonnet and front doors were identical to those of the smaller car.

Since MkII prices have gone sky-high the S-Type is now starting to gain a following as people begin to recognise its many fine qualities. The 420s, especially in Daimler form, are even cheaper, and deliver all the S-Type's advantages together with performance that is very nearly the equal of the MkII 3.8 – a manual 420 will top 125mph (201kph) and touch 60 (97) in less than 10 seconds.

The S-Type, launched in 1963, was never intended to be a replacement for the MkII. Jaguar reasoned that the latter would always have its followers because it was cheaper and just that bit faster. In the end the MkII, in 240/340 form, actually ended up outliving the S-Type by a year or so.

A longer tail and a flatter roofline gave the S-Type of 1963 a new profile, although the shell was based closely on that of the MkII. It came with the 3.4 or 3.8 litre engine.

NKX 967D

The body style changes were calculated to make the car look a little more impressive. At the front, the MkII's face was still there, but to balance it out against the completely new tail section the headlights, still in the same position, had their surrounds stretched to give a hooded, 'eyelid' effect. The auxiliary lamps were also now set more deeply into the wings. While the MkII's sidelights sat in 'blisters' on the brow of the wings, on the 'S' they were at the bottom of the panel next to new-style wraparound indicator units. The front grille had a thicker surround and centre section.

Like the MkX, the S-Type had shallow-section bumpers front and rear with rather less aggressive overriders than the MkII – these would later also become a feature of the 240 and 340 cars. From the rear door backwards the car was restyled on MkX lines with elongated wing panels, low wheel cut-outs and the same type of slim taillight clusters let into the ends of wings rather than just bolted on MkII-style. Longer and flatter, the bootlid also followed MkX practice and had a similar style of numberplate housing. The boot was also much more roomy, with 19 cubic feet (0.53 cubic metre) of luggage space compared to the MkII's 12 (0.34). All told, the S-Type was 7 inches (178mm) longer than the MkII, but still a good foot (305mm) shorter and much narrower than the bloated, outsized MkX.

A more subtle change was to be found in the new car's roof-line, which was longer and flatter than that of the MkII thanks to a slightly more upright rear window, all in the name of increased rear headroom.

With its purposeful twin tail pipes, the S-Type had its badging and engine size identification on the centre of the bootlid in chrome script, and as with the MkII there was another badge on the grille, announcing the engine size.

Meanwhile, a great deal of chopping and changing had gone on under the

Jaguar S-Type 3.4
1963-68

ENGINE:
In-line six-cylinder, cast iron block, alloy head, hemispherical combustion chambers

Bore x stroke	83 x 106mm
Capacity	3,442cc
Valves	Twin ohc, one inlet, one exhaust
Compression ratio	8:1 (7:1 and 9:1 optional)
Carburettors	Two 1.75in HD6 SUs
Power	210bhp at 5,500rpm (gross)
Torque	216lb ft at 3,000rpm (gross)

TRANSMISSION:
Four-speed manual with synchromesh on second, third and top. All-synchro gearbox from September 1965. Overdrive and automatic optional
Final drive   3.54:1 (manual/auto) or 3.77:1 (overdrive)

SUSPENSION:
Front: independent semi-trailing double wishbones, coil springs, telescopic dampers and anti-roll bar.
Rear: independent lower wishbone/upper drive shaft link with radius arms and twin coil springs
Steering   recirculating ball, 4.7/3.5 turns lock-to-lock

BRAKES:
Dunlop discs front and rear

WHEELS:
Bolt-on 15-inch (381mm) pressed steel, or optional 5K knock-off wire wheels with Dunlop RS5 6.40 x 16 or SP 41 185 x 15 tyres

BODYWORK:
Unitary all-steel construction

LENGTH:	15ft 7in (4.75m)
WIDTH:	5ft 6¼in (1.68m)
HEIGHT:	4ft 7¾in (1.42m)
WEIGHT:	32cwt (1,627kg)

MAX SPEED:	N/a
0–60mph (97kph)	13.2 seconds

PRICE NEW (1963): £1,669 inc PT

Jaguar S-Type 3.8
1963-68

As S-Type 3.4 except:

Bore x stroke	87 x 106mm
Capacity	3,781cc
Power	220bhp at 5,500rpm (gross)
Torque	240lb ft at 3,000rpm (gross)

WEIGHT:	33cwt (1,678kg)
(distributed 53.5% front, 46.5% rear)	

MAX SPEED:	120mph (193kph)
0–60mph (97kph)	10.2 seconds

PRICE NEW (1963): £1,759 inc PT

Jaguar 420 and Daimler Sovereign
1966-69

As S-Type 3.4 except:

Bore x stroke	92.07 x 106mm
Capacity	4,235cc
Carburettors	Two 2in HD8 SUs
Power	245bhp at 5,500rpm (gross)
Torque	283lb ft at 3,750 rpm (gross)

LENGTH:	15ft 7½in (4.76m)
WIDTH:	5ft 7in (1.7m)
HEIGHT:	4ft 8¼in (1.43m)
WEIGHT:	33cwt (1,678kg)
(distributed 55.5% front, 44.5% rear)	

BRAKES:	Girling discs, 11in (279mm) front, 11⅜in (289mm) rear

MAX SPEED:	123mph (199kph)
0–60mph (97kph)	9.9 seconds

PRICE NEW (1966): £1,930 inc PT (Jaguar)

PRODUCTION FIGURES:

3.4S	10,036
3.8S	15,135
420	9,801
Sovereign	5,829

S-Types gripped and handled better than the MkII thanks to Jaguar's superb new independent rear suspension borrowed from the E-Type and MkX. On the S-Type the headlights were hooded slightly to differentiate the car from the cheaper MkII; note also the slimmer bumpers.

skin in order to graft on the independent rear suspension, with the greatest attention being focused on the rear seatpan area. On the MkII the semi-elliptic leaf springs were located in channel-section mountings at the end of the main longitudinal chassis rails. To allow adequately strong mounting of the S-Type's new suspension, these box-section rails were continued over the rear wheel arches to the back of the car, on the way being welded to the double-skinned boot floor. The spare wheel was now mounted in a central well in the floor and there were twin 7-gallon (32-litre) tanks mounted inside each rear wing with a changeover switch on the dashboard.

Under the direction of William Heynes and Bob Knight, Jaguar had seriously begun to think of independent rear suspension for production cars in 1955, although the very first experiments can be traced back to a prototype lightweight army vehicle built by the company in 1944. The systems were tested on MkI and MkII saloons, but the first production Jaguar to use independent rear suspension was the E-Type in March 1961, followed in October by the MkX. The basic design – with numerous alterations – lived on until the demise of the XJ-S coupés in 1996.

The design worked on the double-wishbone principle, although the top wishbone was formed by the fixed-length driveshaft – the S-Type's driveshaft length was somewhere between that of the E-Type and that of the MkX. Big alloy hub carriers were attached to the bottom of the tubular forked lower arms with the driveshafts running into them, and the Salisbury 4HU diff – with its Powr-Lok limited slip device – was rigidly mounted inside a large bridge-type pressed steel subframe. This was especially clever, as it allowed the whole suspension assembly – diff, driveshafts and all – to be removed from the car just by undoing a few bolts. There were two small combined spring/damper units on either side, anchored to the lower wishbone and the top of the subframe. The brakes – Dunlop 10-inch discs – were mounted inboard to cut down on unsprung weight.

Fore and aft location was provided by forward-facing radius arms attached to the lower members and located on the box sections. There was no metal-to-metal contact between the bodyshell and the suspension subframe thanks to the V-shaped Metalastik mountings bolted to reinforced flanges at the outer end of the subframe. These, more than anything else, were responsible for the suspension's superb road shock insulation.

Mechanically, the rest of the S-Type was almost pure MkII: double wishbone and coil spring front suspension, front disc brakes, and either a 3.4 or 3.8 litre engine with the same transmission options. There was no 2.4 litre version of the S-Type, as the baby of the Jaguar engine range would have found the S-Type's 3cwt (153kg) of extra bulk a severe embarrassment.

Where the 'S' did differ technically from the MkII was in its steering. Jaguar had heeded road test moans about the MkII's low gearing and reduced the number of turns lock-to-lock from 4.5 to 3.5. The Burman-built pump had a larger operating ram and there was also a torsion-bar link

between the input shaft and the hydraulic valve, which, by introducing a pre-determined load between the movement of the wheel and the opening of the valve, had the effect of increasing the degree of steering sensitivity. The standard 15-inch (381mm) wheels, usually shod with Dunlop SP41 tyres, now had wider 5½-inch (140mm) rims, thus increasing the track of the S-Type by a useful inch or so over the MkII. Knock-off wire wheels, a rare S-Type option, actually reduced the rear track by 1¼ inches (32mm).

The interior of the S-Type was a mixture of MkX and MkII. The centre panel of the dash was veneered instead of black leathergrain, and there was a new centre console and parcel shelf. The front seats were thinner and there were no rear picnic tables, but they did benefit from armrests.

The 420 was the ultimate variation on Jaguar's compact saloon theme, designed to fill the gap while the largely new XJ6 was developed. The grille and four headlights echoed the MkX, and at the time it was considered the best-looking car in Jaguar's saloon range.

The cabin of the S-Type had an upmarket air, more MkX than MkII in most of its details. The dashboard, still richly veneered, had a new larger type of centre instrument panel trimmed in wood rather than the MkII's leathergrain. Underneath there was a full-width parcel shelf with a padded edge and a pull-out picnic table under the central switch panel, perhaps as some kind of consolation for the lack of picnic trays in the backs of the front seats. There was a new centre console, of a more rounded, integrated design than that of the MkII, which provided a home for the pull-out ashtray, heater controls and optional radio. Heating and ventilation arrangements were again borrowed from the MkX and were alleged to be greatly improved over the MkII, which frankly would not have been difficult, but they still could not match cheaper cars such as the new Ford Cortina.

There was still wood on the doors and cantrails and the usual high standard of interior lighting with lamps on the centre pillar on each side plus a map-reading light and two-position dimmer switch for the panel lights.

Leather was still a feature of all the seat facings, but the S-Type had a semi-bench type of front seat rather like that of the V8 Daimler – it was actually two separate front seats that met in the middle. There was a more elaborate type of swinging link adjustment, whereby the front of the seat lowered in an arc, and the back was raised whenever the seat was adjusted forward. The back rests reclined as standard on the 'S' and each of the passengers had a separate fold-down centre armrest. Less padding in the rear seat squabs meant a few welcome inches of legroom for rear passengers, while a thinner squab, with an extra 1½ inches (38mm) of rake, took full advantage of the increased headroom afforded by the new roofline and more upright rear window.

At £1,669 for the standard 3.4, and £1,758 for the 3.8, Jaguar priced the S-Type precisely between the MkII and MkX. Power steering added £55 while the Borg-Warner DG automatic transmission would have lightened the buyer's wallet by a further £126. Overdrive was a worthwhile fitting at £56.

The S-Type was well received on both sides of the Atlantic, and was welcomed as a major improvement over the MkII, which had nonetheless won the 'Best Imported Car of the Year' title for a number of years on the trot. Some of the critics had a bad word or

The S-Type was well received on both sides of the Atlantic and was a major improvement over the MkII

two for the car's styling (*Car and Driver* thought that the styling of the front and rear ends was 'somehow mismatched'), but the ever-respectful British journals kept their feelings about its styling to themselves, and had almost nothing but praise for the new mid-range Jaguar.

Everyone regarded its ride as outstanding and *Motor* placed the S-Type among Europe's most comfortable cars, soft but well-controlled and with none of the rattle and shake associated with live-axled cars, together with much-improved stability over poor road surfaces compared with the MkII.

It was almost certainly the best-handling Jaguar saloon up to that time. There was much more roadholding, especially on wet surfaces, and with its higher-geared steering and power assistance it was much easier to place

Italian S-Types by Bertone and Frua

In 1966 Bertone unveiled a two-door coupé, called the Jaguar FT, based on the 3.8 litre S-Type saloon. The idea was initiated by Dr G. Tarquini, an Italian Jaguar importer, who saw the need for a more modern-looking Jaguar saloon with better visibility, engine access and use of space. Styled by Bertone's young protégé, Gandini, the car had a completely new interior with a much improved heating and ventilation system incorporating air-conditioning. Although it weighed about the same as an S-Type, this handbuilt coupé was about 10mph (16kph) faster.

Jaguar gave every assistance with the project but showed no serious interest in producing the car, which was talked of as being sold in Britain at an all-in price of £3,673 – at a time when a 3.8 litre 'S' cost £1,813. There were plans to build 50 FT coupés, but the car remained a one-off.

Frua built a similar two-door coupé (which survives in the UK), in appearance very like the contemporary Maserati Mexico, another Frua design. Again it was a one-off.

Bertone built this handsome coupé on the basis of an S-Type in 1966, when it was displayed at the Geneva show. Frua built a similar car, but neither progressed beyond the prototype stage.

in corners, being responsive to steering torque and not just wheel movement thanks to that torsion-bar link between the input shaft and the hydraulic valve. It was still too light to give any true feel, but a great improvement all the same. The S-Type was no E-Type, of course; there was lots of roll and considerable understeer, not to mention head-turning tyre squeal on corners taken very quickly.

Performance was blunted a little by the extra weight of the new rear suspension, but the S-Type – especially in 3.8 litre manual form – was still a fast car, capable of 125mph (201kph) (manual) and 0–60mph (97kph) in 10 seconds, with 100 (161) coming up in around half a minute from the standstill.

The S-Type changed very little during its fairly short lifetime. The biggest improvement came in March 1965

when the Moss 'box was finally replaced by the all-synchromesh Jaguar-built unit, first seen as an option in October the previous year. It had a cast-iron casing to absorb noise and retain rigidity and there were Warner inertia-lock baulk rings on every forward gear to prevent them being engaged before synchronisation was complete.

A high proportion of S-Types came equipped with automatic

transmission, either the ageing DG unit or later (from 1965 onwards) the much more up-to-date Model 35, both built in England by Borg-Warner.

Power losses in the torque converter, not to mention a little extra weight, took their toll on the automatic S-Type's performance. A 3.8 S-Type equipped with the earlier DG 'box achieved 116mph (187kph) and 0–60mph (97kph) in 11.8 seconds in *Motor*'s 1964 test. They noted the roughness of its full-throttle up-changes from low to second, although that could be overcome by using the 'hold' switch on the dash. Through the gears acceleration was little affected if good use was made of the kickdown, but that kind of treatment sent the fuel consumption figures plummeting. *Motor* only achieved 12mpg in that appraisal, making the

S-Type almost as thirsty as the original Series One XJ12.

The S-Type range suffered the same downgrading treatment as the MkII in the autumn of 1967. They lost their wing-mounted fog lights, while occupants sat on Ambla seats and had ordinary tufted carpets rather than Wilton underfoot. On the plus side there were savings of between £100 and £140 compared with the previous cars, increasing the price gap between the S-Types and the new 420.

Introduced in October 1966 to supplement rather than replace the S-Type, the 420 was a kind of upmarket S-Type or, put another way, a downsized MkX in appearance and equipment. It was designed as a holding operation while the XJ6 was

Inside, the 420's dash was topped by a padded roll of black vinyl with an electric clock in the centre.

bores also had to be siamesed. Total capacity was 4,235cc, and with the new SU HD8 carbs total (gross) power was a claimed 245bhp at 5,500rpm, with 283lb ft of torque at 3,750rpm. The 420s gained a crossflow radiator together with an alternator and negative earth electrics, the latter now being employed on all Jaguars.

As on the S-Type there was the option of the new all-synchro manual 'box – with or without Laycock overdrive – or a new Borg-Warner Type 8 automatic transmission, a beefier gearbox to cope with the 4.2 litre's increased torque. The Type 8 was imported from America and as with the Type 35 had manual hold on the column for second gear.

Marles Varamatic power steering was optional on the 420. A variable ratio system, it was low geared on either side of the straight, but became more sensitive as lock was wound on, there being three turns lock-to-lock overall. Brakes were now produced by Girling and the 420 had the welcome innovation on a Jaguar of twin hydraulic circuits front and rear.

Inside, the 420 looked a little more up-to-date than the S-Type, and it took far more notice of safety requirements. It had a padded vinyl-covered roll on top of the dashboard, and vinyl on the tops of the door trims where there had once been wood, although there was still a slim garnish rail between the glass and the trim at the very top. There was a new style of electric clock mounted in the centre of the padded roll on the dash rather than in the rev counter, which was now electric.

Introduced at the same time as the 420 was a badge-engineered Daimler version of the car called the Sovereign – the first Daimler-badged car to use a Jaguar engine. The only differences were the traditional fluted radiator grille and rear numberplate lamp, although Sovereign buyers got overdrive and power steering as part of the package. The Sovereign broke the

The Daimler Sovereign was purely a badge-engineering job on the 420, as it was mechanically identical. However, unlike the 420 the Sovereign had power steering and overdrive as standard if buyers opted for the manual version.

under development. Certainly the most modern saloon that Jaguar had on offer at the time, it faced an onslaught of very up-to-date offerings from continental makers, who were beginning to catch up on – and in some cases exceed – Jaguar's standards of refinement.

From the front screen pillar backwards the 420 was pure S-Type, but at the front Lyons had decided to go for a new, squared-off look with twin 7-inch (178mm) and 5½-inch (140mm) diameter lights and an upright, square MkX (or 420G as it had now become) grille and dummy air vents. It has been said that this was the style of front end that the S-Type would have had from the beginning, had Jaguar had the time to incorporate it.

Under the new-style wider bonnet was a two-carb (rather than three-carb, as on the 420G and E-Type) version of Jaguar's biggest 4.2 litre engine, first seen in October 1964. For this unit, really the limit of expansion left in the XK engine, the designers had re-spaced the bore centres, moving the two end bores outwards and the centres of the two middle bores together, allowing an enlargement of the bore size from 87 to 92mm. To keep the block at its existing size, the

£2,000 price barrier, while the basic non-overdrive 420 came in at £1,930 including Puchase Tax.

The S-Type and 420 have always been the unsung small Jaguars, living in the shadow of the technically inferior but faster and better-looking MkII. That the all-independent car had no significant sporting pedigree probably has a lot to do with its underdog status.

The extra weight of the independent suspension muted the S-Type's performance somewhat, and certainly an automatic S-type will not provide blistering straightline pace – expect family saloon acceleration from the 3.4 litre version. On the other hand, a manual 3.8 litre 'S' will not feel significantly slower than a MkII (you would need a stopwatch to tell the difference) and any 420 variant should still feel quick with such a torquey engine, although it will not have the sweetness of the 3.8 unit.

It is in their steering, ride and roadholding that the S-Type and 420 really score over the MkII. The steering provides just that bit more feel and sensitivity than the MkII (most S-Types and 420s were assisted) and the tail will hang on longer through turns, especially the bumpy variety, by which the independent rear is not easily upset – unlike the MkII's live axle. Ride comfort is still generally excellent, particularly for rear-seat passengers who enjoy a smooth absorbent ride that cushions them from all but the most violent potholes.

All the same, to put the Jaguar in perspective it is an inevitable truth that the S-type 420 – derived, after all, from a design originally seen in 1955 – feels desperately outdated. Understeer is very strong with such a hefty engine up front (although the power steering masks its worst excesses), there is more roll than most press-on drivers would feel comfortable with today, and a combination of thin tyres and lots of torque to the rear wheels means cautious progress on wet roads.

Buying Hints

1. Most of the corrosion problems are as described for the MkII. Look at the sills (inner and outer), jacking points and floors; damp carpets are a big giveaway.

2. Structural considerations for the S-Type/420 are also similar to the MkII, so check the front valance under the bumper, the 'crows feet' that support the front of the wings, the bonnet hinges and the wheel arch lip. Door-bottom rot is also as described for the MkII.

3. The rear skirt under the bumper catches road dirt, and this can also lead to rust – and thus leaks – in the side-mounted fuel tanks. Look at the seams in the boot floor and the spare wheel well.

4. Underneath check the mounting points for the suspension radius arms.

5. On the move look for 40psi oil pressure at 3,000rpm with a warm engine (ideally not less than 15psi at tickover). Worn valve guides will give themselves away by a smoke haze. The XK is a fairly leaky engine, but one that leaks oil from the back indicates a weeping rear main bearing oil seal; this is an engine-out job, as is a clutch replacement.

6. Parts for the early Moss gearbox are difficult to find. Automatics are more robust, but there are some spares problems on the DG unit.

7. Look for perished radius arm mountings and check the condition of all rubber bushes on the rear-end independent suspension. Four dampers and four springs mean that refurbishment of the suspension is expensive. The diff can clonk and the bearings in the alloy hub carrier can fail.

8. The inboard rear brakes can give trouble when they pick up oil from a leaking differential. Look for rusty discs if the car has been standing for some time.

Few tears were shed when the S-Type and 420 were finally laid to rest in the late 1960s. The sensational new XJ6 was coming on stream, offering more performance and better handling and refinement in a beautiful new shape. Quite simply it was the world's best saloon and these later developments of Jaguar's successful compact line were looking distinctly elderly.

The S-Types were given the chop straight away in 1968 after more than 26,000 cars had been produced since 1963. The 420 went at the same time, after a short 9,800-car run, making this underrated variant one of the rarest '60s Jaguar saloons. The Daimler Sovereign hung around until 1969, by which time Browns Lane had created a Sovereign variant of the XJ6.

The XJ6
series I *and* II

W hen Jaguar launched the XJ6 in 1968 they rewrote the luxury car rule book, not with radical new concepts – the XJ was a conventional front-engine, rear-drive, coil-sprung saloon – but by fine-tuning existing components to near-perfection. The talented Browns Lane team brought together in one design standards of ride comfort, silence, handling and roadholding – qualities previously thought incompatible in a luxury car – that eclipsed the best in Europe and set the pace for the next 20 years.

On its plump tyres, specially designed for it by Dunlop, this new British world-beater would out-corner Jaguar's own E-Type but had a ride that was softer and quieter than a Rolls-Royce. This was the world's most beautiful saloon, too, a car with a feline aggression and organic muscularity that proved amazingly enduring. The last XJ saloons, built in 1991, looked embarrassingly more attractive than 1986's XJ40, and it came as no surprise when the new car was facelifted along the lines of the old XJ in 1994.

The XJ6, announced in 1968, was the best-looking saloon car yet from Jaguar. Squat and muscular, yet dignified and elegant, it retained strong visual links with previous models but had a purity and balance all of its own.

Jaguar XJ6/ Daimler Sovereign 4.2 Series I 1968-73

ENGINE:
In-line six-cylinder, cast iron block, alloy head, hemispherical combustion chambers

Bore x stroke	92 x 106mm
Capacity	4,235cc
Valves	Twin ohc, one inlet, one exhaust
Compression ratio	8:1 (7:1 and 9:1 optional)
Carburettors	Two HD8 SUs
Power	245bhp at 5,500rpm (gross)
Torque	283lb ft at 3,750rpm (gross)

TRANSMISSION:
Four-speed manual with synchromesh, overdrive and automatic optional

Final drive	3.54:1 (manual/auto), 3.77:1 (overdrive)

SUSPENSION:
Front: independent semi-trailing, double wishbones, coil springs, telescopic dampers and anti-roll bar
Rear: independent lower wishbone/upper driveshaft link with radius arms and twin coil springs

Steering	rack-and-pinion with power assistance

BRAKES:
Discs front and rear

WHEELS:
Steel, with Dunlop SP sport E70 VR 15 tyres

BODYWORK:
Unitary all-steel construction

LENGTH:	15ft 9½in (4.8m)
WIDTH:	5ft 9¼in (1.76m)
HEIGHT:	4ft 6in (1.37m)
WEIGHT:	33cwt (1,678kg)
MAX SPEED:	124mph (200kph)
0–60mph (97kph)	8.8 seconds

PRICE NEW (1968): £2,254 inc PT

Jaguar XJ6 2.8 1968-73

As XJ6 4.2 except:

Bore x stroke	83 x 86mm
Capacity	2,791cc
Power	180bhp at

Torque	6,000rpm (gross) 182lb ft at 3,750rpm (gross)
MAX SPEED:	117mph (188kph)
0–60mph (97kph)	11 seconds

PRICE NEW (1968): £1,897 inc PT (De Luxe)

Jaguar 4.2 XJ6, XJ6 L and XJC Series II 1973-79

As XJ6 4.2 except:

Power	170bhp at 4,500rpm (DIN)
Torque	231lb ft at 3,500 rpm (DIN)
LENGTH:	16ft 2¾in (4.95m) (XJ6 L)
WHEELBASE:	9ft 4¾in (2.86m) (XJ6 L); 9ft 1in (2.77m) (XJ6 and XJC)
WEIGHT:	34cwt (1,729kg) (XJ6 L); 33cwt (1,678kg) (XJ6 and XJC)
MAX SPEED:	125mph (201kph)
0–60mph (97kph)	8.6 seconds

PRICE NEW (1973): £3,674 inc PT (XJ6)

Jaguar XJ6 3.4 1975-79

As XJ6 4.2 SII except:

Bore x stroke	83 x 106mm
Capacity	3,442cc
Power	161bhp (DIN) at 5,000rpm
Torque	189lb ft at 3,500rpm
MAX SPEED:	117mph (188kph)
0–60mph (97kph)	10.9 seconds

PRICE NEW (1975): £5,198 inc PT

Jaguar XJ12 Series I 1972-73

As XJ6 4.2 SI except:

ENGINE:
V12 all-alloy sohc per bank

Bore x stroke	90 x 70mm
Capacity	5,343cc
Compression ratio	9:1

Carburettors	Four Zenith
Power	253bhp (DIN) at 6,000rpm
Torque	302lb ft (DIN) at 3,500rpm
WEIGHT:	35cwt (1,780kg)
(distributed 53.8% front, 46.2% rear)	
MAX SPEED:	140mph (225kph)
0–60mph (97kph)	7.4 seconds

PRICE NEW (1972): £3,726 inc PT

Jaguar XJ12 L, XJ12 C Series II (with injection) 1973-79

As XJ12 SI except:

Power	285bhp at 5,750rpm
Torque	294lb ft at 3,500 rpm
LENGTH:	16ft 2¾in (4.95m) (XJ12 L); 15ft 9in (4.8m) (XJ12 C)
WHEELBASE:	9ft 4¾in (2.86m) (XJ12 L); 9ft 1in (2.77m) (XJ12 C)
MAX SPEED:	147mph (237kph)
0–60mph (97kph)	7.8 seconds

PRICE NEW (1973): £4,702 inc PT (XJ12 L)

PRODUCTION FIGURES:

Series I:	
2.8	19,322
4.2	59,077
4.2 (lwb)	874
XJ12	2,474
XJ12 (lwb)	754
Sovereign 2.8 (swb)	3,233
Sovereign 4.2 (swb)	11,522
Sovereign 4.2 (lwb)	386
Double Six (swb)	534
Double Six (VP)	351

Series II:	
XJ6 2.8	170
XJ6 3.4	6,990
Sovereign 3.4	2,341
XJ6 4.2 (swb)	12,147
Sovereign 4.2 (swb)	2,435
XJ6 4.2 (lwb)	57,804
Sovereign 4.2 (lwb)	14,351
XJ6 4.2 coupé	6487
Sovereign 4.2 coupé	1,677
XJ12 (lwb)	16,010
Double Six (lwb)	2,608
Double Six (VP, lwb)	1,726
XJ 5.3 coupé	1,855
Double Six coupé	407

The badge on the bootlid denoted the engine size. Most XJs came with the 4.2 litre engine found in the 420, but there was a cheaper 2.8 litre version built to compete in continental markets where cars of over 2.8 litres were heavily taxed.

Initially using the six-cylinder XK engine – the V12 for which the car was designed did not arrive until 1972 – most XJs were Borg-Warner autos and all had power steering. Jaguar also built a few with a short-stroke 2.8 litre engine to beat European tax laws, but this proved unreliable – it could hole its pistons under certain conditions and is rare today. A four-speed manual was available in either version, which, with optional overdrive, made the 4.2 litre car into a superbly high-geared 125mph (201kph) express.

Like all Jaguars before it, the XJ was a bargain, often undercutting the nearest comparable Mercedes by more than half. From day one, buyers were queuing to get hold of a new XJ, one angry group from Switzerland staging a protest for the benefit of BL boss Lord Stokes to complain about

the waiting list. As production accelerated, the four-door XJ began to spawn other variants: the inevitable badge-engineered Daimler, the short-lived XJC coupé, the V12, and, of course, the XJ-S, which we will look at in a separate chapter.

When the XJ6 was launched in 1968 at the London Motor Show, it was destined to banish every other Jaguar saloon to the history books, and also provide the basis for the next generation of Jaguar sports cars. Four years in development and costing an estimated £6 million, the XJ6 was the first completely new Jaguar saloon since the MkX, and was certainly the most complex. Great efforts had been made to improve perceived areas of weakness – steering and heating and ventilation in particular. It was a huge improvement over its forebears, yet obviously still a Jaguar. So confident of the car's identity were the people at Browns Lane that nowhere on the car did it say 'Jaguar'.

Although the unitary body (lighter, lower, shorter and stiffer than that of the MkX) was new, much of what was underneath was familiar, albeit thoroughly re-worked. Most impressive was Bob Knight's suspension, where much attention had been paid to the banishment of noise and vibration thanks to the use of rubber-mounted subframes as a first-stage isolator. A combination of coil springs and wishbones (similar to those found on the MkX except that now the damper was mounted outside the spring, allowing a greater capacity) and the familiar Jaguar double-wishbone rear end with its quad dampers made for a car that handled every bit as well as it looked. The Adwest rack-and-pinion steering

– a first on a Jaguar saloon – added greatly to the feeling of agility, being responsive and accurate but perhaps a bit too light for the most sporting of tastes.

The car rolled very little thanks to the wide track, and had enormous grip on its Dunlop tyres, which were carefully designed to avoid the road noise and thump associated with radials. In fact, the ride was uncannily good, combining softness with resilience, yet with none of the wallow associated with lesser luxury cars of the period. Combine this with low levels of engine noise (the bulkhead was double-skinned) and wind noise and you had a car that had no peers in the refinement stakes – not even Rolls-Royce. Perhaps only the NSU Ro80 – a radical rotary-engined saloon introduced in 1967 – came anywhere near matching the XJ's all-round standards.

If the XJ looked good, it handled, and rode, even better. Jaguar tweaked existing suspension components to produce a car that set new standards with its combination of cornering agility, smooth ride and lack of noise from either engine or body.

transmission being smoother, stronger and with more logical selector detents.

Despite the fact that Jaguar had virtually designed the XJ around its heating and ventilation system, it still fell short of expectations and not everyone was appreciative of the dashboard, which looked impressive but did not prove ergonomic with its confusing line-up of lookalike tumbler switches. Yet none of these gripes was serious enough to put off buyers.

The engine was entirely smooth and virtually silent from inside and stayed that way on the move

There was immediately a long waiting list for the car, with low-mileage used XJs fetching new prices on the open market.

The much-rumoured XJ12 arrived in 1972 using the aluminium V12 5.3 litre engine first seen in the SIII E-Type the year before. Jaguar chose a V12 because of the cachet it gave them, particularly in the American market where even ordinary cars had large V8 engines. A V12 would be perceived as smoother and – since it was the trademark of exotic marques like Ferrari and Lamborghini – more sophisticated.

Jaguar V12s had been in preparation since the early 1960s. Four-cam (with hemispherical combustion chambers) and two-cam (flat-head) prototypes had both been tried in MkX 'mules', but Jaguar had decided on the latter; the four-cam had enormous top-end power but lost out dramatically to the single-cam-per-bank version in terms of low and mid-range torque – which was what mattered in a luxury car. Additional points in favour of the

Inside, the dashboard of the Series I XJ6 and XJ12 was familiar yet different. Efforts had been made to improve on the ventilation of previous models, but Jaguar eschewed modern ergonomic notions for a fascia that simply looked impressive.

The long-stroke 4.2 litre engine perhaps felt a little rough when pressed near its modest red-line, but with such prodigious torque there was rarely any need to extend it. The manual 'box suffered from a heavy clutch and long, sticky lever movements, but most buyers would have opted for the automatic at the cost of more high-speed fuss and bigger fuel bills. Initially a Borg-Warner Model 8, the automatic became a Model 12 during 1970, the new

single-cam engine were lightness, cost and lesser bulk – the four-cam would have been a tight fit under the bonnet of the XJ.

Power was 253bhp (which appeared to be no better than the E-type/MkX but was expressed in more honest net terms), and thanks to the light alloy construction the V12 was only 80lb heavier than the XK straight-six.

Four Stromberg carbs delivered their mixture through long induction pipes (there was no room to mount the carbs in the vee) and the engine boasted Lucas Opus electronic ignition. Apart from beefed-up brakes (vented front discs) and higher-spec Dunlop tyres the XJ12 was much like the XJ in the rest of its internals, and indeed there was little other than a

new grille and some discreet badging to tell the two apart. Aside from some new armrests the interior was much as before, too.

Only by starting the car would you have told the difference – the engine was entirely smooth and virtually silent from inside, and it stayed that way on the move, endowing the XJ with prodigious 146mph top-end urge and effortlessly swift acceleration, despite the obligatory automatic transmission. From 0 to 60mph (97kph) took 7.4 seconds, with 100mph (161kph) coming up in 19 seconds. Fuel consumption was equally dramatic on these carburetted models, averaging 11mpg on road tests with the weekly journals, yet the car still received rave reviews and was blessed with handling and ride that

The first of the V12 saloons was seen in 1972. Fast, quiet and agile, this was the finest saloon in the world in its day, although its 11mpg fuel consumption raised a few eyebrows even in those pre-fuel-crisis days. Only the front grille set this model apart from lesser six-cylinder versions.

were every bit as good as its six-cylinder sister model.

There was a Daimler Double-Six version of the XJ12, and this was joined in September 1972 by a long-wheelbase top-of-the range Daimler model, the Vanden Plas. Trimmed at the VP works at Kingsbury, each car received a posher, thicker paint job, a vinyl roof and even more upmarket interior fittings. More importantly, the Vanden Plas came as standard with a wheelbase 4 inches (102mm) longer, answering critics who said that the XJ was a little cramped in the rear. It was joined the following month by longer-wheelbase versions of the other XJ models, badged XJ6/XJ12 L and sold alongside the regular-wheelbase cars.

The Series I V12 XJs would prove to be short-lived models, being replaced in September 1973 by the Series II XJs in six- and 12-cylinder form. Outwardly these had a new, higher front bumper line – to satisfy Federal crash-protection requirements – and a shallower grille. Inside there was a completely re-thought heating and ventilation system comprising an air

blending rather than a water-valve heating system with more air capacity and sophisticated electric servo operation of the controls. An improved air-conditioning unit meant a redesign of the bulkhead, which was now single-skinned rather than double-skinned. The dash was new, still veneered but featuring stalk controls for the lights and wipers and a more ergonomic grouping of the smaller dials in front of the driver behind a new, more padded steering wheel.

Mechanically the engines had been de-rated. Emission controls had taken the 4.2 down to 170bhp (DIN) at 4,500rpm and the V12 to 250bhp, although the torque of the latter remained unaltered. The 2.8 litre model was dropped as the 'base' model; it was a sweet, free-revving engine, but its reputation for holing pistons was now well known and it was hardly any more economical than the 4.2. The 2.8 is the rarest of the Series IIs, with only 170 produced.

The most interesting Series II development was the coupé, a handsome pillarless two-door built to

Perhaps the ultimate among classic XJ saloons is the Vanden Plas Double-Six with the V12 engine. Not only swift, smooth and utterly silent, the VP V12 was specially finished at that company's Kingsbury factory with a better paint job and a then fashionable vinyl roof. The interior, too, was even plusher and the cars came only in the long-wheelbase shell.

The Broadspeed Racers

In March 1976 Jaguar announced that they were to re-enter motor racing with an XJ12 coupé. Heavily modified by Ralph Broad, the cars were designed to challenge the dominance of the CSL BMWs in the European Touring Car Championship. Leyland Cars viewed it as a fine publicity tool for the flagship marque of their group and had commissioned Broad to build the car using the XJC as a base rather than the XJ-S, whose internal dimensions were a little too small for the car to be accepted as a Group Two saloon. Nobody ever bothered to ask if Jaguar actually built a manual version of the XJ12 for the public, which, strictly speaking, it should have done for the car to be eligible in Group Two.

The car displayed to the public that March was far from ready for track action, although it was extensively modified. The engine had been bored out to 5,416cc and with Lucas injection, Cosworth pistons and modifications to the sump to counter oil surge (dry sumps were not allowed according to the rules) it was said to be producing 500bhp or more.

After a series of delays, the car made its debut at the Tourist Trophy race at Silverstone in September. It showed early promise in the hands of Derek Bell and David Hobbs until a driveshaft failed and put the car out of contention. Leyland bosses dismissed it as bad luck – but such 'bad luck' was to dog the XJ racer for the whole of its brief career.

The coupés did not come out again until 1977 when two XJCs appeared at Monza with tail spoilers and a new livery. They were a little lighter now but still too heavy – although on this occasion it was oil starvation that spoiled the cars' chances while well ahead of the BMWs, which they could out-drag on the straights. Although only one BMW lasted the race, it won easily.

It was driveshaft problems again at Salzburg and the coupés missed the next two rounds while Jaguar tried to cure it. Things looked better at the Brno circuit in Czechoslovakia, its long fast straight well suited to the 550bhp, 170mph (274kph) Jaguars. They went superbly in practice, putting Bell and Fitzpatrick on the front row, but a seized gearbox, burst oil delivery pipe, then a blow-out that damaged the rear suspension resulted in a 16th overall and a third in class – but at least they finished.

Dire problems in practice at the Nurburgring round did not bode well for the coupés' hopes, but on the day Fitzpatrick was very quick. Sadly his engine failed on lap 2, leaving Bell and Rouse to finish the race for Jaguar, who took second overall. This was no disgrace, although it should be pointed out that the BMWs were in equal mechanical disarray yet still took the flag.

Now dry-sumped, just one XJC appeared at Zandvoort. The team were showing pace – Rouse brought the car into the lead from the second row at the end of lap 1 – but there were problems with the Cosworth scavenge pump during Tim Schenken's drive, then the diff disintegrated when Rouse took over, leaving the field open to the CSL of Dieter Quester.

Perhaps the XJC's most exciting showing was at Silverstone that year. Rouse was leading the BMW of Quester when he handed over the coupé to Derek Bell. He increased the lead to 27 seconds, then handed back to Rouse on lap 75. Sadly, the car was caught out by the drizzle when Rouse put it against the barriers while making up time lost in the pits.

There was more engine and gearbox trouble at Zolder, but by then Leyland had announced their intention not to continue to sponsor the adventure.

The XJC coupé was beaten by the tyrannies of excess weight – which put too much stress on braking and suspension components – heavy fuel consumption (which meant more time-consuming pit stops than the thriftier but slower BMWs), and oil surge generated by the high cornering forces that they could achieve. Yet they were fast and the results show that, with more time and money, the car could have been a winner; in eight races it had led them all and qualified fastest five times.

The Broadspeed-developed XJ coupés showed promise in Group 2 touring car racing but were dogged by poor reliability.

Launched in 1973, the Series II models gained a slimmer grille, new interior and many detail changes to bring the cars up to date in the face of newer German opposition.

challenge the BMWs and Mercedes coupés that were selling so well at the time. Available as a 4.2 or a 5.3 (and as either a Daimler or a Jaguar) it was based on the standard wheelbase with doors 4 inches (102mm) longer and an open-plan side aspect when the glass was wound down. A vinyl roof disguised the extra width of the rear pillar, but problems with window sealing delayed production until 1975. Legroom inside was unaffected, although obviously entry and exit of the rear seats was less gracious because the front seats had to be tipped forward.

There were no short-wheelbase versions of the four-door V12 models in SII form, and in fact the long wheelbase was standardised on all the saloons at the end of 1974.

With the departure of the 2.8 the XJ range lacked an economy entry-level model, a slot filled by the introduction of the 3.4 in Jaguar and Daimler form in April 1975. Although the capacity was the same as the old 3.4 engine – last seen in the 340 saloon – this was in fact a de-stroked version of the 4.2 engine with its offset bores and straight-port head. It came only as a four-door saloon and featured a more downmarket velour-trimmed interior. Good for 161bhp, it was still quite a quick car – it would do 117mph (188kph) and up to 20mpg with gentle driving. What is more, the 3.4 engine was rather smoother than the 4.2, with a higher rev limit.

A more uplifting development was the introduction of fuel injection on the V12 cars. At the same time power was boosted from 250 to 285bhp and fuel economy was improved. The Lucas electronic system also allowed the V12 to meet US emission regulations more easily. The new cars were distinguishable from their forebears by a 'Fuel Injection' badge on the bootlid, a black vinyl roof and a chrome waist trim. On all versions badging now denoted engine capacity, so the XJ6 became the XJ3.4, XJ4.2/XJ4.2 C, and the V12 the XJ5.3/XJ5.3 C.

If there had been any doubts that this was the finest all-round luxury saloon in the world, the introduction of injection dispelled them. The car's smoothness was uncanny, and its performance truly crushing in the luxury class with 0–60mph (97kph) in 7.6 seconds, 100 (161) coming up in 18 seconds, and the top end now touching 150mph (241mph).

Drive an XJ today and perhaps the most remarkable aspect of its behaviour is its ride. Few cars, even in the late 1990s, feel as cosseting and soft as an XJ. Today's executives, weaned on harder-riding German machines, expect to be able to feel something of the road, yet the XJ manages to combine silky smoothness

The most intriguing Series II XJ development was the coupé or XJC, built to take on the Germans at their own game. It was something of a pet project of Sir William's, but was delayed by two years after the 1973 launch as engineers struggled to get the pillarless side glasses to seal properly.

Electronic fuel injection brought even more refinement and power to the V12 engine, although not that much more economy.

with resilience. If the springs and dampers are healthy there is little that will disturb its poise, and the lack of road noise and thump from the tyres is uncanny. You sit lower than in earlier Jaguar saloons, in a car that seems to be in another world of sure-footedness and grip after, say, a MkII or an S-Type. In the dry the adhesion is excellent, but it takes surprisingly little to break away the tail in the wet – and if the steering feels light by modern standards, then to some degree that is all part of this car's laid-back charm. Early 4.2s still feel quick, even sporty, with the slightly sticky manual gearbox, and there is

something special about the interior of the Series I with its old-style rocker switches and foot dip-switch – a comforting link with 1960s Jaguars in a car that drives 'Seventies'.

If you can afford the petrol, an SI V12 must be some kind of ultimate among luxury saloons. That giant powerhouse – curiously characterless yet fascinatingly smooth – gives the XJ a mechanical feel that matches the silken action of its other components, and somehow an automatic seems the only appropriate transmitter of power in such an effortless device. The V12 did not receive the automatic it deserved until the introduction of the GM 400 'box announced on the injected SII versions in April 1977, but at least on this rather more garish later model you can expect fuel consumption somewhere in the low teens thanks to the injection. The smoothness, of course, remains sublime, and the power delivery turbine-like in a car that – if all is well with its window seals – should be as quiet at 120mph (193kph) as it is at half that.

The last Series II saloons were built in 1979, dropped to make way for the gently reworked Series III. Since May of the previous year, the 4.2 straight-six had been fitted with fuel injection for the American market in an attempt to retrieve some of the power lost to emissions equipment. A Lucas/Bosch L-jetronic set-up, it enabled Jaguar to run a higher compression ratio on the 4.2, which in US form now produced 175bhp, up from 161. Economy was up too, from 14 to 16mpg.

The coupé, a favourite of William Lyons himself, had proved a short-lived variation on the XJ theme. Problems with sealing the side glasses had never been truly resolved and it took valuable production capacity away from the popular saloon for which there was still a waiting list despite increasing quality problems.

Some argued that the pretty coupé made a better all-round sporting flagship than the controversially styled XJ-S, but in the interests of rationalisation it was dropped in 1977. Since then the XJC has been continually tipped for top collector status – particularly the rare V12 version of which just 609 were built – but somehow it has never quite achieved it: the SI 4.2 remains the XJ to have.

Buying Hints

1. SIs were better finished than the SIIs, but all models suffer badly structurally and cosmetically. Check the front wings around the headlights, the wheel arch lips, the rear bottoms of the wings behind the wheels, the A posts and the front and rear valances under the bumpers. The sills – both inner and outer – are crucial and vulnerable, as are the suspension mounting points. Look also for rust around the petrol filler caps.

2. Coupés need special care when being inspected as the rear wings and many other parts special to the model are difficult to obtain now. The heavier doors are more prone to drop. Also check for rust under the vinyl roof on the coupé.

3. All opening panels are vulnerable. Doors rot along the bottoms, bootlids along the edges.

4. None of the chrome is of particularly good quality – especially on the Series II bumpers – and some items, such as grilles on the Series Is, are difficult to find now.

5. Remove the spare wheel to check the well for rust, a favourite spot on the XJ.

6. Interiors wear fairly well but the SIs had better wood. Leather problems will be obvious. Beware of leaking heaters on the XJ – most of the dash will need to be dismantled to sort out the trouble.

7. Electrics are always suspect on the XJ, especially on the more sophisticated high-spec SII models. The complex electrics operating the heating and ventilation flaps are often troublesome.

8. The 4.2 and 3.4 engines suffer all the maladies of the earlier XKs, but the SI engines seem to be more durable than the SIIs. Look for overheating, evidence of bore wear, and the usual low oil pressure. Take heed of timing chain rattle – particularly from the bottom one as it is much more complicated to replace. Do not take a leaky rear main bearing oil seal lightly, either; as for the 2.8, it should not now give problems if driven with care.

9. If anything, the V12 is even stronger than the XK. Overheating is, however, usually fatal, as the heads weld themselves to the block and warp. Water pumps need to be watched. As on any car, the V12's fuel injection can give trouble and you may experience problems with the amplifiers in the ignition system.

10. Check the power steering for play, leaks or a noisy pump. The air-conditioning usually suffers from lack of use but can generally be revived when recharged with gas.

11. Of the transmissions, the GM400 used on the V12s from the mid-1970s is the strongest. On all the autos look for rough, snatchy changes and dirty fluid, and be aware that spares for the earlier Borg-Warners are now difficult to obtain. The manuals are strong, and most desirable when fitted with overdrive, but are relatively rare.

12. The front springs sag with age and use, which can sometimes lead to the tyres fouling the arches. At the rear there are four expensive springs and dampers to replace, together with often neglected inboard disc brakes.

13. Exhausts are difficult to fit and often bang irritatingly on the bottom of the car if not hung properly.

The XJ6 *series* III

The Series III XJ6 was intended to be an interim measure while the new XJ6 (known to Browns Lane insiders as the XJ40) was in preparation, and would never have been conceived had its replacement, caught up in company politics, been on schedule. In the event the basic Series III design served for 13 years and was still among the most refined saloon cars in the world when it finally deferred to the XJ40 in 1992.

Launched in March 1979, it was the result of a £7 million investment. There were no basic engineering changes – the 3.4, 4.2 and 5.3 engine options remained more or less unchanged – but instead Jaguar had concentrated on updating the labour-saving ancillaries that had fallen behind the times since the introduction of the XJ range ten years earlier.

The bodyshell was 'refreshed' by Pininfarina of Italy, the first time that Jaguar had gone to an outside stylist, and most people agreed that it looked even better. A new higher roof-line gave the XJ a sleeker look while increasing the headroom in the rear. Screen pillars had more rake, the rear screen was slightly flatter

The 1979 Series III was intended to be a stop-gap while the XJ40 was in preparation, but it became one of Jaguar's most successful models, lasting in V12 form until 1992. Clever restyling of the Series II body was by Pininfarina of Italy.

and there was more glass area generally. The profile was cleaner thanks to the deletion of the front quarter lights and – because the roof panel itself was thinner – there was more 'tumblehome' to the side windows.

Other details prepared the bodyshell for the 1980s. There were flush-fitting door handles and black injection-moulded bumpers with chrome caps and flush-fitting indicator lights. The steel road wheels were of sportier design, although the GKN alloys were still available as an option on all models except the basic 3.4, which was aggressively marketed as an entry-level Jaguar.

The specification inside was upgraded with cruise control on the options list for the first time for automatic versions, more supportive seats with optional electric adjustment, thicker carpets, intermittent wiper operation and wash-wipe for the headlights. Warning lights updated the dashboard, and the toolkit now came in a posh, lined briefcase – a nice touch.

Mechanical changes were few. Lucas Injection was now standardised on the 4.2 (it was first seen on later US-bound SII 4.2 saloons), and it had fuel cut-off on the over-run as an economy measure. It made 200bhp and with the new Rover five-speed gearbox fitted it was a rapid car – acceleration was the equal of the hotshot 3.8 MkII manual of two generations earlier. Top speed of the manual was 131mph (211kph), the Borg-Warner automatics around 128mph (206kph), much faster than any previous automatic XJ. The 3.4 continued to the end of production with twin SU carburettors.

Press reaction to the car was extremely favourable; the V12 was still the quietest, smoothest engine you could buy, and the ride/handling compromise the best in the industry, even if the new Pirelli P5 tyres were

Jaguar XJ6 Series III 4.2
1979–87

ENGINE:
In-line six-cylinder, cast iron block, alloy head, hemispherical combustion chambers

Bore x stroke	92 x 106mm
Capacity	4,235cc
Valves	Twin ohc
Compression ratio	8.7:1
Fuel system	Lucas/Bosch injection
Power	200bhp (DIN) at 5,000rpm
Torque	236lb ft (DIN) at 2,750rpm

TRANSMISSION:
Five-speed manual or three-speed automatic

Final drive	3.07 or 3.31:1

SUSPENSION:
Front: independent semi-trailing, double wishbones, coil springs, telescopic dampers and anti-roll bar
Rear: independent lower wishbone/upper driveshaft link with radius arms and twin coil springs

Steering	Adwest rack-and-pinion with power assistance

BRAKES:
Discs, vented front

WHEELS:
Steel, with Pirelli P5 tyres

BODYWORK:
Unitary all-steel construction

LENGTH:	16ft 2¾in (4.95m)
WIDTH:	5ft 9¼in (1.76m)
HEIGHT:	4ft 6in (1.37m)
WEIGHT:	35.4cwt (1,800kg)
MAX SPEED:	128mph (206kph)
0–60mph (97kph)	9.6 seconds

PRICE NEW (1979): £14,609

Jaguar XJ6 Series III 3.4
1979–87

As XJ6 Series III 4.2 except:

Bore x stroke	83 x 106mm
Capacity	3,442cc
Valves	Twin SU
Power	161bhp (DIN) at 5,000rpm
Torque	189lb ft (DIN) at 3,500rpm

MAX SPEED:	116mph (187kph)
0–60mph (97kph)	11 seconds

PRICE NEW (1979): £13,259

Jaguar XJ12 Series III 5.3
1979–92

ENGINE:
All-alloy sohc per bank, 60 degree V12

Bore x stroke	90 x 70mm
Capacity	5,343cc
Compression ratio	9:1 (HE 12:1)
Fuel system	Lucas/Bosch injection
Power	285bhp at 5,750rpm (HE 299bhp at 5,500rpm)
Torque	294lb ft at 3,500 rpm (HE 318lb ft at 3,000rpm)
Final drive	2.88:1

WEIGHT:	37.8cwt (1,922kg)

MAX SPEED:	148mph (238kph)
0–60mph (97kph)	7.5 seconds

PRICE NEW: (1979) £17,627

PRODUCTION FIGURES:

3.4	5,799
4.2	97,349
Jaguar Sov. 4.2	27,261
Daimler Sov. 4.2	20,315
Daimler Sov. 4.2 VP	1,953
XJ12	5,403
Jaguar Sov. 5.3	9,129
Double Six	9,628
Double Six VP	401

All 4.2 litre XJ SIIIs had a fuel-injected version of the now venerable XK engine, which boosted power, response and economy. A few were built with the Rover SD1 five-speed manual gearbox.

not as quiet as the old Dunlops. Performance was still remarkable, with mid-range urge rivalled only by much more expensive luxury saloons such as the Aston Martin Lagonda at more than twice the price of the Jaguar.

There was a sense, however, that the opposition – effectively BMW and Mercedes – was beginning to catch up with, if not eclipse, the XJ's standards. Certainly the Germans had Jaguar licked when it came to quality. The new Castle Bromwich paint shop, built at a cost of £15.5 million, was proving troublesome. Completely painted shells had to be transported to Browns Lane from Castle Bromwich, which was a difficult task if they were not to be damaged in transit. Inevitably the quality suffered

and despite Jaguar's efforts to inhibit corrosion on the Series III, paint on the early cars was poor.

Over the next six years the XJ6 and XJ12 – together with the Daimler Sovereign and Double-Six/VP versions – received many detail changes mostly aimed at uprating the specification and broadening its appeal in an ever more competitive marketplace. The most technically important change was the introduction of the HE version of the V12 in 1981. In search of increased fuel economy potential, Jaguar adopted Michael May's unique 'Fireball' combustion chamber design. The young Swiss engineer had created a special two-chamber system with the inlet valve recessed in a collecting zone and the exhaust valve located higher up in a 'bathtub' into which the spark plug projected. A swirl-inducing ramp connected the two chambers, and when the mixture was pushed from the inlet valve zone to the combustion chamber on its compression stroke, it created a low-turbulence, concentrated charge around the spark plug, thus enabling rapid and complete burning of the highly compressed and very lean mixture. Now the higher-geared V12s could turn in 15mpg around town and over 20mpg on a run – better in fact than the equivalent Mercedes S-Class. At the same time the V12s got fatter tyres and the VP version of the Daimler even more standard equipment – cruise control, more lavishly upholstered seats and veneered door fillets.

New names came in 1982 for the 1983 model year. The Daimler marque was dropped for Europe, replaced by the Jaguar Sovereign, and this version was shortly available in the UK as well, replacing the VP version of the 4.2. Sovereigns came with air-conditioning, electric mirrors, rear head restraints and electric front seats. All XJs had a revised interior with a new centre console with figured or burr walnut inlays and a thicker steering wheel rim.

XJ12 HEs received 'pepper pot' perforated alloys and there was a Sovereign version of the Jaguar V12 that included VP levels of equipment – electric mirrors, headlamp wash/wipe and a more upmarket radio/cassette.

Quality had improved dramatically by this time and the Series III was spearheading a renaissance for the company under John Egan. In

Jaguar's new body plant at Castle Bromwich produced many quality problems at first: early SIII models are best avoided. . .

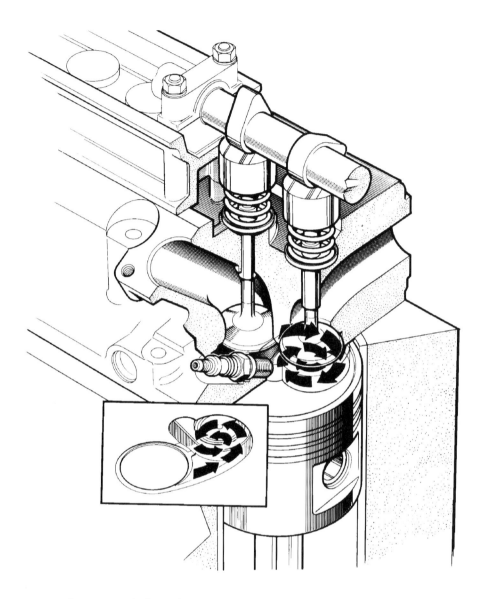

for 1986 now came with wool-blend tweed cloth on the seats (Daimlers and Jaguar Sovereigns continued with leather) and all versions received more wood on the centre console and door tops. Rear seat belts and tinted glass were now standard on all the 'sixes'. Badging was simplified on all versions with the 'HE' and engine capacity badges dropped. More upmarket scripted plates replaced the plastic scripts used on earlier models.

By the end of its life it was a car trading on its old-world charm; wood and leather had strong appeal

The last six-cylinder XJs were built in May 1987 as the new 'XJ40' XJ6 got into its stride as the mainstay of Jaguar saloon car production. The XJ12 followed suit in 1991, by which time it was virtually being made to order on the XJ40 pilot production line. The last Daimler Double-Six was built exactly one year later in 1992.

The Sovereign name had been dropped in 1989 and for the last couple of years the V12s had ABS to bring them into line with the XJ40s, and a catalyst-equipped exhaust system in the name of cleaner emissions.

By now the opposition had truly caught up with, if not entirely overtaken, all the standards set by the now 22-year-old XJ series. The balance between handling and ride comfort had perhaps tipped towards the latter as Jaguar struggled to accommodate the ever more weighty labour-saving electrics expected by the market. Yet the V12 was still swift and exceptionally smooth and quiet,

The May 'Fireball' combustion chamber design brought new economy to the thirsty V12 models in SIII form, promising up to 20mpg if driven carefully. The diagram shows the swirl-inducing combustion chamber and swirl pattern.

America particularly the car was more popular than ever and Jaguar was setting new production records for the XJ almost every month.

The six-cylinder Jaguars and Daimlers received their final update in 1985, the year Jaguar came fifth in the North American JD Power Customer Satisfaction Index. This was a major achievement for the company, whose fortunes had been at a low ebb in the States for some years.

Standard XJ6 3.4 and 4.2 litre saloons

Series III quality:
what went wrong and what they did about it

Under BL, morale at Jaguar sank to an all-time low in the late 1970s, with dire effects on the quality of the product. When John Egan took over in March 1980 he was charged by Sir Michael Edwardes with turning Jaguar around. If he failed, there was a chance, said Edwardes, that Jaguar could cease to exist within a couple of years as sales were falling together with the company's prestige in the marketplace. Egan quickly learned that the basic product was excellent, that talent was in abundance at Browns Lane, but that the cars needed to be built properly.

He moved quickly to establish Japanese-style quality circles between workers and managers to identify problems, and immediately tackled the Castle Bromwich body assembly and paint factory. Perhaps more crucially, he put pressure on suppliers to improve the quality of the components they were selling – those that did not improve were dropped.

There were redundancies – there were too many people making too few cars – and dealers were told in no uncertain terms that they had to improve the service they were giving to customers or risk losing their franchises. Some ignored the warnings and lost their dealerships.

In America, dealers felt that they had been forgotten and presented Egan with a litany of problems – mostly electrical – that made the XJ nearly unsaleable in a market used to the reliability of German luxury cars.

Slowly Egan began to arrest the company's downward spiral. Sales rose dramatically from 1983 onwards – particularly in the States – and gradually loss turned to profit. Jaguar regained control of its marketing and in 1984 the company was hived off from BL and floated with notorious success on the stock market. Egan got a knighthood for his trouble and the success of Jaguar was heralded by the Conservative Government as a shining example of Margaret Thatcher's ideology of privatisation. William Lyons lived to see the rebirth of the company he had spent a lifetime building, but would have been deeply disappointed to see it stumble again in the late 1980s and fall into the hands of Ford.

John Egan was appointed Chairman of Jaguar in 1980. Under his guidance Series III quality improved dramatically in the early 1980s.

although the upcoming XJ40 could almost match it in those areas too. By the end of its life it was a car trading largely on its old-world charm; wood and leather had strong appeal, separating the Jaguar from the cold efficiency of its German rivals. What it lacked was the internal dimensions – legroom and headroom – and the sort of boot capacity expected in a car of its type, but many buyers were willing to put up with this for a body shape that was still the most beautiful in its class.

The Series IIIs do not have quite the classic appeal of the earlier XJs, but they are undoubtedly better cars. Injection makes the 4.2 six-cylinder models both more driveable and livelier, particularly in five-speed manual form where full use can be made of the engine's torque, thanks to that excellent Rover five-speed gearbox; not only that, but better than 20mpg can be achieved on a gentle, long run.

The much more numerous automatic suits the car's character better and generally even the self-shifters feel very lively with smoother gearchanges than the earlier automatic versions. Steering feel improved during the life

of the Series III – less assistance, more weight – even if the damping was not quite as efficient on this heavier car. All models make superb motorway express material, particularly the V12, which in HE form drinks nothing like as much fuel and provides the benefit of modern luxury touches such as electric seats and proper air-conditioning systems, and even ABS on the last of the 5.3s.

In 1982 the Ladbroke Motor Group offered this Avon Estate version of the XJ at a cost of £20,000.

As quality improved, sales of the XJ series increased dramatically, particularly in North America. Here Graham Whitehead, President of BL's American offshoot Jaguar Rover Triumph Inc, poses with a Series III XJ6 in 1981. Sales of the car in North America rose 50 per cent that year.

Buying Hints

1. Jaguar did not begin to get a grip on the quality of the Series III until 1981, so if you are looking for one it is definitely a case of the later the better.

2. Really poor early SIIIs must be nearly extinct now, and rust protection towards the end of the 1980s had become quite good. Check the front wings around the headlights, the wheel arch lips, the rear bottoms of the wings behind the wheels, the A posts and the front and rear valances under the bumpers. Sills – both inner and outer – are crucial and vulnerable, as are the suspension mounting points. Look for rust around the petrol filler caps. All opening panels are vulnerable: doors rot along the bottoms, bootlids along the edges.

3. Series III six-cylinder engines are not as durable as earlier XKs and most seem to need a rebuild before 100,000 miles. Look for poor oil pressure, oil smoke and evidence of overheating. Take heed of timing chain rattle – particularly from the bottom one as it is much more complicated to replace. Do not ignore a leaky rear main bearing oil seal.

4. If anything, the V12 is even stronger than the XK. However, overheating is usually fatal as the heads weld themselves to the block and warp. Water pumps need watching. Listen for timing chain noise from the front end (a grating sound). As on any car, the fuel injection can give trouble and problems might be experienced with the amplifiers in the ignition system.

5. Remove the spare wheel to check the well for rust, a favourite spot on the XJ.

6. Interiors wear fairly well. Leather problems will be obvious but beware of leaking heaters on the XJ; most of the dash will need to be dismantled to sort out the trouble.

7. Electrics were always suspect on the XJ but improved over the years on the SIII.

8. Check the power steering for play, leaks or a noisy pump. New mounting bushes for the rack will improve the feel. Stiffness can be caused by bearing failure in the upper part of the column, seized ball joints in the suspension, or just a lack of fluid in the system. Air-conditioning usually suffers from lack of use and can usually be revived when recharged with gas.

9. Of the transmissions, the GM400 used on the V12s from the mid-1970s is the strongest while the Borg-Warner 'box in the 'six' is at the limit of its capacity. On all the autos look for rough, snatchy changes and dirty fluid. Whining, whistling and whooshing noises are indicative of the imminent failure of the front pump in the gearbox.

10. Front springs sag with age and use, which can sometimes lead to the tyres fouling the arches. At the rear there are four expensive springs and dampers to replace, together with often neglected inboard disc brakes. All rubber bushes and mounts are subject to deterioration. Check the V mounts that locate the rear suspension cage by jacking up the car at the back – the wheels should not stay on the ground. . .

11. Hollow rear radius arms can get so rusty that they break up, and the front suspension subframe is also vulnerable to rust behind the spring towers.

12. Brakes should pull the car up square. A pulsing pedal usually means a cracked or distorted front disc.

13. Exhausts are difficult to fit and often bang irritatingly on the bottom of the car if not hung properly.

The XJ40 *series*

The internal code name for the new generation of XJ series Jaguars was XJ40. Their development had become so famously protracted (the first ideas had been laid down in the early 1970s) and their introduction so keenly anticipated that the code name leaked and became general knowledge long before the cars appeared in the autumn of 1986. Today these cars – now in a restyled and very heavily revised third generation with new V8 engines – are still known as 'XJ40' in the trade, if only to differentiate them from the model that came before.

This all-new Jaguar, easily the most complex the company had ever built, had a formidable task ahead of it. Not only was the XJ40 expected to improve upon the world-class standards set by its predecessors, but in designing it Jaguar's engineers also had to comply with a new set of expectations regarding safety and reliability – particularly reliability – that simply had not existed when the original XJ6 had been announced in 1968.

The new XJ had to be better built, easier to service and cheaper to run than its forerunner, as well as a better drive. Bear in mind that its counterparts from BMW and Mercedes had been through two model changes while the original XJ6 had remained fundamentally as it had been on

The long-awaited new XJ6 finally appeared in 1986. This is the entry-level 2.9 litre version with the single-cam 165bhp engine. The shape was reminiscent of the old model, which survived in V12 form, but it was not quite so elegant.

introduction. On top of all this the new XJ had to remain essentially a Jaguar in looks and feel.

On announcement, the new cars were only available in six-cylinder form, as the Series III V12 was to stay on for another five years as Jaguar's top-of-the-range model.

The entry-level XJ40 was the 165bhp 2.9 single-cam (effectively half the V12 with the same bore spacing, camshaft and 'May' head) while higher-spec models had the four-valve 3.6 litre AJ6 twin-cam engine first seen in the XJ-S in 1983, developing 221bhp. The new engines shared the same basic aluminium block and featured Lucas/Bosch injection with mapped, digital ignition.

Power was deployed through either a Getrag five-speed manual gearbox or a new ZF four-speed automatic whose unique 'J' gate offered a second plane of operation for sporty manual shifting.

Much thought was put into the rear suspension of the new car. Conceived by engineering boss Jim Randle, it retained the driveshaft doubling as an upper link, but the lower link's inner mounting was designed to promote fore-and-aft movement, allowing the tyres of the car to 'ride back' when impacting with bumps in the road. Combined coil spring and damper units were used, but only one each side this time. Discs were outboard now – so no more cooked differential seals familiar to owners of the previous model – and ABS and electronically controlled self-levelling featured on the posher Sovereign 3.6 and Daimler models. The subframe was rubber-mounted to the body to attenuate road and differential noise.

At the front, as on the original XJ6, there was anti-dive geometry for the double wishbone suspension, which shared a subframe with the engine mounts and the power steering rack,

Jaguar XJ6 2.9
1986–90

ENGINE:

In-line six-cylinder, alloy head and block	
Bore x stroke	91 x 74.8mm
Capacity	2,919cc
Valves	sohc
Compression ratio	12.6:1
Fuel system	Bosch injection
Power	165bhp (DIN) at 5,600rpm
Torque	176lb ft (DIN) at 4,000rpm

TRANSMISSION:
Five-speed manual or four-speed automatic
Final drive   3.77:1

SUSPENSION:
Front: double wishbones, coil springs, telescopic dampers and anti-roll bar
Rear: independent lower wishbone/upper driveshaft link with radius arms and single coil springs
Steering   rack-and-pinion with power assistance

BRAKES:
Discs, vented front, solid rear

WHEELS:
Steel, Dunlop TD Sport 220 65 VR 390 tyres

BODYWORK:
Unitary all-steel construction

LENGTH:	16ft 4.4in (5m)
WIDTH:	6ft 6.9in (2m)
HEIGHT:	4ft 6.3in (1.38m)
WEIGHT:	32.7cwt (1,663kg)

MAX SPEED:	117mph (188kph)
0–60mph (97kph)	9.9 seconds

PRICE NEW (1986): £16,495

Jaguar XJ6 3.6
1986–91

As XJ6 2.9 except:
ENGINE:

Bore x stroke	91 x 92mm
Capacity	3,590cc
Valves	dohc, 24 valve
Power	221bhp (DIN) at 5,000rpm
Torque	248lb ft (DIN) at 4,000rpm max

SPEED:	137mph (220kph)
0–60mph (97kph)	7.4 seconds

PRICE NEW (1986): £18,495

Jaguar XJ6 3.2
1991–94

As XJ6 2.9 except:

ENGINE:

Capacity	3,239cc
Valves	dohc, 24 valve
Bore x stroke	91 x 83mm
Power	200bhp at 5,250rpm
Torque	294lb ft at 3,500 rpm

MAX SPEED:	132mph (212kph)
0–60mph (97kph)	8.5 seconds

PRICE NEW (1991): £25,850

Jaguar XJ6 4.0
1991–94

As XJ6 2.9 except:
ENGINE:

Capacity	3,980cc
Valves	dohc, 24 valve
Bore x stroke	91 x 102mm
Power	223bhp at 4,750rpm
Torque	278lb ft at 3,650rpm

WEIGHT:	33cwt (1,678kg)

MAX SPEED:	138mph (222kph)
0–60mph (97kph)	7.6 seconds

PRICE NEW (1991): £28,850

Jaguar XJ12 6.0
1993–94

As XJ6 2.9 except:
ENGINE:

sohc 60-degree V12	
Capacity	5,994cc
Bore x stroke	90 x 78.5mm
Power	318bhp at 5,350rpm
Torque	335lb ft at 2,850rpm

MAX SPEED:	155mph (249kph)
0–60mph (97kph)	6.8 seconds

PRICE NEW (1993): £48,800

PRODUCTION FIGURES:

XJ6 2.9	14,148
Daimler 3.6	10,314
Jaguar 3.6	9,349
Jaguar Sovereign	50,291
Federal 3.6	13,319
Jaguar/Daimler 3.2	13,053
Sport 3.2	3,117
Jaguar Sov. 3.2	3,487
Gold 3.2	1,499
Jaguar 4.0	13,576
Daimler 4.0	8,876
Jaguar Sovereign 4.0	50,336
Federal 4.0	12,846
Sport 4.0	500
Gold 4.0	23
Long-wheelbase 4.0	121
Jaguar Sovereign 6.0	1,243
Daimler Double Six	985
Jaguar 6.0 (export)	1,521
Long-wheelbase 6.0	50

The twin-cam AJ6 was first seen in the 3.6 litre XJ-S. It was lighter and more powerful than the XK engine and certainly less thirsty, but never delivered the refinement expected in this class.

the latter giving 2.8 turns lock-to-lock.

The shell was lighter and stronger than its predecessor and better able to absorb noise generated by the engine or suspension before it got into the cabin. It was made up of fewer panels and, claimed Jaguar, was much more resistant to rust and easier to repair.

As for the styling, this was only partially successful. Some were disappointed by its similarity to the Series III – echoed in the haunches over the rear wheels – others that it was too squared-up after the elegant curves of its predecessor. Either way it did age rather quickly and, no matter how Jaguar tried to dress it up,

it looked slightly awkward and unfinished. Bertone, Pininfarina and Ital Design had all been hired to produce alternatives, but the in-house design, approved by Sir William Lyons himself, was felt to be the best compromise.

The 2.9 and 3.6 XJ6s came with four round front lamps, the better-trimmed Jaguar 2.9 and 3.6 Sovereigns and the Daimler 3.6 with big rectangular lights.

Inside, Jaguar was fairly successful in mixing the usual veneers with modern technology in a roomier cabin. If not everybody approved of the digital bar gauges that surrounded the conventional circular speedometer and rev counter, at least the heating and ventilation finally matched that of the Germans. Cheaper models got tweed trim, Jaguar Sovereigns part-leather, and there was full leather for the Daimlers, which had special separate rear seats.

The critics were impressed. This all-new Jaguar was faster, quieter and nimbler than the car it replaced, not to mention more frugal thanks to ultra-high gearing, less weight and a

more efficient engine. Pitched against ordinary mass-market executive cars such as the Rover 800 and Granada Scorpio, the entry-level 2.9 seemed an amazing bargain at £16,500 and was, if anything, over-qualified for its task even if the performance – 117mph (188kph) – was a little lack-lustre.

Jim Randle's careful attention to springs and damping had produced a

In 1990 the capacity of the AJ6 engine was taken out to 4 litres, boosting torque rather than power. This is the 150mph (241kph) XJR with its matt-black grille, spoiler and sill skirts.

Wood, leather and chrome – traditional interior touches continued for the XJ40 series. This car is a Jaguar XJ6 Gold, a limited-edition model issued just before the end of production in 1994.

car with a superb ride/handling compromise with poise to match the best that BMW and Mercedes could throw at it, and a ride to eclipse even Rolls-Royce. The 3.6 litre models – with engines much smoother and quieter than those that had first appeared in the 3.6 XJ-S three years earlier – were good for 137mph (220kph) in manual form and just over 130mph (209kph) as an automatic, this transmission coming as standard, incidentally, on Sovereigns and the single Daimler variant.

With its sights set on BMW's superb M5, Jaguar quickly added to the range the 3.6 XJR, modified by Tom Walkinshaw's JaguarSport and fitted with sports suspension, a tweaked

engine and some none-too-tasteful skirts and spoilers, as was the fashion in the mid-1980s.

Sales boomed in 1987, reaching 47,000 cars (most of them XJ40s), and such was the popularity of the new XJ6 – despite some initial teething troubles – that there was soon a black market in second-hand cars as the factory struggled to meet demand. The new XJ6, crucial to the future of the newly independent company, was deemed a success, although Jaguar did not rest on their laurels.

In search of more power, the 200bhp 3.6 was upgraded to a 223bhp 4 litre in 1989, with re-profiled camshafts and timing and digital engine management, along with a new ZF electronic automatic transmission system linked to the engine management system. The ABS was improved and, inside, the digital instruments, which customers had never liked, were replaced by conventional analogue dials.

This all-new Jaguar was faster, quieter and nimbler than the car it replaced

Later came a new 200bhp twin-cam 3.2 litre to replace the 2.9, which had been panned for its lack of urge if not its free-revving smoothness.

There was no lack of urge from the 6-litre V12 model, announced in March 1993. Here at last was the super-smooth alloy V12 in Jaguar's modern saloon body, giving 318bhp in new longer-stroke form for an artificially limited top-end of 155mph (249kph) and a 0–60mph (97kph) time of 6.8 seconds. The cylinder head, inlet valves and cam profiles were all new, and power went through a new four-speed switchable GM gearbox with a lock-up clutch to improve take-off. The car was as velvety smooth and cosseting as you would expect – although in certain aspects of refinement and accommodation it could not match the latest Mercedes S Class. It came with all the luxuries and labour-savers that could be imagined, including mirrors that automatically dipped when reverse was selected and picnic tables in the backs of the front seats.

If more room was required, there were always the Majestic and Insignia

The Majestic was a special-order long-wheelbase model offered from 1993 to take the place of the old DS420 limousine.

Birth pains of the XJ40

The first proposals for a replacement for the original XJ6 were laid down in 1972 after the departure of Sir William Lyons – although with the current car selling so well there was no great pressure to come up with something new. At that stage, any new XJ6 would have been a development of the existing one, but with a new wider bodyshell on the existing floorpan and suspension. Power would have come from the then new V12 or a slant 'six' made on the same tooling.

Clay styling models were generated within Jaguar's styling department but the designs were rejected by the BL board as not being 'different' enough. Pininfarina, Ital Design and Bertone were commissioned to come up with proposals, but all were rejected on the grounds of being 'un-Jaguar'.

Meanwhile, problems with the giant British Leyland conglomerate were slowing the process. Jaguar's future within BL was looking uncertain and funds needed to engineer the new car were not forthcoming.

Managing Director Bob Knight fought hard to keep Jaguar

Engineering within Jaguar, which meant that when the board finally gave the go-ahead for the car in May 1980 (a month after the appointment of John Egan) the company was in a position to do the job itself. By then, any ideas of using components from the old model had been forgotten and Knight – who retired in 1980 – had encouraged Jaguar's stylists to give the car a more 'Jaguar' look, hence the curved waistline and prominent front grille. The success of the Series III (thanks to Egan's quality drive) bought more time for the development of the XJ40, easily the most complex and most thoroughly tested new Jaguar up to that point; 400 development vehicles were built on a special pilot production line that helped Jaguar to ascertain the most efficient way of building the cars, while the development XJ40s themselves were subjected to 5½ million miles of testing in all kinds of conditions. This one had to be right first time, no excuses . . .

Development of the XJ40 began in the early 1970s but a lack of funding held the project up and the final go-ahead for development was not granted until the end of the decade.

long-wheelbase models available from 1993, which were 5 inches (127mm) longer and became a familiar sight outside 10 Downing Street as ministerial transport.

In their twilight run-out years, the final first-generation XJ40s were offered in a series of limited editions, designed to entice younger executives. The 3.2 S had sports suspension, rosewood veneer and alloys, while the even cheaper XJ6 Gold featured special colours and extra leather trim to raise it from base model status.

These were end-of-season bargains, of course, to clear the path for Jaguar's extensively redesigned XJ6 – codenamed X-300 – launched in 1994. If the XJ40 in its various forms had not been the most charismatic of Jaguars, then at least it retained the Jaguar 'feel' and provided a sound basis for this next generation of large saloons, funded by Jaguar's new owners Ford.

Buying Hints

1. Early XJ40s now come very cheaply, but it is always advisable to go for the best you can afford, preferably with a dealer service history. Obviously, high-specification, low-mileage cars are the ones to buy, if only because they will be easier to sell. Steer clear of under-endowed 2.9s and anything without leather or air-conditioning. Metallic paint is also preferable.

2. Rust does not attack these cars as it did the SIIIs, but certain cosmetic areas are worth looking at, particularly the bootlid and the edge of the bonnet, which can rust quite badly on early models if stone chips have not been treated early.

3. Ex-police XJ40s need not be rejected if the price takes into account the holes in the dash and roof and the lack of certain creature comforts. The mechanicals will certainly have been well looked after.

4. Rear door handles can be troublesome and replacement kits from Jaguar are expensive – some specialists do kits for about half the price. The central-locking solenoids are also troublesome, together with the switches for the electric windows.

5. There was an early recall on the brake accumulator, which used to leak, and these can still play up.

6. The engines are strong and capable of high mileages: look for oil leaks and smoke, and evidence of overheating. Thanks to the digital instrumentation, mileometer 'clocking' is difficult with the XJ40.

7. Inside, leather should be free of rips, and the headlining good; reject cars showing major problems with either. Look for a leaky heater and non-functioning air-conditioning.

8. Differentials can get noisy with age, and the self-levelling on some models fails to do its job. Specialists sell conversion kits.

The epitome of Jaguar luxury and style: an American-specification Vanden Plas version from the 1992 model year.

The X-300 *and* XJ8

In 1994 the XJs were cleverly re-styled in the mould of the old XJ saloon. Every panel was new; in fact, only the floorpan of the old model was retained. Not only did this model – code-named X-300 – look better, but it was also cheaper to make and had better panel fit.

Although it was clearly based on the outgoing XJ40, the 1994 X-300 saloon – bank-rolled by Ford to the tune of £200 million – was effectively a new car. For the next eight years this vehicle and its replacement, the XJ8, would give Jaguar a viable presence in the large luxury saloon sector that gave nothing away to its German competitors in terms of speed, refinement and, for perhaps the first time, build quality.

Outside, every panel was new on a body that was easier to make and had tighter panel gaps. Styling chief Geoff Lawson's award-winning design

recalled the classic Series III XJ6 with four lamps on all models, a sculptured bonnet and new tail lights of more SIII-like shape. In Italy the X-300 was voted 'the most beautiful car in the world', although it remains to be seen how long its retro look will remain fashionable.

There were five different suspension packages, although the basic engineering was carried over from the old car. The new supercharged XJR was firmer, and the top-of-the-range Daimler Double-Six cossetingly soft for tired tycoons. The unreliable self-levelling had gone and basic models were given 20 per cent stiffer front

Jaguar XJ8 3.2
1997–

ENGINE:
All-alloy 90-degree V8	
Bore x stroke	86 x 70mm
Capacity	3,248cc
Valves	dohc
Compression ratio	10.5:1
Fuel system	sequential injection
Power	240bhp (DIN) at 6,350rpm
Torque	233lb ft (DIN) at 4,350rpm

TRANSMISSION:
Five-speed automatic	
Final drive	3.27:1

SUSPENSION:
Front: double wishbones, coil springs, telescopic dampers and anti-roll bar
Rear: independent lower wishbone/upper driveshaft link with radius arms and single coil springs
Steering	rack-and-pinion with power assistance

BRAKES:
Discs, vented front and rear

WHEELS:
8 x 16-inch (406mm) alloys with 225/55 ZR 16 tyres

BODYWORK:
Unitary all-steel construction

LENGTH:	16ft 4.4in (5m)
WIDTH:	6ft 6.9in (2m)
HEIGHT:	4ft 6.3in (1.38m)
WEIGHT:	32.7cwt (1,663kg)
MAX SPEED:	139mph (224kph)
0–60mph (97kph)	7.9 seconds

PRICE NEW (1998): £34,475

Jaguar XJ8 4.0
1997–

As XJ8 3.2 except:
ENGINE:
Capacity	3,996cc
Power	290bhp at 6,100rpm
Torque	290lb ft at 4,250rpm

WHEELS:
8 x 17-inch (432mm) alloys with 235/50 ZR 17 tyres

MAX SPEED:	150mph (241kph)
0–60mph (97kph)	6.9 seconds

PRICE NEW (1998): £40,975

Jaguar XJR 4.0
1997–

As XJ8 4.0 except:
Fuel system	sequential injection, Eaton supercharger
Power	370bhp at 6,150rpm
Torque	387lb ft at 3,600rpm
MAX SPEED:	155mph (249kph)
0–60mph (97kph)	5.3 seconds

PRICE NEW (1998): £50,675

PRODUCTION FIGURES (up until 2001):
3.2 4Q	9,047
3.2 long wheelbase 7Q	687
3.2 Sovereign 4S	1,936
3.2 Sovereign lwb 7S	325
3.2 Sport 4N	3,678
4.0 4R	7,463
4.0 long wheelbase 7R	123
4.0 Sovereign 4T	32,264
4.0 Sovereign lwb 7T	11,448
4.0 s/c 4H	14,235
4.0 VDP 4P	1
4.0 VDP lwb 7P	19,783
4.0 VDP s/c lwb 7E	643
Daimler V8 4.0 4U	59
Daimler V8 4.0 lwb 7U	2,070
Daimler V8 4.0 s/c 4G	76
Daimler V8 4.0 s/c lwb 7G	2,269

anti-roll bars. Traction control was standard on the XJR and the V12s, and the ZF power steering was new, with more feel and a better-looking wheel.

A more sculptured dashboard with a new binnacle gave the X-300 a more modern flavour inside, but door casings were as before. Seats were new and rear passenger legroom had improved, although it still lagged behind the Mercedes opposition in this respect. Long-wheelbase models had been to special order in the case of the superseded range, but for X-300 they became a showroom model, with the lengthened body being standardised on the Daimlers in 1995. The Double-Six versions came with electrical adjustment for the individual rear seats, and announced in October was a commemorative Daimler Century – celebrating 100 years of the marque – with special badging, and equipped to be the plushest X-300 of them all.

Under the bonnet the AJ6 had been reworked to become the AJ16, with revised induction porting, new cam profiles, a higher compression and new pistons. The result was 8 per cent more power for the 3.2 (219bhp) and 10 per cent more for the 4 litre (249bhp). If that was not enough, there was always the creamy smooth but thirsty V12 (unchanged) or the new 326bhp supercharged 3.2 litre XJR with an Eaton M90 blower. Boosting at 10psi, this belt-driven device gave the XJR a broad and progressive power band and very healthy torque, of 378lb ft at 3,050rpm.

Five-speed manuals would sprint to 60mph (97kph) in 5.5 seconds and the top end was a restricted 155mph (249kph). More importantly, here for the first time was an XJ with really involving handling. No longer was the steering slightly remote in feel, and the cornering poise slightly floaty, yet Jaguar had managed to maintain a

ride that was marvellously smooth, especially considering the massive 255/45 ZR17 tyres. In that department, at least, it had its German rivals licked.

A mesh front grille distinguished it from other XJs, along with massive 17-inch (432mm) alloys, a body-colour rubbing strip and, inside, more supportive sports seats than in the standard 3.2 and 4 litre versions. Otherwise it was the same elegant car as the standard X-300 XJ6 – the days of ugly TWR body kits for the sporty XJs had long gone, thank goodness. Later would come special editions, like the XJ 3.2 Executive of April 1996 with climate control and leather-faced sports seats. Later that year the rear bench was reshaped to take three passengers, although the legroom remained poor. It was perhaps in response to this widespread criticism that Jaguar made the long-wheelbase body standard on Sovereign models.

The six-cylinder Jaguar engine was radically revised for the new X-300 to become the AJ16. The top-of-the-range model had a supercharger and delivered 326bhp.

At the time of the X-300's launch in the autumn of 1994, Jaguar engineers privately admitted that time was running out for the straight-six, which lacked the smoothness and ultimate silence of the best V8s from Mercedes, BMW and Audi (with its new A8), not to mention the new benchmark Lexus from Japan.

Sure enough, in 1997 came an even more radically revised XJ, the XJ8. Outwardly it did not look all that different apart from bigger bumpers, yet underneath was a car that relied heavily on the new XK8 coupé for its engineering.

Out went the 'sixes' and the venerable V12, and in came the 90-degree, sequentially injected V8 in 3.2 and 4 litre form, the latter with an even bigger Eaton supercharger in XJR guise. At 370bhp – produced at 6,000rpm – this was Jaguar's most powerful production engine yet, also used in a top-line Daimler version called the Super V8.

There were no manuals now as there was nothing available that could take the power. Supercharged cars had a Mercedes five-speed automatic, lesser versions the electronic five-speeder from the XK8. All models came with ASC stability control, which used the anti-lock braking to check wheelspin and reduced torque by automatically retarding the ignition. On all but the 3.2 litre, traction control featured, in conjunction with ASC – using the rear brakes to provide a kind of limited slip differential. The brakes themselves were better than ever, with bigger vented discs at the front.

A new double-wishbone front suspension – from the XK8 –

Hearses and limousines

With the demise of the DS420 Daimler's limousine offerings have gone down the 'stretch' route, and are built by officially sanctioned coachbuilders who are otherwise independent of the factory. The North-West of England seems to be the heartland of limousine building, so it comes as no surprise to find that the current XJ8-based cars are built in Bolton, Lancashire, by Eagle Specialists Vehicles, although they are distributed by Wilcox Limousines of Buckinghamshire.

Hearse and six-door limousine versions are available (the latter with occasional seats),

mechanically identical to the standard factory offerings. The £76,000 Daimler has the 4.0 litre V8 and there are £8,000 cheaper Jaguar versions with the 3.2 litre engine. They come with everything that standard wheelbase saloons have but there are several special options, such as manual or electric divisions and flag masts. As well as the lengthened wheelbase there are extensive changes to the roof line on the limousines, which are much higher and more formal. The hearse model was used to take the Queen Mother – a life-long Daimler buyer – to lie in state when she died in 2002.

sharpened the steering of the V8s and improved refinement, while the rear suspension was tweaked to reduce squat and lift under braking.

The interior, still short on rear legroom compared with its German rivals, was restyled along XK8 lines with a new, swoopy dash, recessed dials and a new centre console.

All these cars were effortlessly quick, with much faster throttle response than on the 'six', and muscular mid-range thrust from a whisper-smooth V8. Auto 'boxes were slick, and refinement and build quality of the stiffer bodyshell world class.

At the top of the range the supercharged XJR, at £50,000, was simply magnificent. Heroic acceleration was on hand from virtually any engine speed and with no lag from the blower. Cracking 60mph (97kph) in 5.3 seconds and 100mph (161kph) in 12.8, it was limited to 155mph (249kph) although ungoverned test cars had touched 170mph (274kph).

Again Jaguar had arrived at a ride/handling compromise that eclipsed even the standard-setting M5 BMW, mixing sensational grip from aggressively wide 255/40 Pirellis with superb poise and balance for a big saloon. Only the steering fell short of ultimate standards, lacking a little in feedback.

There have been few changes to the car since its launch, other than minor steering modifications and the introduction of a sports suspension option on the Sovereign.

Whether V8 saloons will ever be regarded as collectable classics remains to be seen, but they certainly introduced levels of quality never previously thought possible on a Jaguar, particularly the post-X-300 cars, which have come near the standard-setting Lexus in the influential American JD Power

Buying Hints

1. On earlier cars front wheel bearings wear prematurely, but this shortcoming was solved with a later modification.

2. Later cars suffer from brake judder: Jaguar may have changed its supplier of discs at some point.

3. These are heavy, fast cars shod with expensive rubber, so you should check the tyres for excessive and uneven wear.

4. The 3.2 can suffer from some engine problems, but this is a known fault. As a consequence, Jaguar may honour engine changes after the car is out of warranty, as long as the car has a main dealer service history. Bore 'wash' from over-fuelling is the problem, causing lack of performance and poor fuel consumption.

5. The instrument pack has some soldering on the back that can break down, meaning that the unit has to be renewed – which means the car resumes with a mileage reading of zero. Hence it is important to buy a car with a full service history in which such work has been documented.

6. On six-cylinder X-300 cars, rear shock absorbers may be worn and are expensive to replace – the sound may make you think the spare wheel is loose. A heavy load in the boot will silence the rattle . . .

7. On higher-mileage cars, you may find some slack and 'shunt' in the differential.

8. The consensus in the trade is that these cars are very close to German standards of fit and finish, so the interior should be in good condition and there should certainly be no rust.

Customer Satisfaction Index. Here was a Jaguar fit to be compared with the best, a car that no longer had to rely on its beauty or quaint appeal as the charming old SIII had done. It was a car you could buy with your heart and your head.

The later X-300 models, a 2002 model XJ8 is shown here, featured the muscular 90-degree, injected V8 engine used in the XK8. The quality and finish of these cars surpassed that of all previous XJs.

The X-350 series

The X-350 first appeared as Jaguar's flagship in 2003. The curvaceous styling linked the car to the earlier X-300.

In the 2003 XJ, coded X-350, Jaguar finally had a big saloon that could square up to the best and latest from BMW, Mercedes and Audi. The XJ40 and its X-300 descendants had finally been laid to rest after a long and successful run. The creators of the X-350 had been able to draw from the beginning on the much deeper resources of Ford to build a big Jaguar for the 21st century, cast recognisably – perhaps too recognisably – in the mould of its ancestors but new in almost every detail.

Its German rivals had evolved at least twice during the 1986–2003 lifespan of the XJ40/X-300 series. The X-350, drenched in new technology, was a car that could match them on every level with no excuses.

A new big car rival had emerged in the form of Audi's A8 with its much-touted aluminium spaceframe. The new XJ even had the measure of this technocrat with an aluminium chassis and body 40 per cent lighter and 60 per cent stiffer than its predecessor. In construction it was similar to a steel body but with its stressed underbody sections bonded rather than welded, using aerospace grade epoxy adhesives plus 3,200 self-piercing rivets. At 3,390lb (1,541kg), the Jaguar was 600lb (273kg) lighter than the Audi. Jaguar calculated that the bare XJ body weighed about the same as a complete BMW-MINI. The designers claimed it was easier and thus cheaper to repair than an equivalent steel body. All subsequent new Jaguars would use similar body construction technology.

The curvy styling was a link with the previous XJ, and older models from the '60s, but the 'six light' roof was dispensed with. It was a handsome, imposing car but many felt it looked too safe and frumpy and didn't present an aesthetic advance over the old model. The S-Class Mercedes and Audi A8 had successfully blended edgy visuals and a commanding presence with a contemporary flavour, a trick that was eluding Jaguar stylists who were still locked into a cycle of uninspired retro designs.

On the plus side, interior space was more generous than before in head and legroom, but with the proper cosseting and cosy Jaguar feel. Double-glazed side windows added to the atmosphere of serene isolation in a car that rode all surfaces beautifully with masterful filtration of road noise. The boot was bigger, although still rather shallow overall.

The leather and walnut flavour remained inside and, again, it was

widely felt that the treatment was too traditional. A rather unsubtle slab of burr walnut, satin walnut, or elm veneer (or aluminium) across the facia looked like a slavish nod to the XJs of the past. It was probably smarter than it looked in that it incorporated the car's myriad labour-saving gadgets and features in a rational way that was intuitive to use. Jaguar intended that the XJ be simple and straightforward to drive, with few distractions. It was well-crafted inside with only the occasional Ford-sourced piece of switchgear spoiling the opulent mood.

Technically, the cars were superbly developed, right first time and priced to undercut the opposition in the true Jaguar tradition. The range was initially comprised of two 4.2 petrol V8s – supercharged and normally aspirated giving 300 and 400bhp respectively – and an 'entry-level' 3.0 V6 with a very adequate 240bhp. Europe but not Britain was also offered a 3.5-litre V8 with 262bhp,

The X-350 featured an aluminium monocoque, with a stressed floor-pan bonded with epoxy adhesive and self-piercing rivets, making it far lighter and stiffer than its predecessor.

while a torquey and refined 2.7-litre bi-turbo diesel would follow in 2005 in the rather clumsily named XJ TDVi.

This last engine was one of the best diesel installations on the market and in some ways the pick of the new XJ range, a 35mpg luxury saloon every bit as fast and effortless as its petrol equivalent that also qualified for lower company car tax and was exempt from the three per cent diesel

The 2.7-litre bi-turbo diesel proved to be one of the best diesel installations on the market, providing smooth power delivery and high mid-range torque.

surcharge because it met Euro IV emission standards.

With nearly half of all large luxury car sales now diesel, Jaguar knew it had to offer an oil burner, but not until it could produce a car that set new standards of refinement. Jointly developed with Peugeot, the V6 ran higher injection pressures than the equivalent unit in the S-Type for more precise combustion and throttle response. Electronic engine mounts reduced vibration – particularly at idle – and the bonnet sealing was more comprehensive. From the inside, a secondary bulkhead filtered out almost any trace of harshness under acceleration. This really was a diesel that matched the smoothness and refinement of its petrol equivalent. At 204bhp it was less

Driving the XJ (X-350)

There are no 'weak' versions of the XJ. Be it a thrifty V6 diesel or a throaty supercharged V8, all XJs are consummate mile-eating executive luxury cars, faster, quieter and roomier than the XJs that came before yet perfectly capturing the silky relaxed feel that has always been at the heart of what makes the big Jaguar saloon such a special drive.

The 240bhp V6 is free-revving (to 6,900rpm), thoroughly sweet and very fast, yet the bi-turbo diesel is equally accomplished with, if anything, even stronger mid-range punch and levels of refinement that will astonish. For once you really would have to strain your ears to satisfy yourself you were in a

diesel-powered car thanks to sophisticated and thorough isolation and clever management of vibration plus a flawlessly smooth yet responsive automatic gearbox.

This ZF unit, common to all models, is one of the keys to the XJ's silky drivetrain and is refreshingly free of paddle shifts and other distracting modes and gadgets. The V8s are super strong and very refined with acceleration that snaps the car off the line and wafts it urgently yet serenely to a cruising speed of 130 or 140mph. The supercharger adds another layer of aggression to that delivery with an almost alarming rate of acceleration to challenge any four-door car in the world.

There is a magic and subtlety to the car's cosseting and quiet air-sprung ride that outranks the German opposition and there is no trade-off in the handling which, thanks to that light, stiff bonded aluminium shell, feels agile and incisive through the Servotronic power steering. The XJ feels much smaller than it is, in fact, when you drive it hard it never loses its composure.

The XJ is a car remarkably free of weak points. It has no build quality problems or driving problems, only an image problem – the unremarkable styling makes it seem something of an old man's car. It is a shame this has clouded perceptions of what must be one of Jaguar's best achievements to date.

powerful than the petrol V6 but the secret of its crushing mid-range overtaking ability was its 321lb ft of torque, peaking at just 1,900rpm.

Beautifully made and very fully equipped, even the entry-level Sport models (later renamed Executive) came with a long specification that included air suspension, anti-whiplash 12-way power seats (and pedal adjustment), cruise control, rain-sensitive wipers, parking sensors and a superb ZF six-speed automatic gearbox. Dual-stage front side and head airbags were used across the range as part of the XJ's 'adaptive restraint' technology that sensed the position of the seats. All the doors locked automatically at speeds over 5mph.

The SE (Sovereign from 2006) added 16-way power front seats, soft grain leather, a touch-screen satellite navigation system, xenon headlamps and bigger 19-inch alloy wheels to that equipment list. You could have the SE/Sovereign as a V6 diesel or petrol or a naturally aspirated 4.2 V8. The Supercharged V8 was a stand-alone model with bigger brakes and satellite navigation as standard.

The ZF Servotronic speed-sensitive power steering was calibrated to each engine and suspension combination and the low weight of the aluminium-bodied XJ made it an extraordinarily agile car for its size and class. Self-levelling air suspension, replacing steel springs, was used on all four wheels – these spring/damper units had height sensors feeding information to an electronic computer module that kept the ride level at all times, regardless of load. When parked for long periods it even re-energised itself every 24 hours to level the car.

Jaguar's two-stage adaptive ride system, working on the dampers, was standard on the XJ. With the 300bhp V8 there was the possibility of a long-wheelbase body offering a metre of legroom to rear-seat passengers, who

could work on their laptops on 'business trays' and luxuriate in individual climate control and powered seat adjustment.

Only the V8 XJs were sold on the North American market. The top version for 2006 was the Super V8 Portfolio, the most expensive Jaguar saloon up to that point and built in a short run of 145 cars which, even at $120,000, immediately sold out. With V8 power, boxwood veneer inlays and huge 20-inch alloys, the Portfolio came only as a supercharged long-wheelbase car, a true hot rod limousine that could hit 60mph in 5.0 seconds.

Jaguar was sensitive to criticisms of the XJ's body style and cleaned the

shape up in 2006 with flush glass and fewer trim mouldings. There were a number of sound-deadening measures introduced at the same time.

At the Geneva show in 2007, the styling of the XJ, now offered in Executive, Sovereign, Sport Premium and XJR, was refreshed. At the front there were new grilles and bumper, plus new side vents, lower side sills, door mirrors with integrated

The interior of the long-wheelbase X-350 provided a high degree of luxury and equipment.

indicators and a small rear spoiler. Executive-spec models now came with 19-inch Carelia wheels, while Sovereign versions got the new Polaris design. The supercharged XJR gained aluminium-finish vents and black-painted brake callipers. Revisions to the interior included redesigned heated front seats as standard. Executive models gained a heated front windscreen, and XJRs an 'R' gear knob and heated front seats with ventilation (optional in other versions). All models had an upgraded Bluetooth system allowing for the connection of up to five mobile phones.

By 2008, sales of the XJ, never that strong, had dipped. For 2009 Jaguar reduced the engine range to just the 2.7 diesel and supercharged 4.2 V8, and it became an open secret that a new model, the X351, was under development, with much more dramatic styling but probably based on the floor pan of the existing car. When that car appears in 2009 the modern Jaguar line-up will be complete.

Daimler

Jaguar continues to value its Daimler brand but has struggled to find much of a role for it in recent years. Always perceived as Jaguar's more patrician stablemate, and a rare example of shameless badge-engineering in the world of luxury cars, it looked like the name might be put on ice

The X-350-based Daimler Super V8.

for good when the X-350 series of XJs appeared in 2003 with no Daimler alternative on offer. This initial hesitance may have been a reaction to the requirements of the American market where Daimler was unknown and might anyway have been confused with Daimler-Benz products. Yet the name still had a chic cachet, particularly in Germany and Belgium, and was revived after a three-year break on a long wheelbase X-350

saloon called the Daimler Super V8, replacing the Jaguar Super 8 at the top of the XJ range. It came with the supercharged V8 and could be recognised by its fluted Daimler grille and boot plinth, chrome rear light surrounds and special 19-inch alloy wheels. Its high spec interior had all the features of other long wheelbase models plus heated rear seats and a multimedia system that played DVDs and ran TV and games.

Jaguar XJ 2.7 V6 TDVi diesel Executive 2008-

ENGINE:
60 degree V6 (diesel)

Bore x stroke	81 x 88mm
Capacity	2720cc
Valves	24 valve DOHC
Compression ratio	17.3:1
Fuel system	Common rail injection
Power	204bhp at 4000rpm
Torque	321lb ft at 1900rpm

TRANSMISSION:
6 Speed ZF automatic

SUSPENSION:	Front: unequal length wishbones, air springs
STEERING:	ZF Servotronic rack and pinion

BRAKES:
Ventilated discs front and rear

WHEELS:
18-inch alloys, optional 20-inch

BODYWORK:
Bonded aluminium monocoque

LENGTH:	
Standard wheelbase 16ft 7in (5,055mm)	
Long wheelbase 17ft 01in (5,207mm)	
WIDTH:	6ft 2.3in (1,887mm)
HEIGHT:	4ft 9in (1,448mm)
WEIGHT:	
Standard wheelbase 3,657lb (1,662kg)	
Long wheelbase 3,671lb (1,669kg)	

MAX SPEED:	141mph
0–60	7.8 seconds
MPG:	35mpg combined
PRICE NEW:	£51,520 (Sovereign)

Jaguar XJ 3.0 V6 (petrol) 2003-2009

As XJ 2.7 except:
ENGINE:
60 degree V6 (petrol)

Bore x stroke	89 x 79.5
Capacity	2,967cc
Valves	24 valve DOHC
Compression ratio	10.5:1
Fuel system	Fuel injection
Power	240bhp at 6,000rpm
Torque	221lb ft at 4,106rpm
Weight	3,393lb (1,542kg)

MAX SPEED:	145mph
0–60	7.8 seconds
MPG	26.9 combined
PRICE NEW:	£43,540 (Executive)

Jaguar XJ 4.2 V8 2003-2009

AS XJ 3.0 except:
ENGINE:
V8

Bore x stroke	86 x 90.3
Capacity	4,196cc
Valves	DOHC
Compression ratio	11:1
Fuel system	Fuel injection
Power	300bhp at 6,000rpm
Torque	310lb ft at 4,100rpm

WEIGHT:	
Standard wheelbase 3,547lb (1,612kg)	
Long wheelbase 3,560lb (1,618kg)	

MAX SPEED:	155mph (limited)
0–60	6.3 seconds
MPG	24.8 combined
PRICE NEW:	£58,040 (Sovereign)

JAGUAR XJ 4.2 Supercharged 2003-

As XJ 4.2 litre except:

Compression ratio	9:1
Power	400bhp at 6,100rpm
Torque	408lb ft at 3,500rpm

MAX SPEED:	155mph (limited)
0–60	5.0 seconds
MPG:	23.4 combined
PRICE NEW:	£60,150

The S-Type
and X-Type

F or Jaguar to thrive as a luxury car manufacturer in the 21st century, Ford concluded that the firm needed vastly to increase its output. Achieving this meant a move downmarket, to face the harsher realities of the mid-range executive sector held in the steely grip of the benchmark BMW 5 Series. This was the car Jaguar had to beat, or at least match, if it was to gain credibility in this viciously contested sector of the market.

Enter, in 1999, the X200 – or S-Type, to give it its proper showroom title, the first medium-sized Jaguar since the demise of the 240/340 MkII-based saloon in 1969. The S-Type moniker was revived so as to avoid the confusion surrounding the MkII, although it is to the latter car that the X200 most obviously pays homage.

Technically it owed very little to any existing Jaguar model. Indeed, its genes were almost as American as

The new S-Type saloon with its inspiration, the MkII, and the original 1963 S-Type. Other than the pastiche grille, the shape lacked character and did not receive universal praise.

Jaguar S-Type 3.0 V6
1998–2008

ENGINE:
All-alloy 60-degree V6

Bore x stroke	89 x 79.5mm
Capacity	2,967cc
Valves	double ohc, 24 valves
Compression ratio	10.5:1
Fuel system	injection with electronic management
Power	240bhp (DIN) at 6,800rpm
Torque	221lb ft (DIN) at 4,500rpm

TRANSMISSION:
Five speed manual/six-speed auto

SUSPENSION:
Front: independent double wishbones, coil springs, telescopic dampers, electronic stability control, CATS adaptive damping optional
Rear: independent double wishbone and coil springs, anti-roll bar, electronic stability control, CATS adaptive damping optional

Steering	rack-and-pinion with power assistance, 2.6 turns lock-to-lock

BRAKES:
Vented discs, ABS

WHEELS:
Alloy, with 205/60 ZR 16 tyres

BODYWORK:
Unitary all-steel construction

LENGTH:	15ft 11.4in (4.86m)
WIDTH:	5ft 11.6in (1.82m)
HEIGHT:	4ft 8.9in (1.44m)
WEIGHT:	32.8cwt (1,670kg)

MAX SPEED:	235kph (146mph) (141mph auto SE)
0-60mph (97kph):	6.9 seconds (8.0 seconds auto SE)

MPG (combined):	29 (manual), 27 (auto)

PRICE NEW (2002)	V6 Sport £29,950 V6 SE £31,400

Jaguar S-Type 2.5 V6
2001–2008

As S-Type 3.0 except:
ENGINE:
V6

Bore x stroke	81.65 x 79.5mm
Capacity	2,497cc
Power	201bhp at 6,800rpm
Torque	184lb ft at 4,000rpm

WHEELS:
Alloy, 7.5 x 17in, 235/50ZR17 tyres

WEIGHT:	31.9cwt (1,622kg)

MAX SPEED:	142mph (228kph)
0-60mph (97kph)	8.2 seconds

MPG (combined):	29.6 (manual)

PRICE NEW (2002):	£25,495–£28,900

Jaguar S-Type 4.2 V8
2001–2008

As S-Type 3.0 except:
ENGINE:
V8

Bore x stroke	86 x 90.3mm
Capacity	4,196cc
Valves	double ohc, 32 valves
Compression ratio	11:1
Power	300bhp at 6,000rpm
Torque	310lb ft at 4,100rpm

TRANSMISSION:
Six-speed automatic

WHEELS:
Alloy, 235/50 ZR17 tyres

WEIGHT:	34.2cwt (1,737kg)

MAX SPEED:	155mph (249kph)
0-60mph (97kph)	6.2 seconds

MPG (combined):	23

PRICE NEW (2002):	£36,000

Jaguar S-Type R 4.2 V8 (supercharged)
2001–2008

As S-Type 4.2 except:
ENGINE:
V8, Supercharged

Power	400bhp at 6,100rpm
Torque	408lb ft at 3,500rpm
Compression ratio	9:1

WEIGHT:	35.4cwt (1,802kg)

WHEELS:
Alloy, 8 x 18in front, 9.5 x 18in rear, 245/40 ZR18 tyres front, 275/35 ZR 18 rear

MAX SPEED:	155mph (249kph) (governed)
0-60mph (97kph)	5.3 seconds

MPG (combined):	22.5

PRICE NEW (2002):	£47,400

they were British, the S-Type having been developed in tandem with Ford USA's Lincoln LS. The two cars shared underbody components, suspension design and many hidden parts, making the S-Type badge rather appropriate: that original 1963 car, with its blend of MkII and MkX styling and E-Type rear suspension, was distinctly cross-pollinated too. Nevertheless, sensitive to comparisons with the Lincoln, Jaguar was keen to point out that the S-Type would have turned out just the same even if it had been developed alone.

The new model was to be built at Jaguar's refurbished Castle Bromwich factory in Birmingham. During the war this plant had built Spitfires and Lancaster bombers, but much of it had been mothballed since Leyland

days and trees were even growing through the assembly tracks.

Funded by Jaguar itself rather than Ford, it was hoped that the new car would double Jaguar's sales volume in the first full year of production. The company predicted that 40 per cent of all S-Types would go to the USA, eight per cent to Germany and five per cent to Japan, with the remaining 20 per cent for the home market.

Styled under the authority of Geoff Lawson, the S-Type's body was viewed as controversial. Rather than a modern interpretation of a classic saloon car shape, the car was dismissed by some pundits as a cynical retro pastiche, particularly the front with its caricature oval grille, which was actually more like a MkI

The S-Type's swoopy dashboard, unlike that of any previous Jaguar saloon, features voice-activated controls for the telephone, stereo and interior climate.

because it lacked the central dividing bar of the MkII. The influences didn't stop there. The curvy bonnet, rounded roofline and ovoid rear window were clearly inspired by the MkII. All this may have passed muster if the tail of the car hadn't been so nondescript: from the back the S-Type looked unnervingly like a big Daewoo saloon.

Unfavourable comparisons were drawn with the Rover 75 launched at the same time (the 1998 Birmingham show), a much more elegant design in many ways. The first S-Type designs had resembled a smaller, rounder XJ, but Jaguar was looking for a car with a different identity rather than a scaled-down version of what it already had.

The second prototype had an XK8 air intake and an even more rounded roofline and looked like an XK turned into a saloon. It was abandoned as being 'not Jaguar enough' in favour of a MkIII with an upright slatted oval grille and horizontal lights and droop-line along its flanks, to echo the profile of

the original MkII while retaining a decently-sized boot. Still, it was felt the tail wasn't right.

Enter the S-Type MkIV, which had the definitive front end but was too long and looked too American. In the end, the adopted design had the front of the MkIV, the profile of the MkIII, and a totally new tail. Perhaps Lawson, who died not long after the car was introduced, might have produced something more daring if he had not had to answer to the Detroit boardroom.

Before committing to the car's body tooling, Jaguar had to send the final clay model to the Ford HQ in Dearborn. On the way the airline company lost it for a while – it was eventually discovered on a runway in Tel Aviv, Israel!

Perhaps the S-Type was a better car to drive than it was to look at. Certainly all S-Types were meaty performers. The V8 auto would swish

From the back there is little to say that this is a Jaguar. The side window line echoes that of the '60s cars but the waistline crease seems fussy.

to 60mph (97kph) in 6.6 seconds and top 150mph (241kph), and the manual V6 – perhaps the best variant for keen drivers – wasn't far behind. As a sports saloon it was a worthy adversary for the 5 Series, though it still fell short of top honours. In its 4.0-litre version the V8 was a cracker, but many didn't like the over-light throttle action or the lack of mid-range punch in the V6 which, perhaps, was not as refined as some of its rivals.

The chassis had lots of grip and good steering combined with a supple silken ride that could only be that of a Jaguar. The almost 40-year-old XJ-type rear suspension was totally abandoned for the S-Type in favour of an entirely new design front and rear. The front used two subframes and carried the variable-ratio steering rack. The single rear subframe carried aluminium wishbones each side, the pivot axes angled to reduce dive and squat under braking. The Lincoln LS had all this too – the differences came in the all-important areas of damping, springs and bushing. Dynamic Stability Control, to supplement the traction control, was an option, using sensory information

from steering wheel movement, lateral acceleration, rate of change in direction of travel, wheel speeds and brake pressure.

Drivers sat higher in the S-Type than in other Jaguars, so visibility was better, with clear instrumentation in the otherwise bloated, unattractive dashboard that many felt was plasticky and unappealing despite the generous use of maple walnut veneer with chrome highlights. The half-wood, half-leather steering wheel was also of questionable taste. Still, you could tailor a good driving position thanks to powered front seats that were standard in all models, with a memory pack in more upmarket versions.

The base 3.0 model came with velour, all the rest with full leather. All the cars had an impressive specification for their price, with air-conditioning and cruise control coming as standard. They also had side airbags in all doors as well as the usual driver and passenger ones. There was a unique-fit, RDS-equipped stereo – not reckoned to be as good as some of the competition – while a multi-disc CD, with a handy changer in the

glove box, was an expensive £1,040 option.

Considering the amount of standard equipment not found in many rivals, and the performance, the S-Type wasn't overpriced in its class. It was much better packaged than its forebears and had all the head, leg and elbow room one expected in this class. The boot was well shaped and the rear seats split 50/50 and folded flat.

On its release the range spanned three models, starting with a £28,000 V6 manual, then the slightly more opulent V6 automatic SE, and finally the V8 five-speed automatic using a modified version of the XK8 engine slightly detuned to 280bhp. This featured new continuously variable valve timing and double-skinned exhaust manifolds to keep the heat inside, thus allowing the catalysts to fire up more quickly. Inside were such niceties as satellite navigation, a

The buying public loved the looks of the S-Type even if styling gurus were unsure. The big 18-inch wheels seen here certainly gave it a tougher look.

built-in GSM telephone, automatic rain-detecting windscreen wipers and, for the first time on a production car, full voice activation for the telephone, air-conditioning and sound system.

The V6 engine was an all-aluminium unit, good for 240bhp at 6,800rpm (the highest peak power speed ever on a production Jaguar). This was based on the Ford family of V6s rather than a shortened Jaguar V8, but Jaguar was keen to point out that there was very little left of the original Mondeo engine (just the block casting and crank).

Built by Ford USA in Cleveland, but developed by Jaguar engineers, it was a four-cam 24-valve engine with lightweight aluminium bucket tappets with variable inlet valve timing. The manual gearbox – with its not at all Jaguar-like lightweight clutch action – was built by Getrag in Germany, the five-speed automatic by Ford in North America.

At least initially, the S-Type proved every bit as successful as Jaguar – and Ford – hoped, with 75,000 sold. A revised model was unveiled in January 2002 with an altered suspension set-up and a much more attractive interior including optional touch-screen telematics. The automatic version was now a six-speeder. The range was also expanded, with a new 2.5-litre entry level model (still good for 140mph and 0–60mph in 8.2 seconds) and, more excitingly, a 400bhp supercharged V8 version. Named S-Type R, this was the most potent Jaguar saloon ever, for which the company claimed 0–60mph in 5.3 seconds and a governed top speed of 155mph (249kph).

The V8 was slightly bigger at 4.2 litres (as it was in lesser V8 versions) and was matched to Brembo brakes, higher-rate springs and CATS adaptive damping, which stiffened the rear dampers an instant ahead of the fronts to give sharper turn-in. You

Ford Mondeo genes are certainly not evident in the rounded lines of the X-Type, which is less self-consciously retro than its big brother, the S-Type.

could recognise the Type R on the outside by its different-sized wheels and tyres (8x18s running 245/40ZR tyres at the front with 275/35ZRs at the rear). At £47,500 it was more than £11,000 more expensive than the 300bhp normally aspirated V8, but was still 10 per cent cheaper than its nearest rival, the BMW M5.

If the S-Type marked Jaguar's return to a market that it had abandoned with the demise of the MkII, then the X-Type was a move in a totally new direction and represented a major gamble. From its secure but small niche in the prestige car market, Jaguar now turned to confront cars such as the BMW 3 Series and the Audi A4 head-on, with a model designed to capture a younger market.

The 2008-model S-Type R had an imposing presence sitting on its 18-inch alloys and, at the time, was the most potent Jaguar saloon yet built.

Visually this new car was deemed to be more successful than the somewhat cartoonish S-Type, its four-headlight nose, wide grille and shapely side profile borrowing details from the big XJ saloon. Jaguar managed to disguise the chunkiness of the car's rising wedge, but it still fell some way short of genuine grace. Nevertheless, to their credit, the designers managed to make it more roomy than the S-Type inside, while mixing German standards of ergonomic excellence with a traditionally warm Jaguar feel.

Not only had the 2001 X-Type been developed in record time – a mere two years from board approval to production – but it was to be built at Ford's reorganised Halewood plant, away from Jaguar's traditional Midlands base.

As part of Ford, Jaguar had access to unrivalled research and development expertise and resources to develop the X-Type. To compete in the premium compact market sector, this ability to use volume-produced Ford

parts was crucial to the project's success. Jaguar's ability to pick and choose amongst Mondeo parts for the X-Type allowed the economies of volume production without compromising the end product.

Much emphasis was placed upon telematics, with class-leading navigation, entertainment and information systems available throughout the range. Their sophistication and complexity meant that these could not be ad hoc additions but had to be integrated into the design and structure of the car's electronics. It was envisaged that perhaps 15–20 per cent of customers would opt for the full package and Jaguar clearly saw these features as important to the new generation of potential buyers.

To meet the expectations of its traditional discerning customers as well, Jaguar sought to find technical solutions which provided the traditional 'feel' of the brand in a 21st-century car. Given the complex and intangible nature of Jaguar's traditional appeal this was no easy task. In its attempt to meet this target, the designers brought a new

Jaguar X-Type 2.0 V6 (front-wheel-drive) 2003–2007

ENGINE:
Transverse V6
Bore x stroke	81.6 x 66.8mm
Capacity	2,099cc
Valves	double ohc, 24 valves
Compression ratio	10.75:1
Power	157bhp at 6,800rpm
Torque	148lb ft at 4,100rpm

TRANSMISSION:
Five-speed manual/five-speed auto

SUSPENSION:
Front MacPherson struts, multi-link rear
Steering	rack-and-pinion with power assistance

BRAKES:
Disc front and rear with ABS

WHEELS:
Alloy, 6.5 x 16in, 205/55 R16 tyres

LENGTH (Saloon):	15ft 3.8in (4.67m)
WIDTH (Saloon):	5ft 10in (1.78m)
HEIGHT (Saloon):	4ft 6.7in (1.39m)
WEIGHT (Saloon):	28.5–29.2cwt (1,451–1,486kg)

MAX SPEED:	130mph (209kph) (manual)
	127mph (204kph) (auto)
0–60mph (97kph)	8.9 seconds (manual)
	9.4 seconds (auto)

MPG (combined):	28–30

PRICE NEW (2002):	£19,995 (2.0 V6) to £23,495 (2.0 V6 Sport Auto)

Jaguar X-Type 2.5 V6 (four-wheel-drive) 2000–2007

As X-Type 2.0 except:
ENGINE:
V6
Bore x stroke	81.6 x 79.5mm
Capacity	2,495cc
Compression ratio	10.3:1
Power	194bhp at 6,800rpm
Torque	180lb ft at 3,000rpm

TRANSMISSION:
Five-speed manual/five-speed auto

WEIGHT:	30.6–31.4cwt (1,556–1,596kg)

MAX SPEED:	140mph (225kph) (manual)
	137mph (220kph) (auto)
0–60mph (97kph)	7.9 seconds (manual)
	8.5 seconds (auto)

MPG (combined):	29 (manual)
	27 (auto)

PRICE NEW (2002):	£22,000–£25,500

Jaguar X-Type 3.0 V6 2000–

As X-Type 2.5 V6 except:
ENGINE:
V6
Bore x stroke	89 x 79.5mm
Capacity	2,967cc
Compression ratio	10.5:1
Power	231bhp at 6,800rpm
Torque	205lb ft at 3,000rpm

TRANSMISSION:
Five-speed manual/five-speed auto

MAX SPEED (Saloon):	143mph (230kph) (auto)
	146mph (235kph) (manual)
0–60mph (97kph)	6.6 seconds (manual)
	7.1 seconds (auto)

MPG (combined):	27

PRICE NEW (2002):	£26,500–£27,750

Jaguar X-Type 2.0 Diesel 2000–

As X-Type 2.0 except;
ENGINE:
Four-cylinder
Bore & Stroke	86 x 86mm
Capacity	1,998cc
Compression ratio:	18.2:1
Power	128bhp at 3,500rpm
Torque	243lb ft at 1,800rpm

TRANSMISSION:
Five-speed manual

MAX SPEED (saloon):	125mph (201kph)
0–60mph (97kph) (saloon)	9.5 seconds

MPG (combined):	50.0

PRICE NEW:	(2009, saloon) £21,058–£28,898

Jaguar X-Type 2.2 Diesel 2000–

As X-Type 2.0 except;
ENGINE:
Four-cylinder
Bore & Stroke	86 x 94.6mm
Capacity	2,198cc
Compression ratio:	17.5:1
Power	155bhp at 3,500rpm
Torque	266lb ft at 1,800rpm

TRANSMISSION:
Six-speed manual/six-speed auto

MAX SPEED (saloon):	137mph (220kph) (manual)
	129mph (208kph) (auto)
0–60mph (97kph) (saloon)	8.5 seconds (manual),
	9.5 seconds (auto)

MPG (combined)	47.1 (manual), 41 (auto)

PRICE NEW:	(2009, saloon) £22,537–£30,269

This ghosted cut-away shows the transverse V6 engine and four-wheel-drive system. Through careful design and use of lightweight materials, there is only a small weight penalty over a conventional two-wheel-drive car of comparable size.

level of refinement to what might be called the synthetic 'driver's car'. Through its sophisticated systems, the X-Type channels and simulates the mechanical 'feel' associated with classic high-performance cars without the adverse intrusions of noise and vibration. Even more importantly it offers the enjoyment and excitement of a responsive car whilst minimising the dangers.

The X-Type has exceptional balance and composure on demanding roads, and steering that gives the kind of feel and feedback that inspires confidence. This is a car that feels solidly planted, with deep reserves of roadholding, whatever the weather. It sets out to flatter the driver, as well as to protect him.

Key elements in this attempt to reinterpret Jaguar marque values for a new century are the sophisticated power units. All-alloy V6 engines of

2.5 and 3.0 litres are linked to an all-wheel-drive system with viscous coupling and rearward-biased torque distribution. Jaguar's designers concluded that driver enjoyment, safety and response all pointed to the four-wheel-drive route, but they also demanded that the vehicle have the feel and response of a rear-wheel-drive car. Fortunately careful design and the extensive use of alloy castings minimised the weight penalty of the all-wheel-drive set-up, designated Traction-4 by Jaguar. The X-Type tipped the scales at a mere 88lb (40kg) more than comparable two-wheel-drive BMW models.

What the Traction-4 system, along with anti-lock braking and dynamic stability control, gave was almost unprecedented levels of stability and security. On the promotional video, a mischievous Eddie Irvine (who at the time drove for Jaguar in Formula One), one hand on the wheel, guides the X-Type through a water-soaked slalom at high speed: "If you tried that in a BMW," he observes, "you'd be in trouble."

This exceptional road behaviour was a joint product of traditional high-quality chassis engineering and high-tech electronic control systems. For Jaguar a starting point had to be a stiff body shell and the designers claimed figures for chassis stiffness 30 per cent up on the current best in class.

ZF provided the Servotronic 2 power steering system, which had undergone extensive development. Perhaps because this was an area in which Jaguar had received criticism in the past, great attention had been devoted to the system's valving. It used electronic control of the assistance curve, which was speed related, and provided what engineers judged to be appropriate feel. Other innovations included a new form of low friction two-piece top bearing for the front strut. The objective was to

preserve a consistency of steering feel in different conditions. At the rear, the modified double-link Mondeo Estate suspension, insulated on a subframe, was both compact and effective.

The four-cam V6 in 2.5 and 3.0-litre form was a development of the S-Type unit. With variable valve timing and variable length inlet tracts the engines had all the features that one would expect. Drivers noticed the unit's free revving characteristics, along with a very flat torque curve. The 2.5 and 3.0 V6s offered above-average power and torque for their size, making the X-Type a brisker machine than its rivals.

However, on the road it wasn't all good news. The 3.0 was pretty effortless, but you needed to make good use of the gears to get the best out of the 2.5. Both engines sounded moderately harsh and strained towards the top end of their rev ranges, failing to match the cultured feel of the straight-six and V6 units of

BMW and Alfa. Here, the Jag betrayed its Ford roots.

In automatic form the X-Type proved disappointing – gearshift quality was often less than smooth, and the 'box frequently indecisive about which gear it should be in.

Quoted power outputs of 194bhp and 231bhp put the Jaguar at the front of its class. Yet simple power and drivability was not enough to meet Jaguar's requirements for the X-Type. It also had to make the appropriate Jaguar sound. To achieve that, intake trunking and exhaust system specifications were adjusted to ensure that this medium-size cat had an appropriate class-leading growl.

Another key to the rapid development of the X-Type was the use of the very latest solid modelling techniques. Jaguar benefited from Ford's C3P systems, which allowed prototype development to be undertaken at great speed. The IDEAS three-dimensional modelling SDRC package

Jaguars at Halewood

When Jaguar moved into the Halewood on Merseyside, management took the view that offering opportunity to the workforce would be a key element in transforming the plant into an environment suitable for the manufacture of Jaguar cars. Indeed, when asked of which aspect of the X-Type's development the company was proudest, then-MD Jonathan Browning had no hesitation in responding that it was the work done with the Halewood workforce and the response that was received.

Managers were at pains to stress that not only had they embarked on the kind of detailed training necessary to ensure that the

workforce had the skills and motivation to achieve the required quality levels, but they had gone several steps further. In particular they took the view that awareness of the product and of the Jaguar tradition, alongside social skills training to build and broaden team working, would be a crucial part of the workforce development.

Working with local colleges through the Education Business Partnership, they were able to deliver a range of educational opportunities to staff alongside more conventional training. The objective was to ensure that the workforce identifies with the Jaguar brand and develops an enhanced involvement and pride in its work. The educational programme has been

an important part of the Jaguar transformation effected at Halewood, and has attracted attention throughout the industry.

Part of the extensive upgrade of the Halewood plant included the provision of a 65-acre supplier park within the site, where many of the company's key suppliers are represented. The plant, which had previously been used to build the Escort, was extensively rebuilt and upgraded to suit the requirements of the new product. This included the construction of a complete new paint shop.

Today the X-Type is built at Halewood alongside sister company Land Rover's Freelander, which commenced production at the plant in 2007.

The X-Type cabin has all the expected wood and leather, and is perhaps more tastefully executed than the S-Type's. Clever packaging results in slightly more room than is found in the S-Type.

proved important in design and development. Colin Tivey, Chief Project Engineer for the X-Type, put it simply: "The car would not be so good, and certainly could not have been developed in such a short timescale, without these systems." They allowed complex issues such as wheel movement and wheelarch design to be resolved with great precision and flexibility.

Talking to the engineers, it is clear that such new tools and technologies allowed design innovation and creativity to flourish. Integration of the four-wheel-drive system in the floor pan and the accommodation of items in the transmission tunnel were also areas where the modelling capacity of these systems proved vital during the design phase.

Jaguar was particularly concerned with robustness during development of the X-Type. It built upon its existing

practices to engineer new levels of integrity and sturdiness into every component, conscious that the car's success would revolve around competing with the industry's benchmarks for quality.

But Jaguar's objective was not just to achieve and exceed the quality levels displayed by its competitors, but also to offer a product that embodied the spirit of Jaguar. This involved more particular attention to integration of design and production. A lot of effort was devoted to seemingly mundane issues such as driveshaft angles, propshaft and diff alignment, and the development of assembly procedures to ensure repeatability in manufacture. This effort was essential if the expectations of traditional Jaguar customers were to be met.

Jaguar devoted unprecedented resources to the marketing and launch of the X-Type and the pundits

seemed to agree it had produced a
fine saloon worthy of the Jaguar
name.

At launch there were eight four-
wheel-drive models, from a 2-litre V6
at under £20,000 through to the
231bhp V6 Sport at almost £27,000,
via a mid-range 2.5 car. In 2003 a
diesel X-Type of two litres became
available plus a 2-litre V6 petrol,
both with front-wheel drive, a
shocking first for Jaguar. A 2.2 diesel
further expanded the range in 2005.
Perhaps the best-looking X-Type was
the estate version launched in 2004,
redesigned from the B pillar
backwards by Ian Callum. The first
production Jaguar estate, it was a
compact 'lifestyle' wagon rather than
a load lugger but Jaguar claimed
best-in-class load space. Neat
features included handsome chrome
roof bars and a rear luggage window
that lowered independently of the
hatch door itself.

By 2008, the X-Type had evolved into
a 20-car range spanning £21,000 to
£31,000 but was now quite an old
design, out-paced in most areas by
competitors such as the Mercedes
C-Class, Audi A4 and, of course, the
BMW 3 Series. The styling had not
aged well, despite a gentle makeover
that year, but until the arrival of the
XF the X-Type was Jaguar's best-
selling car. Having said that, it had
nowhere near matched Ford's
ambitions for it of 100,000 sales a
year. X-Type production peaked at
50,000 units in 2003 and shows no
signs of rallying. US sales were ended
in late 2007, and the X-Type range cut
back to the two diesel engines and
the 3.0 V6, the last only available as
an Estate. The car's probable demise
in 2010 will likely mark the end of
Jaguar's adventure in the realm of
volume car making.

Meanwhile the S-Type was usurped by
the XF in 2008. It had evolved into a

The X-type Estate was launched in
2004 – the first production Jaguar
estate.

good driver's car – it always was –
and sales were buoyant if not strong
enough to worry BMW with its class-
leading 5 Series. A gentle redesign in
2004, including a modified front grille
and a remodelled tail, sustained
interest as did an excellent 2.7-litre
diesel option, but it was hard to
ignore the fact that the styling just
didn't work. The world was ready for
a truly modern-looking Jaguar saloon
that respected the history and spirit
behind the name and reinterpreted it
without cherry-picking the retro cues.

The X-type Estate was without doubt one of the best-looking estate cars on the market.

Jaguar's best-selling car, the X-type underwent a mild facelift in 2008.

Ian Callum: new design guru

In August 1999 Jaguar announced that Ian Callum had succeeded the late Geoff Lawson as Director of Styling, although he was to continue to be responsible for future Aston Martin styling too.

'Funnily enough,' he recalls, 'when I was a kid all I used to do was design Jaguars all the time. I was stunned, like everybody was, by the E-Type, and the XJ6. So I've sort of landed my dream job – so long as I end up designing them and not just managing people. . .' Callum loved the original Jaguar XJ6 and can still remember where he was when it came out. 'I was 12 and I was on holiday in Aberdeen. I can still remember going into our local Jaguar dealer to get the brochures.'

As far as foreign cars were concerned, Porsche and Ferrari were the big influences. 'I occasionally saw a Porsche 356, such a pure looking car,' says Callum, whose all-time favourite design is the Ferrari 250GT short wheelbase, which he still draws for 'relaxation'.

After getting a master's degree in Industrial Design at the Royal College of Art in 1978 Callum spent the next 12 years globetrotting around Ford design studios in Britain, Japan, the United States, Australia and Germany, before being appointed Design Manager responsible for the Ghia Studio in Turin. You'll see his work on the Fiesta, the Mondeo, the RS 200 mid-engined sports car, the Escort RS Cosworth and the Probe.

On returning to Britain in 1990 he became General Manager and Chief Designer at TWR, but undoubtedly his finest moment up to now has been the DB7, star of the 1993 Geneva motor show and named 'one of the most beautiful cars in the world' by a panel of Italian art world high-brows. It has now entered the history books as the most successful Aston Martin of all time. To follow-up the much-fêted DB7 Callum also penned the V12-powered DB7 Vantage, Aston's Project Vantage concept car, and the Vanquish.

At Jaguar he is hoping to top his success at Aston, and significant evidence of that is the XF, the most talked-about Jaguar for decades and a model that has quickly become the brand's best seller. 'I've got big ambitions for the job, obviously. I want to design cars that can recreate the impact that the E-Type and XJ6 had for me. They'll look nothing like them, and that's probably the secret: I'm a bit tired of all this retro, looking-behind-us styling. You have to do it to a certain degree, but with respect rather than plagiarism. We've got to look to the future again with great optimism. A Jaguar will never lose its elegance as far as I'm concerned, but it might take on a different form of elegance.'

The XF *series*

Jaguar's survival as a builder of luxury cars rests on the success of the XF and as these words are written it is fulfilling all expectations. It is already outselling its predecessor, the S-Type, two to one with 30,000 built in less than 12 months. Buyers are embracing the XF as a viable BMW 5 Series and Mercedes E-Class alternative in a way they did not with the S-Type.

Even so, Jaguar has readjusted its volume ambitions as a BMW/Audi/ Mercedes rival, building 200,000 cars a year. The plan now is to become a more 'niche' maker turning out premium cars in lower numbers. One benefit of this approach could be a stronger resale value for Jaguars – it is widely predicted that the XF will retain more of its value at two years old than any of its rivals.

Developed at Jaguar's Whitley headquarters and built at Castle Bromwich in Birmingham, the XF was launched at the Frankfurt show in 2007 with the first cars delivered in March 2008.

The C-XF concept car, shown at the 2007 Detroit show provided a preview of the modern, athletic saloon to come.

Previewed as the C-XF concept car shown at the Detroit show in 2007, the XF is a thoroughly modern, athletic-looking saloon and the most important new Jaguar for years. It manages to cleverly blend established marque virtues of refinement and performance with a new kind of high-tech 21st century elegance. It is the car Ian Callum, Jaguar's Design Director, has been wanting to create for a long time:

"It's the most difficult car I've ever worked on and the most satisfying. It's a very clever car. I don't think people fully appreciate how well proportioned it is given that it is a five-seater. It is the biggest challenge I've ever faced. I think we pulled it off."

The XF is a five-seat, four-door saloon with the low-slung profile of a coupé, an elegant rising wedge with a low nose dominated by a deep woven mesh grille that evokes the original 1968 XJ6. With a cd of 0.29, the XF is the most aerodynamically efficient Jaguar ever, more slippery even than the XJ220 and with zero front-to-rear lift.

With its big wheels, up to 20-inch on the highest specification cars, bi-xenon headlamps and sculptured tail lamps the shape is in fact a complete departure from the retro design cues that were becoming an increasing showroom turn-off for buyers in the S-Type class.

The low-slung, swooping curves of the XF are evident in this view.

The XF's build quality and detailing would do justice to any of its benchmark German rivals. In fact, for some time now, Jaguar has rated higher in the JD Power customer satisfaction survey than either Mercedes or BMW.

The shell, built from the latest high-strength, high-carbon steel, features excellent panel fit and although heavier than the alloy-bodied XK sibling, is the most torsionally stiff in its class. This allowed Jaguar's chassis

engineers to work their magic on the suspension and drivetrain, which is essentially carried over from the S-Type and XK with lightweight anti-dive unequal length wishbones at the front and multi-links at the rear. The body is slightly longer than the S-Type to meet predicted crash safety requirements.

The result is a superbly agile rear-drive saloon that offers a sublime ride/handling compromise – perhaps the best to be found in any saloon car in the world – and outstanding refinement. Wonderful high-speed bump absorption qualities and a cosseting feel maintain Jaguar's reputation for building supple-riding

saloons that feel more 'special' than the sometimes wooden Teutonic rivals. CATS (Computer Active Technology) is a system of sensors linked to the XF's adaptive damping that monitor and adjust the damping to the requirements of the driver's style.

At launch three versions – Luxury, Premium Luxury and SV8 – embraced four different engine options from a thrifty 143mph 2.7-litre twin-turbo diesel to a supercharged petrol 4.2 V8 limited to 155mph. In the mid-range was a 3.0-litre V6 petrol adapted from the Ford Duratec engine available in Luxury and Premium Luxury form. It had more

The 502bhp supercharged XFR V8.

power than the diesel but, in the real world, the huge torque of the oil burning engine made it the quicker car.

The AJ V8 – 420bhp supercharged, 300bhp without – was carried over from the previous models and the XK/XKR, a compact all-aluminium V8 with quad camshafts and variable valve phasing. With its rotor-type supercharger, the 420bhp version in the SV8 delivered 80 per cent of its 413lb ft of torque from 2,000rpm to its 6,500rpm redline, yet some felt the naturally aspirated V8 XF, available only in Premium Luxury trim, was the quieter, smoother drive and the better package. While Europe gained the full

range of engines, the North American market only received the V8 XF models.

On the 37mpg diesel, which was expected to account for 70 per cent of XF sales, noise and vibration were dealt with by special engine mountings, tuned exhaust and a double thickness bulkhead. Jaguar claimed it was the quietest diesel in its class and also the lightest. It was a Euro IV Compliant 24-valve unit with common rail injection.

By the spring of 2009 a new Gen III development of the AJD V6, up rated to three litres and up to 272bhp, was scheduled. It dropped the 0–60 to 5.9

seconds but perhaps more importantly for fleet buyers dropped the car's official CO_2 emission ratings. This diesel engine was developed jointly with PSA and also featured in the Land Rover Discovery and Range Rover Sport.

The other major news for the 2010 model year, revealed in early 2009, was the introduction of the latest 5-litre V8 petrol engines into the XF, alongside their fitting to the XK as detailed in a later chapter. The

The aggressive styling of the XFR hints at the raw power under the bonnet.

The styling of the XF interior is far modern than any previous Jaguar model.

supercharged version, with 502bhp, would power a new XFR model.

All XFs use the ZF six-speed automatic gearbox – evolved from the XK/XKR – with paddle shifts, which has been highly praised as one of the smoothest-shifting gearboxes available. There is no manual option.

The 'box uses shift-by-wire technology and is 10 per cent quicker-shifting than before, adapting itself to how the car is being driven. The column mounted 'paddles' offer one-touch manual control while four separate modes on the 'Jaguardrive' selector interact with the car's Dynamic Stability Control system to change engine mapping, transmission shift points and brake intervention depending on whether you are in standard, winter or track mode. Supercharged versions have an additional 'dynamic' mode and it is possible to turn the DSC off all together. All the latest computer-controlled safety systems are incorporated of course, such as Brake Assist for the vented discs, stability

control and electronic brake force distribution plus optional refinements like radar-controlled cruise control, tyre pressure monitoring and blind spot monitoring.

Perhaps the highlight of the car is its interior, a revelation after the clichéd wood and leather treatment of the S-Type. It still uses luxurious traditional materials but ice blue ambient backlighting around instruments, switches and major controls evoke an MP3 player or the mood of a vodka bar. Modern textured finishes such as aluminium and straight-grained oak gives the XF's cabin a distinctive flavour while remaining cosseting.

With the ignition on, the red starter button pulses. Press it, and as the engine fires, the 'JaguarDrive' gear selector wheel rises from the console and the motorised facia air vents are revealed. It's a theatrical touch, but nowhere near as gimmicky as it sounds, although the optional illuminated sill tread plates won't be to everyone's taste.

Jaguar XF 2.7 diesel
2008-2009

ENGINE:

60 degree V6 (diesel)	
Bore x stroke	81 x 88mm
Capacity	2,720cc
Valves	24 valve DOHC
Compression ratio	17.5:1
Fuel system	Common rail injection
Power	204bhp at 4,000rpm
Torque	320lb ft at 1,900rpm

TRANSMISSION:
6-speed ZF automatic

SUSPENSION:
Front: unequal length wishbones
Rear: multi-link

BRAKES:
Vented discs front and rear: electronic parking brake

WHEELS:
17, 18, 19 inch alloys

BODYWORK:
Bonded and riveted aluminium monocoque

LENGTH:	16ft 3in (4,953mm)
WIDTH	6ft 7in (2,007mm)
HEIGHT	4ft 7in (1,397mm)
WEIGHT	3,904lb (1,775kg)
MAX SPEED:	143mph
0-60	7.7 seconds
MPG:	37.6 combined
PRICE NEW:	£33,900

Jaguar XF 3.0 V6
2008-

As 2.7 except;
ENGINE:

60 degree V6 (petrol)	
Bore x stroke	80 x 79.5
Capacity	2,967cc
Valves	24 valve DOHC
Compression ratio	10.5:1
Fuel system	Fuel injection
Power	240bhp at 6,000rpm
Torque	216lb ft at 4,106rpm

WEIGHT:	3,702lb (1,683kg)
MAX SPEED:	148mph
0-60	7.9 secs
MPG:	26.8 combined

Jaguar XF 4.2 V8
2008-2009

As 2.7 except;
ENGINE

V8	
Bore x stroke	86 x 90.3
Capacity	4,196cc
Valves	DOHC
Compression ratio	11:1
Fuel system	Fuel injection
Power	300bhp at 6,250rpm
Torque	413lb ft at 3,500rpm
WEIGHT:	3,856lb (1,753kg)
MAX SPEED:	155mph (limited)
0-60	6.5 seconds
MPG:	25.3 combined
PRICE NEW:	£44,553

Jaguar XFS 4.2 V8
2008-2009

As 2.7 except;

Compression ratio	9:1
Power	420bhp at 6,250rpm
Torque	413lb ft at 3,500rpm
MAX SPEED:	155mph (limited)
0-60	5.1 seconds
MPG:	22.4 combined
PRICE NEW:	£53,753

Jaguar XF 3.0 Diesel
2009-

As 2.7 except;

Capacity	2,993cc
Bore x stroke	84 x 90
Compression ratio	16:1
Power	236bhp (S model 271bhp) at 4,000rpm
Torque	369lb ft (S model 443lb ft) at 2,000rpm
WEIGHT:	4,004lb (1,820kg)
MAX SPEED:	149mph (S model 155mph)
0-60	6.7 (S model 5.9) seconds
MPG:	42.0 combined
PRICE NEW:	£32,900 (S model £36,900)

Jaguar XF 5.0
2009-

As 2.7 except;

Capacity	5,000cc
Valves	32 valve DOHC
Bore x stroke	92.5 x 93
Compression ratio	11.5:1
Power	379bhp at 6,500rpm
Torque	380lb ft at 3,500rpm
WEIGHT:	3,916lb (1,780kg)
MAX SPEED:	155mph (limited)
0-60	5.5 seconds
MPG:	25.4 combined
PRICE NEW:	£49,900

Jaguar XFR 5.0 Supercharged
2009-

As 5.0 except;

Compression ratio	9.5:1
Power	502bhp at 6,000rpm
Torque	461lb ft at 2,500rpm
WEIGHT:	4,160lb (1,891kg)
MAX SPEED:	155mph (limited)
0-60	4.7 seconds
MPG:	22.5 combined
PRICE NEW:	£59,900

Driving the XF

Taken all round, the diesel XF is probably the one to have in the real world, particularly the new one, which is a 149mph saloon that returns 42mpg with refinement that is comparable to the very sweet 3.0 petrol V6. The latest 3-litre diesel is now 2bhp more powerful than the 3-litre petrol XF and a quicker car, taking 6.7 seconds to 60mph compared to the petrol's 7.9.

The V8s add another dimension of course although they exact a penalty in fuel thirst that most buyers won't feel they can justify. Of the two eight-cylinder cars offered at launch, the SV8 satisfied most buyers'

aggressive urges but the supercharged XF was not the model to tempt buyers out of their M5 BMWs or AMG Mercedes. In fact many believed the naturally aspirated 4.2-litre XF was the nicer drive with its near silent engine (at town speeds) that also revved freely and had none of the suggestion of high-end gruffness that slightly hampered the SV8. Whether the new 5-litre engines would make a significant difference was still to be discovered as this book went to press.

A fantastically smooth and responsive automatic gearbox makes the most of the engine in all versions. The XF, in all its forms, 'wafts' like a Jaguar

should. Jaguar has managed to combine the grip and stance of big wheels and very wide tyres with the subtle qualities of a superbly resilient ride, particularly over 40mph. The XF copes with camber changes and mid-corner bumps with a supple distain its rivals, most of them stiffly sprung Germans, just cannot match. The supercharged car trades some, but certainly not all, this ride comfort for increased resistance to body roll but it still rides very well. Inside all XFs are cosseting but very contemporary in feel. The XF saloons are not the roomiest in their class but the glamorous design of the cabin will sell the XF to many buyers.

JaguarSense is an electronic control system that frees you from fumbling for small buttons in the dark – touch the interior light anywhere and it comes on, press the glove box lid anywhere and it pops open. The Bowers & Wilkins eight-speaker sound system option has been hailed as one of the best audio systems to be found in any car and the sophisticated climate control with humidity control and odour and particle filtration is similarly cutting edge. There's a 7-inch touch screen for audio, telephone and (optional) TV functions, reducing mechanical buttons to a discreet minimum.

The embracing sculptured front seats are 16-way adjustable and can be heated or cooled with fan assistance depending on the model. The rear seat, at 6ft 4in (1,930mm) across, is one of the widest in its class. All leather is double-stitched (there's no cloth option) and the XF feels well put together with impressive attention to detail. Among its rivals, all but the Audi A6 are upstaged in terms of interior build quality by the XF. With the low roof and with the front and rear screens at the same angle, headroom in the rear is compromised, as is legroom, but customers who buy into the cars

rakish four-door coupé feel will deem it a price worth paying. The 500-litre boot capacity can be increased by folding down the rear seats or opting for the tyre repair system.

XF prices span £20,000 between the least expensive Luxury version and the highest specification supercharged car and the cars are relatively expensive in their class even compared with the German competition. However, they come well equipped as standard. The Premium Luxury version scores keyless entry, posher soft grain leather, 18-inch wheels and a heated front screen over and above the entry level Luxury specification. The stand-alone SV8 is identified by its 20-inch wheels, metallic paint, powered folding mirrors, oak veneer and tyre pressure monitoring.

Rather than attempt to create an entirely new car, Jaguar has retained established components, honed them where necessary, and concentrated its efforts on getting the look and feel of the XF just right. The results are so shockingly modern that some established Jaguar buyers may even be put off the car. Even so, it seems certain that the XF will attract many more new customers than it upsets old ones.

The TATA take-over

In March 2008, as the first XF buyers were taking delivery of their cars, it was announced that Tata, India's largest automotive company, was acquiring Jaguar and Land Rover from Ford at a cost of £1.25 billion ($2.3 billion) – about half what the American firm had paid for them originally. Jaguar never made a profit for Ford. Tata, established in 1945, is the world's fourth largest truck maker and second largest bus

manufacturer, employing 23,000 people. Around the time of the sale it had recently announced the Nano, the world's cheapest new car priced at £1,250. Tata Motors had been the most likely suitors for Jaguar since January 2008, a firm with a good reputation and viewed as a safer pair of hands than the various private equity firms that had shown an interest in the two businesses. Anthony Bamford of JCB pulled out of talks when it became

clear that any deal had to include Land Rover. The sale of Jaguar and Land Rover, announced in June 2007, was intrinsic to The Ford Motor Company's restructuring plans in the wake of the sooner than expected collapse of SUV sales on the North American Market. As part of the deal, Ford agreed to contribute $600 million to Land Rover and Jaguar pension funds and continue to supply the firms with components.

The XK12.0 *series*

In a war-ravaged Britain starved of motoring excitement it is little wonder that the Jaguar XK120, launched at the Earls Court Motor Show in 1948, was such a sensation. Originally conceived as a low-volume dream car rather than a serious production machine, it was destined to become a great dollar-earner for Britain (most XK120s went to the States) and one of the most celebrated classics of all. After the E-Type its profile is probably the most instantly recognisable of all Jaguars, and the view down its shapely bonnet remains one of the most evocative sights in motoring. It is so beautiful, this car, that most would forgive even its major dynamic shortcomings; that

it still stands up as an enjoyable driver's car is almost a bonus.

First there is the engine. The XK 'six', launched in this model, is at its smoothest and sweetest in 3.4 form and has superb flexibility too, so gear play in the Moss 'box is optional. That is just as well, as clean, quick changes are difficult, although they come with practice, and the clutch is on the heavy side. It is best to let the XK lug in top, which it will do happily from as little as 10mph. Any healthy XK should be good for 80–90mph (129–145kph) cruising; that the car still feels brisk is a pertinent reminder of how mind-blowingly fast it must have been in 1948 when it had more

The XK120's sweeping, full-bodied wingline was inspired by Touring's Mille Miglia BMW 328s, but if anything the Jaguar looked even more elegant. Production of these cars was very slow until Jaguar were tooled-up to produce the car with steel rather than aluminium bodywork.

than twice the performance of the average family runabout.

The steering wheel is of heroic proportions, connected to a steering box that is heavy at low speeds but lightens dramatically on the move. The XK never feels anything less than vintage through corners, with strong understeer and lively axle behaviour, although the degree of roll is certainly post-war in flavour, a corollary of William Heynes's long-travel torsion bar front suspension. Yet it remains safe, forgiving and fun, its poise only eclipsed in its heyday by pure-bred racers or much more expensive foreign makes.

So what if the bench-like leather seats offer little support should you want to corner at all briskly? For budding racers the factory offered buckets (which were apparently worth a second a lap – and you can see why) while others either gripped the steering harder, or backed off. The cramped driving position with the lack of elbow room, the closeness to the chest of the steering wheel, with its bombshell-shaped hub, and the high floor – short legs are a definite plus if you are planning to buy an XK – reveal the show-car nature of the XK's conception.

Yet for the purist this is of little consequence. Later XKs were more comfortable and faster, but none looked quite so delicious as the original, a flowing two-seater roadster that remains a model of elegant purity.

It is hard to exaggerate the impact made by this car when it was first announced. The general public could not believe that it would do 120mph (193kph), while the rest of the industry, dramatically upstaged by Jaguar at that first post-war show, were doubtful that William Lyons could build the car at the price, just under £1,000 before tax. He proved them both wrong with a package that was unbeatable.

Jaguar XK120
1948–54

ENGINE:
In-line six-cylinder, cast iron block, alloy head, hemispherical combustion chambers

Bore x stroke	81 x 106mm
Capacity	3,442cc
Valves	Twin ohc, one inlet, one exhaust
Compression ratio	7:1 (8:1 optional)
Carburettors	Two 1¾in SUs
Power	160bhp at 5,200rpm (gross)
Torque	195lb ft at 2,500rpm (gross)

TRANSMISSION:
Four-speed manual with synchromesh on second, third and top

Final drive	hypoid semi-floating Salisbury 4HA live rear axle

SUSPENSION:
Wishbones, torsion bars, anti-roll bar. Rear live axle with semi-elliptic springs

Steering	Burman recirculating ball

BRAKES:
Girling 12-inch (305mm) drums with servo

WHEELS:
Pressed steel bolt-on 16-inch (406mm) with 5K rim

BODYWORK:
Separate steel body and chassis

LENGTH:	14ft 5in (4.39m)
WIDTH:	5ft 2in (1.57m)
HEIGHT:	4ft 5½in (1.36m)
WEIGHT:	25½cwt (1,297kg)

MAX SPEED   120mph (192kph)
0–60 mph (97kph)   12 seconds

PRICE NEW (1948) £1,263 inc PT

Jaguar XK120 SE
1951–54

As XK120 except:

Carburettors	Two 2in HD8 SUs
Power	180bhp at 5,000rpm
Torque	203lb ft at 4,000rpm
0–60mph (97kph)	9.5 seconds

PRODUCTION FIGURES:

Aluminium roadster	240
Steel roadster	7,374
fhc	2,680
dhc	1,767
Total	12,061

Taking for inspiration the Touring-bodied BMW 328 roadster that had won the 1940 Mille Miglia, the XK, with its slender bumpers, cutaway doors and swoopy profile, was a car at once bold yet somehow delicate. On looks alone it would have sold handsomely, but there was more. Under the long, tapering bonnet was the brand new twin-cam 'XK' straight-six engine, from which the car took its name. Conceived during the war with a specification that echoed 1930s racing car practice, the 3.4 litre

William Heynes was one of the principal architects of the XK120. He moved to Jaguar from Rootes in the 1930s and worked on all models right through to the 1968 XJ6.

XK was, in one form or another, to power everything from Le Mans winners to tanks and fire engines, and was destined to be the cornerstone of Jaguar's saloon and sports car range for the next 40 years. With Harry Weslake's gas-flowed lightweight aluminium head, and a fully counterbalanced seven-bearing bottom end, it mixed strength and stamina with free-breathing sophistication. It developed a smooth 160bhp (among true production engines only the latest ohv Cadillac V8s produced more power), which made sure that the '120' tag was no idle boast. In fact, the XK was for a time the world's fastest standard production car, a point proved by Jaguar when a supposedly standard example – with hood and side screens fitted – managed 126mph (203kph) at Jabbeke in Belgium for the benefit of the previously doubting press. This was pre-war racing car performance at a luxury saloon price.

From the beginning Lyons had told engineers Claude Baily, William Heynes and Walter Hassan that the engine should look good, with elegant detailing that reflected the sophistication within – hence the polished cam-covers and inlet manifold and the enamelled exhaust manifold. The XK engine had a muscular symmetry that promised power. It was no accident that it was making its debut in the XK120 rather than the new MkVII saloon, still a couple of years away; in a relatively low-volume car any problems with this totally new design could be more easily monitored and contained.

There had been plans for a 2 litre, four-cylinder version of the XK 'six' called the XJ, but as it would have cost as much to produce as the bigger unit, plans for a cheaper version of the XK sports car (the XK100) were quietly dropped.

Alongside the new six-cylinder XK120 engine Jaguar displayed a 2 litre, four-cylinder model called the XK100. As the car would have been slower than the six-cylinder version, yet no less expensive to produce, Jaguar saw no future in such a car and the XK100 was canned.

The chassis of the XK120 was fresh in design, shared with the MkV but shortened by 18 inches (457mm) and slightly narrowed to take an alloy two-seater body that had never been intended for mass-production. The torsion bars were stiffened to reduce roll, but the Burman recirculating-ball steering was the same as that found on the MkV, but higher geared. Damping was by telescopics at the front and lever arms at the rear, where the rear axle was both sprung and located by semi-elliptic leaf springs.

Such was the reaction to the car that Lyons soon realised that Jaguar would have to tool up for a big-volume steel body by Pressed Steel, abandoning the traditional ash frame with its alloy outer panels: thus only 240 alloy-bodied XK120 roadsters were ever built and those that survive are much

coveted. In fact, very few XKs emerged from Jaguar before 1950, and those that did were mostly earmarked for the American market.

Steel cars began to come on stream by the middle of 1950 with subtle alterations to the shapes of the headlamp nacelles and the front and rear wings. The bonnet, bootlid and doors were still aluminium, but internally there was a new bulkhead, hollow-section mild steel sills (replacing the composite wood/steel structure), mild steel door shut-faces and boxed-in door hinges. Weight was up by 1cwt (51kg) but performance was little altered.

Those lucky enough to drive, never mind own, an XK120 would have been deeply impressed by its ability, with performance that allowed it to sweep past most other traffic as though it

Not only was the XK120's handling well up to the standards set by the engine, but the car was also comfortable, with an excellent ride.

The XK120 in Competition

The XK120 was a natural for competition and William Lyons was not slow to recognise its potential as a publicity tool. Despite inadequate brakes, its superiority over the competition made it virtually unassailable for a couple of years, particularly in rallying where its ground clearance was useful and the poor brakes mattered less. Moreover, the engine and chassis had great basic strength.

After proving the car's straight-line urge to the press at Jabbeke, Lyons seized upon the new production car race at Silverstone set for August 1949 as the scene of the model's racing debut. In a thrilling event, drivers Leslie Johnson (driving the ex-Jabbeke car HKV 500) and Peter Walker made it a 1–2 victory for the new Jaguar. In fact, it would have been a 1–2–3 had the XK120 of Prince Bira (driving the first XK built, HKV 455) not suffered an unlucky puncture. With spats and wheel discs the cars looked very standard and were reported to be noticeably quieter than the other competitors.

For 1950 six alloy-bodied cars were lent by the factory to private entrants Leslie Johnson, Tommy Wisdom, Nick Haines, Clemente Biondetti, Peter Walker and Ian Appleyard. The headline-making results for which Jaguar were looking were not slow in coming. Walker won a one-hour race at Silverstone and won his class at the Shelsley Walsh hillclimb. Appleyard, married to William Lyons's daughter Pat, who was also his co-driver, won the over-3,000cc class and a Coupe des Alpes for a penalty-free run in the Alpine Rally. Wisdom lent his car to the up-and-coming Stirling Moss, who won the wet and windy Tourist Trophy in what is regarded as the seminal race of his career. Biondetti suffered a broken connecting rod on the Targa Florio and fell victim to overheating on the Mille Miglia, although he still managed a respectable eighth. His was one of a team of factory-sponsored XKs in the Italian 1,000-mile classic that year, although Johnson was the only other finisher, taking fifth. The 120s

were not destined to do well here: the following year they were all out by half distance.

Johnson's XK showed promise at Le Mans in 1950, catching the leading Talbot at a rate that would have seen the XK in the lead before the full 24 hours had elapsed. Sadly, he retired with clutch failure after 21 hours, but the car's performance convinced William Lyons to forge ahead with the C-Type.

The *Daily Express* International Trophy meeting at Silverstone in 1951 saw a field of three factory-sponsored XKs driven by Walker, Moss and Wisdom competing against several private entrants, perhaps most notably Duncan Hamilton, who came in third behind the winner Moss and another private XK driven by veteran Charlie Dodson – who had not raced in 12 years! In fact, XKs took the first five places in the over-2,000cc heat.

Appleyard won the Tulip, Morecambe and RAC rallies in 1951 and repeated his Alpine success, making his white 120 Roadster – registered NUB 120 – perhaps the

NUB 120 was perhaps the most famous XK120 roadster of them all. Driven by Ian Appleyard, son-in-law of Sir William Lyons, it won the Alpine Rally twice outright and on its third attempt gained a first-ever Gold Cup for a third consecutive penalty-free run in the event. Appleyard, with his wife Pat as co-driver, also won the Tulip, Morecambe and RAC Rallies in 1951.

most famous XK of all. The greatest moment for this husband-and-wife team came in the 1952 Alpine Rally when they won the first ever Gold Cup for their third consecutive penalty-free run on the event, although outright victory eluded them that year.

The gruelling Marathon de la Route had never appealed to the Appleyards and it took a Belgian called Johnny Claes – in the factory-loaned HKV 500 – to prove the XK's durability and speed on this notorious car-breaker with a win in the 1951 event followed by private XKs in second and fifth positions.

As if the car's pace and durability needed further underlining, Jaguar took an XK120 fixed-head to Montlhéry in 1952 where, over seven days and seven nights, it was driven non-stop for 168 hours at over 100mph (161kph). There were more visits to Jabbeke too: Norman Dewis was timed at 142mph (228kph) in a Special Equipment roadster in April 1953 and followed it up with an astounding 172mph (277kph) run in October in a heavily modified bubble-topped XK.

In America, future world champion and three-times Le Mans winner Phil Hill was making his name in a lightened 3.8 litre XK120 (although it was the V8-engined Allards that dominated the results in the very early 1950s), together with other soon-to-be famous names such as Richie Ginther, John Fitch, Sherwood Johnson, Don Parkinson and Walt Hansgen.

The XK120 continued to be competitive throughout the 1950s, although factory interest ended, naturally, as the C-Type began to impose itself from 1951 onwards.

were standing still. Only a rarely encountered Allard J2 would have given the Jaguar a run for its money in straight-line acceleration, but the top speed was not as high and neither the looks – nor the comfort – were in the same league and it cost £200 more. At £650 more than the XK, Aston's slower and less accelerative DB2 also looked expensive.

That the XK120 was quick was only part of the picture. Just as pleasing were its docility – the engine would dawdle at 10mph in top – and its chassis, which combined the refined comfort of a saloon with true sports car agility and grip. It did not stop all that well – the poorly cooled 12-inch (305mm) Lockheed drum brakes were prone to a disquieting fade if used hard repeatedly from high speed – but that seemed a mere detail; in fact, few of the magazines that tested the car felt moved to talk about it, so glowing was the tone of their prose. To have mentioned the extremely rudimentary hood, the slow gearchange and the unsupportive seats would also have seemed churlish. In that more patriotic age, *The Autocar* called the XK120 '. . . a prestige gainer for Britain's engineering as a whole and car engineering in particular.' It would

The fixed-head coupé was an attractive and luxurious variation on the XK theme with a more up-market interior similar to the drophead coupé. The roofline echoed the shape of the MkVII.

The C-Type

The XK120 C ('C' stood for Competition), more generally known as the C-Type, was built specifically, and in very short order, for Jaguar's 1951 assault on Le Mans. Mechanically Jaguar made few radical changes to the XK formula, but instead concentrated on making a lighter, more wind-cheating aluminium body – designed by aerodynamicist Malcolm Sayer – on a new triangulated spaceframe. It was immensely stiff, with sills 10 inches (254mm) deep and a single-piece bonnet/wing front end that hinged at the front for access to the engine.

The rear section was a single piece, too, and could be removed to reveal the new rear suspension with its single transversely mounted torsion bar replacing the leaf springs of the production XK. A huge 40-gallon (182-litre) tank fed a tuned, high-compression 204bhp XK engine with improved porting, a new camshaft and a more durable bottom end with indium-coated lead bronze bearings and a crankshaft damper. A lighter flywheel and a one-piece input shaft improved changes on the otherwise familiar Moss four-speed gearbox. The problem of brake fade was also addressed, with automatically adjusting drums and wire wheels to improve the air flow. Out went the Burman steering box, replaced by a more accurate rack-and-pinion system.

Jaguar entered a three-car team for 1951's Le Mans. The C-Types of Moss/Fairman and Biondetti/Johnson retired with oil feed problems while lying in the first two places, but the Walker/Whitehead car somehow escaped the malady and went on to win at an average speed of 93.49mph (150.43kph), and 60 miles

ahead of the nearest Talbot Lago. Later in the year Moss won the TT at Dundrod, breaking the lap record.

Overheating problems, induced by new, more slippery bodywork, robbed the now disc-braked C of victory at Le Mans in 1952, but Jaguar returned again in 1953, determined to make it a double. The 4½ litre Ferrari was the C-Type's

Jaguar entered a three-car team for the 1951 Le Mans. Walker and Whitehead won at an average speed of 93.49mph

main opposition, but the disc brakes were allowing the Jaguars to brake far later without fear of fade. Moss took the lead from the Ferrari of Villoresi just four laps in, but within an hour recurrent fuel starvation problems pushed him down the field, leaving the way open for the winning Hamilton/Rolt C-Type, which set a 100mph-plus average for the first time at Le Mans. The C-Types of Moss/Walker and Whitehead/Stewart took second and fourth. Jaguar had made their point.

Bodily the victorious 1953 cars were much like the originals, but in search of lightness a thinner-gauge tubular frame was used. Mechanically they ran Webers and the rear suspension featured a single cast torque arm and a Panhard rod.

The ultimate in early-1950s sports racers, Jaguar built 54 C-Types, all but 11 of them for private individuals and teams. In 1953 the C-Type was priced at £2,119 including Purchase Tax, hardly a huge premium over the XK120, which in roadster form then cost £1,602 including PT.

Jaguar built the C-Type specifically to win Le Mans, which it did first time out in 1951 and repeated its success in 1953. The windcheating shape was by Jaguar aerodynamicist Malcolm Sayer, and with 204bhp these cars were good for 140mph (225kph) or more. The aluminium body was immensely stiff with sills 10 inches (254mm) deep. The front panel hinged for access to the engine, while the rear section of the body could be removed to reveal the new rear suspension with its single transversely mounted torsion bar.

have made even the least jingoistic enthusiast proud to be British.

The fixed-head coupé joined the roadster in 1951, and was a beautifully balanced design cast in the mould of the Bugatti Type 57 SC Atlantic, with a rounded roof profile echoing that of the MkVII saloon. The theme was increased sophistication, with wind-up windows replacing the side screens, and outside door handles on the new wider doors. The interior was much more opulent than that of the roadster, with a veneered dash and door cappings, proper door trims, a heater, and more cockpit ventilation to answer criticisms from American owners.

Compared to the roadster with its hood in place, the fixed-head was much less oppressive, and the feeling of space was enhanced by moving the dash an inch further back from the seats. Weight was up slightly, but the fixed-head's aerodynamics were better, so the difference in top speed was minimal. This good-looking and refined car was destined to be a rare XK on the British market, as the first right-hand-drive examples were not sold until 1953.

At around the same time as the introduction of the coupé, Jaguar introduced self-adjusting brakes to try to address the fade problems, and many cars were now being fitted with the optional wire wheels, which vastly increased the amount of air circulating around the brake drums.

It was natural that many owners would want to race their cars and to that end the factory was now offering some

The XK120 drophead coupé was a much more luxurious open-bodied XK with a permanently attached and fully lined hood that could be raised and lowered quickly, unlike the rather sketchy affair found on the roadster. It had proper winding windows, quarter lights, and exterior door handles.

Buying Hints (all XKs)

1. XKs have suffered far more than other Jaguars from parts swapping with other models, and non-original components can now devalue cars dramatically.

2. Everything is now available for the XK, even a complete bodyshell or a restored chassis.

3. Rare alloy-bodied early XK120s with ash frames are the most difficult to restore, and there are a surprising number of abandoned projects. Ensure that such cars come complete. It is always cheaper to buy a good car than embark on having a wreck restored.

4. Door drop is common as the well-hidden hinges are almost impossible to lubricate.

5. Surprisingly few components on the early alloy cars are the same as later models. Early 120s have a gearbox mounting behind the main block that is prone to cracking.

6. The ENV axles on early XK120s are notoriously weak, but the later Salisbury axle can be made to fit and is much stronger. Check for broken leaf springs.

7. Chassis outriggers should be checked for rust, as well as the front mounting of the rear spring shackles and the vulnerable and exposed last 2 feet of the chassis. Look for accident damage – a 'concertina' effect behind the front shock absorbers.

8. Rusty sills will cause door shut-pillar problems and could indicate trouble with the front inner wings and bulkhead side members.

9. On the body look for filler around the headlamps, the sidelight bases, below the bumper valance and along the bottom of the front wings. The rear door shut-pillar is another favourite rot spot. On the roadsters examine the tonneau panel for rust on either side of the beading.

10. Open the boot and check the floor at the sides and the spare wheel well. Inside the car check behind the seats at the forward ends of the inner wheel arches.

11. The strong XK engine has a well-known weakness for oil burning and leaks from the rear main bearing oil seal, which is an engine-out job to rectify. Oil pressure of 35–40psi should be maintained at 3,000rpm

when hot, 15–20 at tickover. Low oil pressure can be put down to worn bearings and/or oil pump. More optimistically, it could just be a faulty sender unit or a problem with the oil pressure relief valve. Timing chain rattle is common; the top chain is adjustable for wear but the bottom one is an engine-out job to replace.

12. The Moss gearbox has slow synchromesh and some spares are now difficult to source, but it is mechanically strong. Change quality can vary enormously from car to car. Beware of a slipping clutch as the engine has to be removed to change it.

13. Lack of regular lubrication can lead to worn ball joints, but otherwise the front suspension is fairly trouble-free. Clonks and rattles will betray worn bushes or ball joints in the front suspension. A clonk as drive is taken up from rest is likely to indicate worn splines on wire-wheeled cars. There should be minimal lost motion in the steering.

14. Rough or non-original interiors will be expensive to put right, particularly on the drophead and fixed-head coupé models with their wood veneer.

tuning parts. High-compression pistons, higher-lift cams, a lightened flywheel and dual exhausts could increase the output to as much as 190bhp, and with stiffened torsion bars and wider brake shoes it was possible to have a chassis to match the power. So equipped, these XKs became known as Special Equipment models.

The drophead coupé of 1953 was essentially a soft-top version of the fixed-head with a superb mohair

three-layer hood that could be raised and lowered with one hand. With the top erect, its rounded contours were those of the coupé from the outside, and it even featured an interior light. The veneered dash, wind-down windows and opening quarter lights echoed the equipment found on the fixed-head. As the fixed-head, this was to be a rare and short-lived variant of the 120 because for Earls Court in 1954 Jaguar were preparing the much improved – if not so pretty – XK140.

The XK140 *series*

The XK140, launched at Earls Court in 1954, might not have been such a pretty car as the XK120 but it was a better one. Sensitive to the demands of the all-important American market, Jaguar had incorporated changes that made the XK both faster and easier to live with – if a little less sporty and a shade heavier.

In retrospect, the styling, with its big bumpers, aggressive overriders, and cast seven-slat grille, lacks the purity of the original, but at the time the car was regarded by most as a welcome improvement. Had there been extra development time, Jaguar had intended to introduce a more radically new sports car, but instead opted to upgrade the existing model.

The SE-specification 190bhp engine was standardised across the three-car XK range with high-lift ⅜-inch (9.5mm) cams. If even more power was required there was always the C-Type head option, which, with its bigger valves and improved porting, liberated a further 20bhp. Only the twin exhausts gave it away from the outside. A new eight-blade fan and a better radiator addressed the XK's cooling problems in traffic. As far as the XK140 was concerned, 'SE' now meant simply wire wheels and Lucas FT 576 fog lamps.

Although all three body styles were retained, Jaguar tarnished the pure original styling with big 'Armco' bumpers (similar to those found on the MkVII and designed to fend off car park maulings from American sedans), which added 3 inches (76mm) to the length overall and were bolted directly to the chassis. The cast grille with fewer, thicker slats

The thicker bumpers, bonnet trims and revised cast grille of the XK140 are immediately noticeable. By this time wire wheels without the rear spat were becoming a more popular option.

than the 17-bar XK120 type was cheaper to make but clumsy in appearance.

Closer inspection revealed other details such as new Lucas J700 headlamps and different front indicators, and, at the back, new style rear lights, numberplate mountings and, for the first time, a bootlid handle. Badging now proclaimed Jaguar's Le Mans wins and the chrome strip that ran down the bonnet continued on the bootlid, which, like the bonnet and doors, was still skinned in aluminium.

The XK140 might not have been such a pretty car as the XK120, but it was a better one

Over and above these cosmetic changes, the basic structure had been altered. On the roadster and drophead coupé the bulkhead was moved forward 3 inches, liberating legroom for taller drivers and, in the dhc, allowing space for two very small rear seats. The dashboard was also lifted by 1 inch to give extra thigh room beneath the steering wheel. On the roadster, which still had only basic amenities, this extra space was utilised to increase the seat travel by a useful 3 inches (76mm). On all models, a single 12-volt battery replaced the twin 6-volts and lived under the bonnet rather than behind the seats.

In the coupé the dash – as with the dhc, still finished in opulent walnut veneer to match the door cappings – was moved forward a further 2 inches (51mm), giving more rear seat room, although the trade-off was a less elegant profile than the earlier model, which had a longer bonnet and bootlid. The doors were wider than

Jaguar XK140
1954–57

ENGINE:
In-line six-cylinder, cast iron block, alloy head, hemispherical combustion chambers

Bore x stroke	81 x 106mm
Capacity	3,442cc
Valves	Twin ohc, one inlet, one exhaust
Compression ratio	7:1 (8:1 optional)
Carburettors	Two 2in SUs
Power	190bhp at 5,000rpm (gross) (210bhp with C-Type head)
Torque	210lb ft at 2,500rpm (gross) (213lb ft at 4,000rpm with C-type head)

TRANSMISSION:
Four-speed manual with synchromesh on second, third and top, optional overdrive

Final drive	hypoid semi-floating Salisbury 4HA live rear axle

SUSPENSION:
Wishbones, torsion bars, anti-roll bar. Rear live axle with semi-elliptic springs

Steering	rack-and-pinion

BRAKES:
Lockheed 12-inch (305mm) drums with servo

WHEELS:
Pressed steel bolt-on 16-inch (406mm) with 5K rim or centre-lock wires

BODYWORK:
Separate steel body and chassis

LENGTH:	14ft 8in (4.47m)
WIDTH:	5ft 4½in (1.64m)
HEIGHT:	4ft 7in (1.4m) (fhc)
WEIGHT:	28cwt (1,424kg)
MAX SPEED:	121mph (195kph)
0–60mph (97kph)	8.4 seconds
PRICE NEW (1954):	£1,598 inc PT (roadster)

Jaguar XK140 SE
(with C-type head)
1954–57

As XK140 except:

Power	210bhp at 5,750rpm
Torque	213lb ft at 4,000rpm

PRODUCTION FIGURES:

Roadster	3,347
fhc	2,798
dhc	2,790
Total	8,935

By moving the engine forward 3 inches (76mm) in the chassis Jaguar liberated extra space inside the XK140 and both fixed-head and drophead coupé models now had small rear occasional seats. The fixed-head coupé interior featured veneers on the dashboard and had more window area than the XK120 fixed-head. The doors were wider, too, and there was more headroom.

before on the coupé, and by extending the top 6¾ inches (171mm) rearwards an extra 1½ inches (38mm) of headroom was liberated. These changes also resulted in the engine being moved forward in the chassis, making the weight distribution almost 50/50 and improving straight-line stability if not the handling.

What it did do was allow room for an optional Laycock de Normanville overdrive unit, which raised the

gearing in top by 12 per cent and effectively gave five forward speeds. It was operated by a switch on the dashboard and gave much more relaxed cruising and the potential for greater economy on a long run – up to 25mpg. Late in the production run of the XK140 a Borg-Warner automatic transmission option was offered, although this was to prove more popular in the car's successor.

New Alford & Adler rack-and-pinion

steering – with a cranked and universally jointed column – replaced the Burman 'box and brought with it a slightly quicker ratio but a mildly reduced lock. The rear dampers were, like the fronts, now telescopic, and the 140s came with the stiffer anti-roll and torsion bars found on the Special Equipment 120s. The brakes had improved fade resistance thanks to a new kind of friction material, were self-adjusting at the front, and reverted to a single brake master cylinder. As before, pressed steel wheels or knock-off wires were available, the hubcaps on the former now having an all-chrome finish.

It might not have been at the cutting edge of technology, but the XK140 still had no rival in sight in the mid-1950s. The Mercedes 300SL was only just entering production in late 1954,

while BMW's 507 did not arrive until two years later; both cars would always be vastly more expensive, and few 507s found buyers. There was no Aston that could match the pace of the XK – particularly in C-Type-head 190bhp form – while road-going Ferraris and Maseratis were virtually unheard of and, like the Aston, much more expensive. It was the success of European sports cars such as the XK that prompted Ford and General Motors to offer their own interpretations of the genre, but neither the wallowy Thunderbird nor the under-endowed original six-cylinder Corvette was fit to be mentioned in the same breath as the Jaguar.

As a driver's car the XK140 loses out a little to its lighter forebear. The extra weight over the nose increases

Ian Appleyard replaced NUB 120 with VUB 140, an XK140 fixed-head coupé. Here he is at Goodwood in 1956, taking part in the RAC Rally.

The D-Type and XKSS

The D-Type, conceived in the early part of 1954, was Jaguar's second attempt at a Le Mans winner, using most of the C-Type's mechanicals in an advanced wind-cheating alloy body designed by Malcolm Sayer. In fact, the D-Types won Le Mans twice, first in 1955 (a rather hollow victory in the tragic circumstances of the famous crash) and again in 1957, with a spectacular 1–2–3–4–6 placing, led by the Ecurie Ecosse team following the works withdrawal from racing the previous year. In a fabulous career, D-Types won nine international events outright and provided the inspiration for the road-going E-Type.

The D-Type was built around a central monocoque tub with full-length sills and a transverse box section for added rigidity. The rear bodywork bolted on to the double-skinned rear bulkhead while at the front the entire nose hinged forward for access to the engine. The tailfin behind the driver's head was a last-minute addition that was found to improve stability. Power went up to 250bhp thanks to improved manifolding and there was dry-sump lubrication to allow a lower engine height and thus a lower centre of gravity than on the C-Type. The 'D' had a better cooling system, an all-synchromesh gearbox and new Dunlop peg-drive alloy wheels, which were stronger than the wires used on the C-Type. The rack-and-pinion

The beautifully styled D-Type was another Sayer creation, schemed in 1954 and conceived with the help of a wind tunnel. Built around a central aluminium monocoque, the tail fin was a last-minute addition found to improve stability. This is a 'short-nose' car: five factory team cars received 'long-nose' styling to improve air penetration. In 1955 the D-Types went into 'production' for private buyers at a cost of £3,878; in all, 68 cars were produced, of which four were dismantled for parts and five destroyed in the 1957 Browns Lane factory fire.

steering and disc brakes were much as before.

For 1955 a separate structure to carry the engine and suspension was created, while at the rear the bodywork became a stressed panel rather than a bolt-on section, improving strength and reducing weight. The factory cars had new 'long-nose' styling to improve aerodynamics, together with a wraparound screen and a longer fin, while engine mods upped the power to 270bhp.

In 1956 the D-Types ran with fuel injection by Lucas, lighter bodywork and a front anti-roll bar. The D-Type

had been included in the Jaguar price list by October 1954, and at the time of that year's Earls Court Motor Show could be bought by anybody with the requisite £2,686 including Purchase Tax. Jaguar even produced a brochure for the model, which latterly proved difficult to sell; dealers are known to have slashed the price by £1,000 to get cars moving. In total 68 D-Types were built, of which four were dismantled for parts and five destroyed in the devastating fire that swept the Browns Lane factory in 1957.

Announced in January 1957, the XKSS was devised by Jaguar when 25 of the original batch of 68 production

The XKSS was a road-going D-Type with the fin removed and improved accommodation. The idea was to use up the remaining D-Type monocoques, but only 16 cars had been built when the factory fire destroyed much of the remaining shells and tooling.

D-Types remained unsold after the factory's retirement from racing in 1956. The real motivation for the XKSS, however, was as a way of making the D-Type acceptable to the Sports Car Club of America as a road machine.

Continued overleaf

The D-Type and XKSS

Michelotti built this handsome body using parts salvaged from a wrecked D-Type and displayed it at the 1963 Geneva show. Later it was stripped of its D-Type components and rebuilt using E-Type parts.

Continued from previous page

The SCCA decreed that 50 of these revised road-going models had to be built if the sports racing Jaguar was to be eligible.

Thus, by removing the head fairing and the central division between the driver and passenger, adding an extra door, a full-width framed windscreen and rudimentary hood with side screen, D-Type became XKSS. The delicate aluminium body was protected on all four corners by slim bumpers cut down from saloon car pressings, with the faired-in lights emphasised by brightwork around the edges. The passenger's entry and exit over the hot exhaust was made safer by a cowling.

Like the D-Type that spawned it, the XKSS was so flexible and tractable that it could be used for shopping (although there was hardly anywhere to put your purchases, without so much as a glove box, never mind a boot), and on its tall, 16-inch (406mm) Dunlop knock-ons it had all the poise and balance of its race-car sibling. All the power, too – yielding 250bhp on triple 45 SCOE Webers, the XK engine was in full, uncompromising D-Type tune, all part of the 'Super Sports' package that was only marginally heavier and less wind-cheating than the original.

With four D-Types being dismantled for spares, Jaguar planned an initial run of 21 XKSSs, but only 16 had been built when the remaining five D-Type shells perished in the factory fire of February 1957.

the understeer, making it less intimidating for the novice but less fun for more advanced students. A little more kick-back is experienced through the rack-and-pinion steering, but at least the wheel, still a huge four-spoke affair, sits at a more comfortable angle in the XK140. What is more, with the increased cabin room there is half a chance of being able to adopt a more comfortable driving position. The steering is quicker but not noticeably more precise than the 120, and indeed most of the other controls will feel much as before including the hefty clutch, slow Moss gearbox, and the drum brakes, which are perfectly adequate in normal driving.

Any good XK140 will still perform strongly, particularly a roadster with the C-Type cylinder head (obviously the lightest of the trio, with its relatively primitive interior trim). Contemporary tests talked of 0–60mph (97kph) in 8.4 seconds, but even more impressive is the sparkling pull in direct and overdrive top where a good car will still waft along at 100mph (161kph) with urge in hand. The dominance over other traffic of a car like this in the mid-1950s must have been incredible.

The XK140 gave way to the XK150, the last of the line, in 1957. Less glamorous than its predecessor, and less sophisticated than its disc-braked successor, the XK140 is the rarest of the XKs by a small margin, particularly in right-hand-drive roadster form – in which guise just 73 were built.

The XK150 *series*

I t was not the way that the new XK150 went or looked that hit the headlines in May 1957, but the way it stopped. At last Jaguar had tackled the braking problems and offered four-wheel Dunlop disc brakes as part of the wire-wheeled Special Equipment package (although it seems almost certain that no drum-braked disc-wheel 'standard equipment' XK150s were ever built), finally banishing the spectre of fade that had afflicted the XK since its introduction almost a decade earlier.

Experiments with disc brakes had begun in 1951 and had continued on

the C-Type racer; they were certainly a major contribution to its success at Le Mans in 1953. The production Dunlop brakes used on the XK150 employed a single calliper containing one cylinder on each side to grip the disc and there was assistance from a Lockheed servo. Now the XK's performance could be used to the full with smooth, swift stopping power on hand no matter how often it was called upon.

Even without the disc brakes, the XK150 was the most radical revision of the XK sports car yet produced. Clever changes to the bodywork had produced a car that not only looked different (without recourse to major retooling) but had a slightly more

By cleverly altering existing tooling, Jaguar gave its now venerable XK sports car a new look with the 1957 XK150. The grille was wider, the flanks more slab-sided than before due to the raising of the waistline, and the scuttle was higher. The front and rear bumpers also wrapped around more.

middle-aged, less sporting image, even though, in its ultimate form, it would prove to be the fastest XK of them all. As usual it was also astonishing value for money at £1,763 17s including Purchase Tax for the 'standard equipment' fixed-head coupé, and, on the other hand, £1,969 7s for the Secial Equipment drophead.

At last Jaguar had tackled the braking problems and offered disc brakes as part of the package

At first there were only fixed-head and drophead coupé versions, priced in 'standard equipment' form at only £52 10s more than the outgoing model. The roadster, initially for export only, followed ten months later in March 1958 with its scuttle moved back 4 inches (102mm) to give a longer, more aggressive bonnet.

Under the bonnet the XK150 retained the 3,442cc 190bhp twin-carb engine of the previous model, although there was now a 'B-Type' head, giving the same 210bhp of the old C-Type head but at a lower 5,500rpm. Moreover, peak torque was now developed at 3,000rpm, 1,000rpm lower than before, which noticeably improved top-gear pick-up. This was achieved in the B-Type head by combining the exhaust valves of the C-Type head with the smaller-diameter inlet throat of the standard head, thereby keeping mixture flow up at low rpm.

Transmission options remained as before: four-speed or four-speed with overdrive Moss manual transmission, or a three-speed automatic from Borg-Warner. The latter was to prove increasingly popular as the XK put on

Jaguar XK150 3.4
1957-61

ENGINE:
In-line six-cylinder, cast iron block, alloy head, hemispherical combustion chambers

Bore x stroke	81 x 106mm
Capacity	3,442cc
Valves	Twin ohc, one inlet, one exhaust
Compression ratio	7:1 (8:1 and 9:1 optional)
Carburettors	Two 2in SUs
Power	190bhp at 5,500rpm (gross)
Torque	210lb ft at 2,500rpm (gross)

TRANSMISSION:
Four-speed manual with synchromesh on second, third and top, optional overdrive

Final drive	3.54:1 (4.09:1 with overdrive)

SUSPENSION:
Wishbones, torsion bars, anti-roll bar. Rear live axle with semi-elliptic leaf springs

Steering	rack-and-pinion

BRAKES:
Dunlop discs front and rear

WHEELS:
Pressed steel bolt-on 16-inch (406mm) with 5K rim or centre-lock wires

BODYWORK:
Separate steel body and chassis

LENGTH:	14ft 9in (4.5m)
WIDTH:	5ft 4½in (1.64m)
HEIGHT:	4ft 7in (1.4m) (fhc)
WEIGHT:	28cwt (1,424kg)

MAX SPEED:	123mph (198kph)
0-60mph (97kph)	8.5 seconds

PRICE NEW (1957): £1,939 inc PT (Special Equipment fhc)

Jaguar XK150 3.4 SE
1957-61

As XK150 3.4 except:

Power	210bhp at 5,500rpm
Torque	213lb ft at 3,000rpm

MAX SPEED:	N/a
0-60	N/a

Jaguar XK150 3.4 S
1958-61

As XK150 3.4 except:

Power	250bhp at 5,500rpm
Torque	240lb ft at 4500rpm
Carburettors	Three 2in SU HD8

MAX SPEED:	136mph (219kph)
0-60mph (97kph)	7.3 seconds

Jaguar XK150 3.8
1959-61

As XK150 3.4 except:

Capacity	3,781cc
Bore x stroke	87 x 106mm
Power	220bhp at 5,500rpm
Torque	240lb ft at 3,000rpm

MAX SPEED:	N/a
0-60	N/a

PRICE NEW (1959): £1,942 inc PT (fhc)

Jaguar XK150 3.8 S
1959-61

As XK150 3.8 except:

Carburettors	Three 2in HD8 SUs
Power	265bhp at 5,500rpm
Torque	260lb ft at 4,000rpm

MAX SPEED:	135mph (217kph)
0-60mph (97kph)	7.2 seconds

PRICE NEW (1959): £2,176 inc PT (fhc)

PRODUCTION FIGURES:

fhc	3,445
dhc	1,903
Roadster	1,297
fhc S	199
dhc S	104
Roadster S	888
fhc 3.8	656
dhc 3.8	586
Roadster 3.8	42
fhc 3.8 S	150
dhc 3.8 S	79
Roadster 3.8 S	36
Total	9,385

middle-aged spread along with its buyers, who, as before, were mostly North Americans.

As for the styling, Lyons had promoted a clever evolutionary rethink on the XK theme with a new, higher front wing-line that ran through to the rear wing, a modern wraparound screen and, in closed cars, a bigger rear screen. Doors were slimmer in section and wore new plunger-type door handles. Although the previous body panel tooling was retained, only the bootlid was shared with the XK140, and the bonnet was now wider, giving easier access to the engine. Almost all XK150s ran wire wheels; spats and steel disc wheels are virtually unheard of, although in theory they could be specified.

The rear bumper ran full width, while the front one had a dip under the new wider front grille, which made a welcome return to the more delicate style of slat used on the XK120. Inside there was more space for the wider seats thanks to thinner doors and, for the first time, a padded top-roll

featured on the dashboard. On all models this was leather-covered, with the layout much as before. The drophead retained its luxurious hood, which made the car virtually as snug as a coupé when it was in place.

The roadster was a much more luxurious machine than the previous two-seater XKs. The windows wound up and the hood was a big improvement over that of the XK120 and 140 roadsters; it was easier to put up and looked much more sleek than before. It also stowed more neatly,

Inside, all models reverted to the leather-covered dashboard of the roadsters. The dash top was padded, the seats softer and wider and the windscreen now wrapped around American-style.

The XK150 was the fastest of all the XKs, particularly with the 3.8S triple-carb engine, but it was becoming dynamically dated by the end of the 1950s.

disappearing behind the seats under a neat cover made from hood material.

To take on the American V8s, Harry Weslake developed a new 'straight-port' head for the XK150. Thus equipped, the cars were badged XK150S, and this option – hiking power up to 250bhp at 5,500rpm and torque to 240lb ft at 4,500rpm – was initially only available on the roadster.

By straightening the ports, Weslake achieved a better flow of mixture at high revs, and to make the best of this improved breathing, 'S' models came with three 2-inch SU carbs on a new inlet manifold. The compression ratio was raised to 9:1, while lead bronze bearings and a lighter flywheel improved bottom-end strength. In top the 'S' could run to an impressive 136mph (219kph) and blast to 60mph (97kph) in 7.3 seconds, which was a good reason for opting for the

Thornton Powr-Lok limited slip-differemtial. 'S' models also came with overdrive as standard, and were not available as Borg-Warner automatics.

The ultimate XK150s were the 3.8 models, offered from Motor Show time in 1959 in all three body-styles and in either normal (220bhp/B-Type head) or 'S' form (265bhp). As an 'S', the 3.8 had a shockingly fine turn of speed, hitting the magic 100mph (161kph) figure in less than 20 seconds. On a bangs-per-buck basis, nothing came close even if the live rear axle with its leaf springs was really on the limit of what it could cope with.

What visitors to that 1959 show could not have known was that the 3.8 option was really intended for a new, much more modern Jaguar waiting in the wings – the E-Type. In fact, very

The drophead coupé was still a popular variant, although even the roadster now featured wind-up windows and proper inside door handles. The hood on the dhc did not fold out of sight, so looked untidy in profile.

By the end of the 1950s the handling of the XK150 was beginning to feel a little dated, but it was still very fast: the 3.8S could touch almost 140mph (225kph), and with the standard four-wheel disc brakes had impressive stopping power, too.

few 3.8S XKs were built: 150 coupés, 89 dropheads and just 36 roadsters.

Forty years on, an XK150 makes a fine, torquey, high-geared touring car, mixing vintage manners with post-war speed and braking power. Inside, the wider seats lack all pretence of side support and you feel as if you are sitting lower than in other XKs, because the scuttle is rather higher and the doors deeper. The coupé models were an early move to an XJ-S kind of car offering relative refinement with the windows wound up and the heater on. As a two-pedal automatic it is closer to a sort of two-door MkIX than the true sports car that the original XK120 had been. The roadster, for all its wind-up windows, is a sports car and, if you find one of the 'S' models, still a very quick one,

with acceleration not that far behind that of an E-Type; I wonder how many owners would risk 136mph in one today. The XK150 cannot be thrown around like a little TR or even a Healey, yet the steering is precise, and advanced students will enjoy slewing the tail out on tight corners, although too much power will have the axle hopping as it struggles to cope with the torque.

The final XK150s, the last separate-chassis Jaguar sports cars, were sold in 1961, overlapping with the first of the E-Types. It was the end of the XK's 11-year reign and the cars would now enter a dark period of low values when rust, and apathy, would claim hundreds before the XK was adopted as one of the darlings of the classic movement in the 1970s.

Most XK150s used the twin cam XK engine in 3.4 or 3.8 form with twin SU carburettors as pictured here. The 3.8S had triple carbs.

Special bodywork on the XK150

Because the standard bodywork was so consistently stylish, few coachbuilders have felt moved to re-body Jaguars. The XK150, however, seems to have lent itself more readily than most.

Bertone did perhaps the most successful re-hash with a series of three fastback coupés in 1958 called, prophetically, XKE. Based on the 265bhp 'S' engine, they differed in small trim details from each other and had a more upmarket two-seater interior in the mould of contemporary Ferrari and Maserati models. One car, registered APC 6, found its way to the UK. The same body featured on a Bertone Aston Martin DB MkIII of the time.

Ghia Aigle, a Swiss offshoot of the better-known Italian house, built a series of special Jaguars in the 1950s based on the MkVII and the XK. Their last-ever project was an XK150 in 1959, to a design by Pietro

Frua who, under his own name, would restyle E-Types and S-Types in the '60s. His XK150, while not unattractive, bore a certain resemblance to his Renault Floride.

Ghia of Turin never seem to have got round to doing an XK150, but they did complete a series of special XK120s with 'Supersonic' bodywork, a design also found on the Fiat 8V styled by Chrysler stylist Virgil Exner. A further three were completed on the XK140 chassis.

Zagato did a couple of XK150 coupés whose profile was surprisingly restrained and elegant, although this coachbuilder was not destined to be a regular user of the Jaguar chassis.

Modifications to the standard body have rarely been attractive. At least three estate XK150s were built by unknown enthusiasts, one using the half-timbered back-end off a Morris

Minor Traveller. Much more elegant, and better known, was Douglas Hull's car, occasionally campaigned in club racing in the 1960s and '70s.

Finally, Martin Brothers of Ealing did a one-off fastback conversion on a fixed-head XK150 in 1960, which was not unattractive.

The E-Type
series I and II

The E-Type, launched at the Geneva show in 1961, was an instant classic. Here was a combination of the cool aerodynamic theory of Malcolm Sayer and the intuitive feel for styling of Sir William Lyons that produced probably the most beautiful sports car of the 1960s. It had the ability to live up to the looks, too. The 150mph (241kph) claimed by Jaguar for the 3.8 E-Type was devastatingly quick in 1961, making the new Jag Britain's fastest production car. Better still, at £2,098 for the roadster, it was probably Britain's greatest motoring bargain, undercutting its nearest British rival – the Aston Martin DB4 – by a third.

That curvy shell, inspired by the D-Type racer, was immensely stiff in both roadster and coupé form. It used a central steel monocoque by the Pressed Steel Company, with deep sills that were attached at their extremities to the scuttle and to a strong box member that ran across the car just ahead of the rear suspension. The transmission tunnel, together with a transverse member that emerged half way along the sills, formed a link between the scuttle, floor and sills. There were further 'top hat' sections in the boot floor for mounting the rear suspension. The whole thing was so strong that the open version needed no further strengthening.

At the front, square-section Reynolds tubing made up a framework that carried the engine, transmission, front suspension, rack-and-pinion steering and big forward-hinged three-section bonnet, and was bolted to the hull at eight points.

Torsion bars and unequal-length wishbones comprised the front

The E-Type caused a sensation in 1961, mixing high technology and great beauty in a car that was not just fantastically fast but also amazingly refined. The fixed-head version shown incorporated a versatile side-hinged tailgate. The covered headlamps allowed good aerodynamic penetration but meant that headlamp beam strength was poor; the glass also tended to mist-up in wet weather.

suspension, with the bars mounted in inner extensions of the chassis as per the D-Type. New and highly sophisticated independent suspension was used at the back, a coil spring and wishbone design Jaguar engineers had been experimenting with for several years. The fixed-length driveshafts cunningly did double duty as the top wishbones, while the tubular forked lower arms supported big alloy hub carriers with the driveshafts running into them.

Providing the power was a 3.8 litre version of the already 13-year-old XK engine, still a stormer and well worthy of the new chassis. In this form it was familiar from the XK150S, developing 265bhp at 5,500rpm with triple 2in SU carburettors on the 'straight-port' head. The cooling system featured a remote header tank and a then unusual electric cooling fan.

The *Autocar*'s road-test 3.8 coupé – the second prototype – pulled 60mph (97kph) in 6.9 seconds and 120mph (193kph) in just 25.9 seconds. What is more, it was 'breathtakingly' flexible in top gear, pulling from 10mph (16kph) without stress, and between 50 and 130mph (80 and 209kph) the top gear urge was incredible.

Running racing tyres and bereft of overriders so as to present a more wind-cheating profile, the coupé topped the magic 150mph (241kph), although it was later revealed that the engine was quite heavily breathed on and the body lighter than standard with an alloy rear door and plastic side windows. Most E-Type owners never saw more than 140mph (225kph), which was fast enough.

If only the Moss gearbox had been a match for the engine. It was slow, notchy and noisy, especially in first gear, which was still 'crash'. Other gripes included the brakes – or more accurately the Kelsey Hayes bellows servo – which gave somewhat delayed assistance at low speeds,

Jaguar E-Type 3.8 Series I
Roadster and Coupé
1961–64

ENGINE:
In-line six, iron block, alloy head, 'hemi'	
Bore x stroke	87 x 106mm
Capacity	3,781cc
Valves	Twin ohc, 12v
Compression ratio	9:1
Carburettors	Three 2in HD8 SUs
Power	265bhp at 5,500rpm (gross)
Torque	283lb ft at 4,000rpm (gross)

TRANSMISSION:
Four-speed manual	
Final drive	3.31:1

SUSPENSION:
Front: ind. wishbones and t. bars
Rear: ind. lower wishbone/upper driveshaft link with radius arms and twin coil springs
Steering	rack-and-pinion

BRAKES:
Dunlop discs with vacuum servo, 11-inch front, 11³/₈-inch rear inboard

WHEELS:
Centre-lock wires with Dunlop RS5 6.40 x 16 or SP 41 185 x 15 tyres

BODYWORK:
Unitary with space frame at front

LENGTH:	14ft 7¼in (4.45m)
WIDTH:	5ft 5½in (1.66m)
HEIGHT (Roadster):	3ft 11in (1.2m)
Coupé:	4ft 0in (1.22m)
WEIGHT (Roadster):	24cwt (1,220kg)
Coupé:	24½cwt (1,246kg)
MAX SPEED:	149mph (240kph)
0–60mph (97kph)	7.1 seconds

PRICE NEW (1961): £2,160 inc PT (Roadster)

Jaguar E-Type 4.2 Series I/II
Roadster and Coupé
1964–70

As E-Type 3.8 except:
Bore x stroke	92.07 x 106mm
Capacity	4,235cc
Power	265bhp at 5,400rpm (gross)
Torque	283lb ft at 4,000rpm (gross)
Transmission	Four-speed all-synchromesh

WEIGHT:	24½cwt (1,246kg)
MAX SPEED:	149mph (240kph)
0–60mph (97kph)	7.4 seconds

PRICE NEW (1964): £1,993 inc PT (coupé)

Jaguar E-Type 4.2 Series I/II 2+2
1966–70

As E-Type 4.2 S1/S2 coupé except:
LENGTH:	14ft 7¼in (4.45m)
WIDTH:	5ft 5¼in (1.66m)
HEIGHT:	4ft 2½in (1.28m)
WHEELBASE:	8ft 9in (2.67m)
WEIGHT:	27½cwt (1,398kg)
MAX SPEED:	139mph (224kph)
0–60 mph (97kph)	7.4 seconds

PRICE NEW (1966) £2,284 inc PT

PRODUCTION FIGURES:
3.8 roadster	7,827
3.8 fhc	7,669
4.2 roadster	9,548
4.2 fhc	7,770
4.2 2+2	5,598
4.2 SII roadster	8,627
4.2 SII fhc	4,855
4.2 SII 2+2	5,326

differing from the usual hydraulic servo by exerting a mechanical pressure on the twin brake master cylinders. The faired-in and deeply recessed lights were not as penetrating as they might have been at high speeds, and tall occupants found footroom at a premium in the earliest 'flat-floor' cars with their very shallow footwells. By the end of 1961 deeper footwells – and greater adjustment for the driver's seat – gave tall drivers a better deal.

Still, these were mere details. Jaguar, who had only planned to build 250 cars, had a hit on their hands and were caught with their corporate trousers down by the strength of demand. Pop stars, racing drivers and royalty jostled for position in an ever-

lengthening waiting list. Lew Grade of ITC wanted to borrow one for his new TV series, *The Saint*, but Jaguar turned him down because they did not want the publicity – they could sell every car they could make.

Despite the demand – especially in America where 80 per cent of production ended up – development continued. The bigger 4.2 engine from 1964 was torquier and came with a much better gearbox and brakes. Retaining the aesthetics of the original 3.8, this model is considered perhaps the best of the family.

For this 4.2 litre unit, really the limit of expansion left in the XK engine, the designers re-spaced the bore centres, moving the two end bores

The roadster had a really good fold-away hood, wind-up windows and a decent boot. It was easily the most glamorous open car on the market in its prime and certainly one of the fastest. This is the famous *The Motor* road test car, clocked at a true 150mph (241kph).

outwards and the centres of the two middle bores together, allowing an enlargement of the bore size from 87 to 92mm. To keep the block at its existing size, the bores also had to be siamesed, but power was unchanged at 265bhp, although it was produced at 5,400 rather than 5,500rpm.

A Lockheed in-line vacuum booster replaced the bellows servo and the 4.2 came with the much improved all-synchromesh Jaguar gearbox, both of which made the car much more driveable. Performance was equally strong. Peaking at 283lb ft at 4,000rpm, the torque curve of the 4.2

was so flat that, between 30 and 120mph (48 and 193kph), no 20mph (32kph) increment in top gear was timed in double figures. A good 4.2 roadster or fixed-head would pull 53mph (85kph) in first, 82 (132) in second, 112 (180) in third, and could be clocking 120mph (193kph) within half a minute. In real-life situations there was rarely any need to exceed 4,000rpm, enough for decisive overtaking response and a smooth, relentless surge of power that can still leave the majority of moderns floundering, never mind the E-Type's 1960s' sports car rivals.

An early 3.8 litre interior with aluminium brightwork on the dash and centre console, together with thin-backed bucket seats. Legroom on the very early 'flat-floor' cars was in short supply.

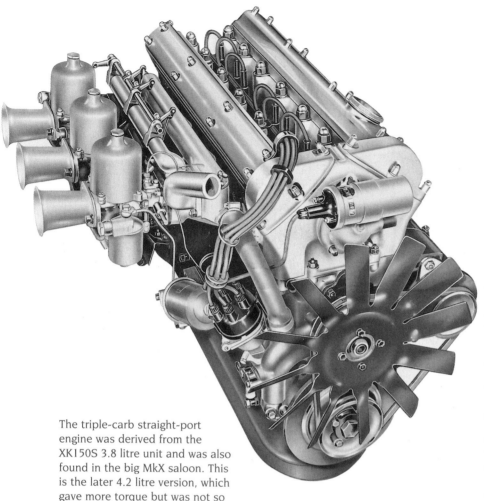

The triple-carb straight-port engine was derived from the XK150S 3.8 litre unit and was also found in the big MkX saloon. This is the later 4.2 litre version, which gave more torque but was not so sweet as the 3.8.

The two-seater E-type's looks began to go as early as 1967 with the deletion of the headlight covers. This took 2 or 3mph (3 to 5kph) off the top speed, but improved slightly the lamps' penetration. These early open-headlight cars are referred to retrospectively as Series 1½, but in fact the factory never made any distinction between the 4.2 litre open-headlight and closed-headlight cars. The former were current for about a year, during which time many of the modifications that were later applied to the full Series II – announced in October 1968 – were introduced, such as rocker switches and earless wheel spinners.

Middle age had apparently crept up unawares on the E-Type; the rot was

Middle age had crept up unawares on the E-Type; the rot was beginning to set in with the Series II

The trim was improved, with new adjustable pleated seats and a hinged armrest/oddments box, while the electrics were enhanced by the replacement of the dynamo with an alternator.

Appeals for a roomier car were answered by a '2+2' version in 1966; by stretching the wheelbase 9 inches (229mm) and raising the screen 1½ inches (38mm), Jaguar made room for a small rear bench seat that was ideal for two children or a sideways-sitting adult. Weight was up by 1.75cwt (89kg) and looks suffered (the 2+2 always looked too top-heavy), but it was still good for 139mph (224kph). There was even an automatic option for the 2+2, as Jaguar tried to reconcile the E's performance image with a need to please buyers in America.

beginning to set in with the Series II. North American safety demands were tarnishing the purity of the Jaguar's styling, and in Series II form, as well as the fussy open lights, the once elegantly clean lines were disfigured by bigger wraparound bumpers and uglier rear lights. Under the bonnet the power of the North American export models was strangled in the Series 1½ and Series II by emission controls on the twin Zenith-Stromberg carbs that were fitted in place of the triple SUs of home-market cars, and which helped to reduce power to 171bhp. By the turn of the decade the car was a shadow of its youthfully vigorous former self. Power steering and air-conditioning were now optional and ugly pressed steel wheels could be ordered to replace the 72-spoke wires.

The 4.2 litre models built from 1964 had a restrained leather-effect dash and more substantial and comfortable seats.

Not all the Series II changes were for the worse, however. Cooling was better thanks to twin electric fans, and the brakes, now by Girling, were slightly bigger.

To drive an 'E' you slide in through slim, light doors and hop over a deep sill into a leather cockpit that has few peers for classic simplicity. The toggle switches – rockers came later with the Series II – sit in a regimented line, the big Smiths rev-counter and speedo are clearly and classily calibrated, and that slim-rimmed wooden steering wheel feels warm and friendly to the touch. Turn the key, press the button and the XK engine shudders instantly to life and idles with a soft purr, the hiss of the triple SUs just discernible. It is smooth and quiet, this big long-stroke 'six', only really stretching its

vocal chords as you move towards 4,000rpm. The distant thunder then rises to a crescendo of chain thrash and double-edged cam whine, the bark from behind throaty but smooth-edged in tone.

Developed to produce lots of torque in the low and mid-rev bands (for the automatic Jags the American market demanded), the 4.2 will lack some of the sweetness and crisp response of the 3.8, but there is not much in it. Blip the throttle and you sense the inertia of heavy pistons moving in a long stroke and an engine that will not enjoy being revved to its red line.

Moving off, the clutch bites progressively, the gearchange – with strong synchro on every ratio in the 4.2 models – is easy and accurate, and the torque is just enormous. You can snick the chunky lever straight over from first to top, should you have a mind, and steam into the 90s in one seamless movement. The 'E' feels neutral and almost roll-free as you toss it into the first curve, its ride supple yet without a hint of wallow. It was this remarkable saloon-car ride that set the 'E' so much apart from its hairy-chested contemporaries. For a sports car it was just so civilised.

Sweeping through roundabouts and country lane curves you sense a superbly rigid shell and instantly get a feel for the brilliant steering, which is light, direct (2.6 turns lock-to-lock), free from shock or significant kickback, yet with all the feel you could ever want.

But it is the controllability that really impresses, the way the 'E' responds so fluidly to correction, loves to be set up and powered aggressively out of the tightest part of the turn – although it will look after the indecisive novice too – and just feels so much handier and more compact than it looks. Pour on the power and you can count on that supple, sophisticated rear suspension to squat and bite hard into the tarmac. Back off and it will just scrub a little at the front.

There is always the potential for breaking the hold of the back tyres in a low gear at the drop of a jaw, even on a bone-dry summer's day, but usually the rear grips far better than those narrow tyres and modest track would suggest. And always there is that tautness, that rigidity about the shell that was at the centre of the design's superiority, and made it so stunningly modern to drive in 1961.

The opening tailgate of the coupé gave access to a surprisingly useful flat load space. This is the 2+2 version, launched in 1965. Its longer wheelbase and higher roofline allowed space for small rear children's seats, and automatic transmission was optional.

The Lightweights

Spurred on by the racing success in 1961 and 1962 of the Coombs and Equipe Endeavour teams (Graham Hill won first time out at Oulton Park against the Ferraris), Jaguar sanctioned the construction of 12 Lightweights for private racing teams.

Although each car differed in specification, they all had an alloy monocoque with a fixed aluminum hard top to contribute to overall strength. Stiffer torsion and anti-roll bars were used at the front with beefed-up dampers and special upper and lower fulcrum housings. At the back, lighter hub carriers and modified wishbones and dampers were used with stiffer mountings and integral bump stops. The discs, callipers and servo were all uprated and wire wheels were eschewed in favour of centre-lock peg-drive wheels much as those used on the D-Type.

The 3.8 litre engine was in a highly developed state compared to the standard road version. It had an alloy block to keep the weight down, while a special wide-angle alloy head with Lucas fuel injection helped the Lightweight to produce between 320 and 344bhp. Most cars used a ZF five-speed gearbox.

Although these cars showed some potential, most memorably at the Easter Goodwood meeting in 1963 when Hill beat Mike Parkes in a Ferrari GTO, they never lived up to this early promise, probably because the factory were never truly committed to the idea of racing the 'E', which, in terms of sales, hardly needed the extra publicity.

Briggs Cunningham, the American team owner, made one assault on Le Mans with three Lightweights, but the enterprise was marred by appalling luck. One car (No 14) retired with gearbox problems, while Roy Salvadori's car spun off on oil deposited from the blown engine of the Aston Martin of Bruce McLaren. Another lost brakes at 165mph (265kph) at the end of the Mulsanne straight and crashed into the straw bales. However, with parts salvaged from No 14, this car managed to limp on and came a creditable ninth.

This is the Lumsden/Sargent Lightweight E-Type with a highly modified low drag body designed by Dr Samir Klat. It was rebuilt in this form after a crash at the Nurburgring in 1963. Its 1964 Le Mans assault ended with a failed gearbox.

From the rear a Series II could be identified by its higher bumper with centre section, re-shaped exhaust pipes, and an anodised panel for the much bigger rear lights.

The six-cylinder E-Type story ends in 1971 when the V12 Series III cars were introduced to complete the sanitisation process. The engine was great but the car was feeling old – the once legendary sex symbol was a flabby spent force, living on old glories, not to mention borrowed time.

It is amazing to think that Jaguar, gearing up for the E-Type's successor,

the XJ-S, had trouble getting rid of the last few in 1975. But that's another story (the Series III will be discussed in more detail in Chapter 18).

It is better to remember the E-Type at its youthful best as Britain's fastest, most glamorous sports car of the 1960s. At twice the price it would still have been a winner.

Buying Hints

1. Search for rot on the bonnet starting with the flanges, around the headlight bowls, and inside the air intake, and check the vulnerable bonnet 'nose' for filler – it is certain to have been touch-parked at some time. Bonnets are expensive but available – repairing a bad one is probably more trouble than it is worth.

2. When inspecting the subframe tubing see if the car has been jacked up in the wrong place (usually the 'picture' frame under the radiator), and check for stress cracks and poorly executed accident repairs.

3. If the bulkhead is rusty, a major rebuild is in prospect – remove the battery and the air cleaner boxes to inspect it properly.

4. The central tub is critical to the car's strength, but rusts liberally from the inside outwards as a result of the moisture-retaining box sections. Check the sills inside and out as well as the floors, and jack up the car on its centre chassis rail to see if the door will still open. The screen pillars rust at their base.

5. At the back, check where the radius arms are mounted, the box sections inside the arches, the bump stop mountings and the anti-roll bar attachment points.

6. On coupés, a water trap between the inner and outer rear wings causes rot around the double-skinned arch with problems continuing underneath the bumper. The leaded joint between the top of the rear wing and the shell can give problems when the lead 'lifts'. The roadster hood's wooden tacking strip retains water, causing corrosion in the top of the rear wing.

7. In the boot, check the fuel tank, spare wheel well and the door aperture on the coupé.

8. The doors rot along the bottom on the folded joint between the skin and frame.

9. The engine is strong but the thin-walled 4.2 block can crack, causing overheating when the head gasket blows. The timing chains should not be noisy and the oil pressure with the engine well-warmed should be a strong 40lb at 3,000rpm. Oil leaks from the cam cover and sump gaskets, and the 3.8 is an oil burner, but be on the look-out for obvious clouds of smoke under hard acceleration.

10. The Moss gearboxes are never silent, but they should not be too noisy in first. Be aware that spares for these are getting rare. The all-synchro 'box used from the 4.2 onwards should have strong synchro in all gears, but remember that changing a clutch is an engine-out job in all versions.

11. Look for worn ball joints in the front suspension. Too much wallow and bottoming on the move indicates worn spring/damper units in the rear suspension. UJs might clonk, and perished Metalastik bushes can detract from refinement and roadholding. Beware, too, of leaking diffs and clicking from a tired limited-slip unit when accelerating on full lock.

12. Loose steering indicates worn UJs in the column or a worn spline. Infrequently lubricated steering may feel stiff. Rack mountings can perish, again resulting in a loose feel.

13. The Dunlop brakes are troublesome, especially if they are not used, resulting in seized callipers, pads rusted to the discs, etc. The 3.8s stop much better with the later booster fitted to 4.2 litre cars.

14. Check the wire wheels for loose spokes and rust. Listen for clunks as the drive is taken up – this could spell worn splines.

15. The interior of the E is less critical than that of the saloons, as kits are available to rejuvenate tired trim, although original condition is always preferable.

The E-Type
series III V12

As a cut-price road rocket the Series III V12 E-Type was one of the bargains of its day. No car before or since has offered the exotic glamour of 12 cylinders and near-150mph (241kph) performance at such an affordable price.

A rapid yet double-cream-smooth drive, the Series III E-Type is still a lot of car in the performance-per-pound stakes 25 years on, especially if you go for the less fashionable but more practical coupé. It has better legroom and access than on the 'six', and more space for luggage. It might not be as sporty as the old 3.8, but the V12 is no sluggard, its 150mph (241kph) speed delivered with an even, steady, unrelenting surge that, in manual form, is easily a match for any straight-six 'E'. In fact, the V12 engine, just 80lb (36kg)

heavier than the old XK due to its alloy construction, knocked 2 seconds off the 0–100mph (161kph) time of the fastest six-cylinder models.

The torque curve should tell you as much: the V12 produces most of its 304lb ft of torque between 1,300 and 5,700rpm, although it should rev cleanly and willingly to over 7,000rpm. However, 5,000rpm is generally more than enough to rocket a Series III past a line of dawdlers, its voice a smooth, quality hum – oddly nondescript – becoming a harder, more gutsy growl as the revs nudge 6,000rpm. It lacks the guttural, aural urgency of the XK straight-six as you wind it through the gears, yet the low, heavily muffled wuffle from the four tailpipes – reduced to two pipes in 1973 – is distinctive and classy.

The clutch is heavy and it is necessary to be decisive with the slightly notchy, but precise, gearchange to get a clean shift before the revs drop away. The

The Series III V12 was the E-Type's final fling, using the magnificent new all-alloy 5.3 litre engine in a mildly reworked long-wheelbase bodyshell. Flared arches filled by fatter tyres gave it a more meaty look than the old car.

ratios seem well spaced, but so massive is the engine's torque that first and top are all you effectively need most of the time. Top seems too low, so even at modest speeds a fifth ratio feels lacking, which means that motorway cruising in what should be a consummate long-legged slogger is fussier than it needs to be. Automatic versions, with just three speeds, are even worse.

The V12 E-type has a superb ride for a 25-year-old sports car, and approaches the levels of silken isolation achieved by the then contemporary XJ6, although generous wheel movement means that the car can bottom easily at both ends and, with its narrower track, it does not really handle as well as the saloon. The

The fixed-head version came only as a 2+2. The bonnet on both versions was totally new, with broad front wings and wheel arches to accommodate the wider tyres, and an enlarged nose intake with a chrome-plated grille.

Jaguar E-Type 5.3 Series III
Roadster and Coupé
1971–75

ENGINE:
All-alloy 60-degree V12
Bore x stroke	90 x 70mm
Capacity	5,343cc
Valves	single ohc
Compression ratio	9:1
Carburettors	Four Zenith 175CD
Power	272bhp at 5,850rpm (net)
Torque	304lb ft at 3,600rpm (net)

TRANSMISSION:
Four-speed manual all-synchromesh or three-speed auto
Final drive   3.07:1

SUSPENSION:
Front: independent wishbones and torsion bars
Rear: independent lower wishbone/upper driveshaft link with radius arms and twin coil springs
Steering   rack-and-pinion, power assisted

BRAKES:
Discs front and rear

WHEELS:
Centre-lock wires or bolt-on steel with 6-inch (152mm) rims, E70 VR 15 tyres

LENGTH: 15ft 6in (4.72m)

WIDTH: 5ft 6¼in (1.68m)

HEIGHT (Roadster):   4ft 1in (1.24m)
(fhc)   4ft 3in (1.3m)

WEIGHT (Roadster):   28¾cwt (1,462kg)
(fhc)   29½cwt (1,500kg)

MAX SPEED:
Roadster: 146mph (235kph)
(fhc)   142mph (228kph)

0–60mph (97kph)   6.4 seconds (fhc 6.8 seconds)

PRICE NEW (1971): £3,139 (roadster), £3,387 (fhc)

PRODUCTION FIGURES:
5.3 SIII roadster	7,990
5.3 SIII 2+2	7,297

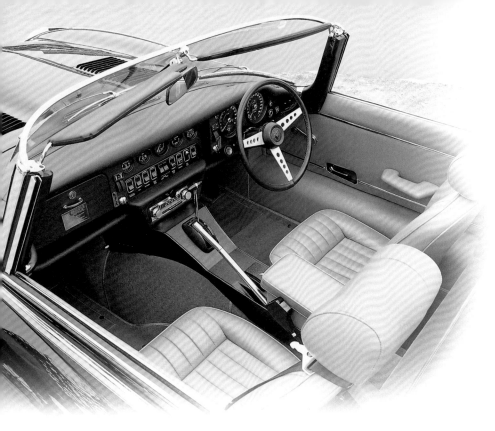

Announced in March 1971 at Palm Beach, Florida (five months after the end of SII production), the SIII took the E-Type in a new direction towards increased refinement at the cost of less aggressive driver appeal. It was also a lower-volume test-bed for Jaguar's new V12 saloon car engine – then the world's only mass-production V12 – still some months away from its intended home in the XJ12 flagship.

The SIII took the E-Type in a new direction towards increased refinement at the cost of less driver appeal

There was no mistaking the Series III for the Series II. The once delicate 'mouth' was now decorated with a chrome grille and the flared wheel arches hinted, rightly, at a wider stance, with a track 2 inches (51mm) wider at the front and 3 inches (76mm) at the back. Steel disc or wire wheels were

Inside, the Series III had a new smaller steering wheel, revised instruments and improved heating, but was otherwise essentially the same as the Series II.

The all-alloy flat-head V12 was first seen in the E-Type before finding its natural home in the XJ12 saloon. Smooth and silent, it made the 'E' as fast as it ever had been with the six-cylinder engine in its prime. Here its designers Harry Mundy (left) and Wally Hassan admire their creation.

power steering is quick enough, but lacks the feel that warns of front-end breakaway, the sort of precision, familiar to owners of the earlier 3.8 and 4.2 E-type, that allows you to set up and place the big car accurately for a bend. Driven briskly on the road, the E feels fast and supple, a sort of sporty XJ12 with more road noise and less ultimate cornering power.

The Tullius and Huffaker racers

In 1974 and '75 the racing teams of Bob Tullius (Group 44) and Joe Huffaker ran V12 E-Type roadsters in the Sports Car Club of America's production racing series. Jaguar were looking for an image boost for its ageing sports car, which in this V12 form had a bad reputation in America for reliability. Many cars stood unsold and Jaguar needed to move them on to make way for the XJ-S. To get maximum possible coverage in this huge market, Group 44 would run the cars on the East Coast, Huffaker on the West Coast.

Understandably the cars were quite radically modified by both teams. Roll cages were fitted not only for roll-over protection but to stiffen the chassis and to accommodate massive new tyres in flared arches that gave the car a low, mean look. There was a front spoiler to reduce front-end lift and blanked-off headlights. While the front suspension remained relatively unchanged, radical things were done with the rear end, including new trailing arms and tweaked geometry. Brakes were vented discs at both ends with bigger slave and master cylinders and an adjustable

proportioning valve so that the bias front-to-rear could be altered at will. The engine featured high-compression pistons, a reworked head and higher-duration cams along with much more efficient manifolding; it was reckoned to produce around 425bhp.

A broken gear lever spoiled a promising start for Tullius at Watkins Glen, but Huffaker won first time out in Seattle. Thereafter the cars, fighting it out with 911s, Daytonas and Corvettes, cleaned up, Tullius winning the next six events. Both teams qualified for an invitation to the run-offs to decide the National Champion at Road Atlanta, but were robbed of victory by tyre problems when the Huffaker car – driven by Lee Mueller – suffered a flat and Tullius's tyres simply 'gave up', allowing him to be overhauled by a Corvette while leading on the last lap.

Revenge came in 1975 when, running on harder compound covers, Tullius

smashed the lap record. Huffaker did fewer events because he did not have such a big budget, but Group 44 were winning everything in sight, pleasing the crowds with a car that was beautifully turned out if heavily out-numbered by the domestic opposition.

Both teams again qualified for the run-offs, and it looked as though the rival Jaguars would finally have a chance to take each other on and see which was quicker. Sadly, on the pace lap, with the two V12s out in front, the Huffaker suffered a jammed differential. With no opposition up to the job, Tullius won by a large margin and became National Champion. With no XJ-S yet available to race, Tullius campaigned the V12 in 1976, by which time it was well and truly out of production.

Late in life the E-Type enjoyed considerable racing success in North America. Bob Tullius of Group 44 and Joe Huffaker both developed cars to compete in the Sports Car Club of America championship for production cars. This is Huffaker in action in a Series III V12 roadster.

available. Perhaps the most important change was the fact that both roadster and coupé were based on the 8ft 9in (2.67m) wheelbase of the old 2+2 version, so there were no more two-seater fixed-heads. It also meant that for the first time buyers were allowed the dubious pleasure of ordering an open E-Type with automatic transmission as there was room for the Borg-Warner Model 12 gearbox in the longer chassis. Top speed was reduced to 135mph (217kph), but it was a telling comment on the sheer torque of the V12 that an auto roadster was as quick to 60mph (97kph) as the original 3.8 model. In all versions fuel consumption was up, 14–15mpg being a road-test norm.

Under the bonnet the subframe was beefed up to take the extra weight and torque of the new engine, which was not the four-cam unit glimpsed in the stillborn XJ13 sports racing car but a simpler two-cam unit built for smoothness rather than ultimate top-end power. At least one Series III was built with a 4.2 engine – indeed, the model was initially catalogued – but this variant was never manufactured.

With single chain-driven overhead camshafts operating in-line valves in flat cylinder heads, the all-new 5,343cc V12 engine was in a relatively 'soft' state of tune, delivering its 272bhp at

5,850rpm with a meaty 304lb ft of torque at just 3,600rpm. If Jaguar had had its way the engine would have been fuel injected, but problems with the Lucas system meant that development was delayed so the production V12 breathed through four Zenith-Stromberg carburettors, two on either side of the 60-degree vee. Lucas OPUS electronic ignition meant that there was no need for any points, a relief no doubt for the technicians who would be servicing this magnificent but complex-looking engine.

To cope with the extra performance, and weight, of the V12, Jaguar specified fat E70 15 radial tyres and vented disc front brakes, with underbody scoops to direct air on to the vulnerable inboard rear discs. The four-speed gearbox remained but featured a more manly, larger-diameter clutch. The suspension was also uprated with the latest anti-dive geometry and the V12 came with power-assisted rack-and-pinion steering as standard, although the assistance was not as intrusive as that of the contemporary XJ6.

Inside, changes were few although the power steering meant that a smaller wheel was possible, a leather-rimmed design with modish satin-finished drilled alloy spokes. The extra space liberated by the longer wheelbase allowed a luggage platform behind the seats on the roadster. On the coupé the floor was lower to provide more

From the rear the biggest Series III tell-tales at the time of its launch, were the new four-piece exhaust tail pipe, the flared arches to accommodate wider wheels and tyres, and the 'V12' badging on the bootlid. In March 1973 the four-outlet exhaust gave way to a twin-outlet item.

legroom, and there was extra footroom for rear passengers thanks to a redesigned seat mechanism. Later cars, from spring 1972 onwards, had better ventilation, but otherwise there were few uplifting developments in the V12's modest four-year life span.

Sales were brisk rather than astonishing, and for the first time Jaguar had to 'push' the car. Dealers became well stocked with Series III V12s and there was no question of having to join a waiting list. Jaguar knew that the car stood no chance of meeting the next set of US Federal crash regulations and began to wind down production in readiness for the E-Type's replacement, the XJ-S.

The coupé bowed out in September 1974 while the roadster struggled on until February 1975. All but one of the last 50 cars were painted black, wore chrome wire wheels and had a dashboard plaque signed by Sir William Lyons stating the car's chassis number. These last cars did not sell as quickly as Jaguar had hoped, and many were discounted.

The last but one car was painted green and stayed in the UK, while the very last car was retained by Jaguar and used for publicity.

The E-Type story was over, and despite promises of a replacement, there has been no true Jaguar sports car since. The XJ-S went down the plush GT route while the XK8, despite paying homage to the 'E' in its retro-styling, is really more a reinvention of the XJ-S.

The V12 had its moment in the sun in the late 1980s when, in the midst of classic car price hype, the last-of-the-line Series III was perceived as the best of the bunch, or at least the most collectable as a long-term hedge against inflation. Now, as cars return to enthusiasts, V12 prices have slipped behind those of the 'sixes' as purity and driver appeal take precedence over any notions of 'investment potential'. That is as it should be.

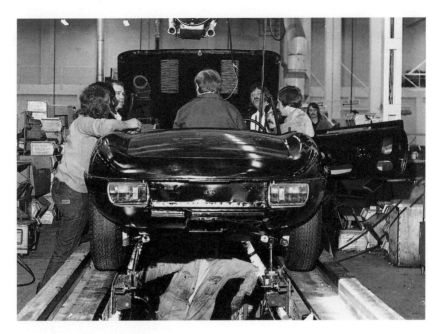

The final E-type having its engine installed on the production line in 1975. The last 50 cars produced had a brass plaque on the dashboard signed by Sir William Lyons. All but one of these cars were painted black.

Buying Hints

1. V12s have the same corrosion problems as the six-cylinder cars: check the bonnet, subframe tubing, rear arches, bulkhead and central tub of the body, concentrating on the sills. The supply of panels is excellent.

2. The V12 is tough but not unbreakable. Huge damage can ensue if the unit overheats (see the next chapter), so beware of water pump problems or any signs of previous overheating.

3. Automatic gearbox changes should be smooth and clean, but these units are not that expensive to service.

4. Very light power steering can mask problems in the rack mountings, and although the V12 rides well the car should not wallow or bottom easily.

5. All-synchro 'boxes should have strong synchromesh in all gears, but be aware that in the V12 it is under considerably greater stress and first and reverse are prone to break. Clutch judder is also a problem with the SIII.

The XJ-S *series*

The XJ-S was a bold break with tradition for Jaguar, with its 'flying buttresses' that swept down from the roofline on either side of a small, upright rear screen. They were not merely ornaments, however, as they helped the car to remain stable in cross-winds.   At the front, big rubber impact bumpers, ellipsoid headlamps and an uncharacteristic grille set the XJS apart from its forebears, but the design did at least have a feel all of its own, which some loved and others hated.

Some see it as the ultimate in medallion-man coupés, others as the best value-for-money supercar of the lot. Whatever you think of the XJ-S, easily the most controversial of all Jaguars, there can be no denying that as a long-distance express it remains hugely impressive. Here is a car that in V12 form wafts rather than accelerates, barely raising its voice above a whisper, and is the smoothest and most seamless of all big-gun coupés. A few were faster, most were better-looking, but none were more refined: at 100 the XJ-S is just loafing and there is still enough silken muscle in reserve to squat the tail even at that speed, 50mph short of its maximum.

It is much more agile across country than might be expected from the initial softness and flabby image of the early cars. Press beyond the wallow and a machine emerges that is predictable and surprisingly poised, the steering quicker and more weighty than on its sibling XJ saloons – although still devoid of true feel on the early models – and grip is entirely ample. Remember that the rear suspension is copybook double wishbone, the tyres plump and sticky. The XJ-S has a stiffer shell than the saloons and the ride is still superbly supple and very quiet.

The XJ-S has a long and chequered production history. As the first Jaguar designed from the beginning as a luxurious close-coupled Grand Tourer – rather than a sports car with a roof tacked on afterwards – it began its career on a rather uncertain footing. Not only were large, inefficiently packaged 14mpg supercars beginning to fall out of favour when it was launched in 1975, but this was also the first Jaguar not to be universally fêted for its styling.

By the end of the 1970s initially buoyant sales had fallen to such a low level that Jaguar considered dropping the model altogether, until a saviour arrived in the form of a more efficient cylinder head design that addressed the old problem of heavy fuel consumption. With the 20mpg XJ-S now a reality, sales picked up dramatically in the 1980s as Jaguar strived to broaden the car's appeal with a firmer, sportier six-cylinder

The XJ-S bounced back to become one of the success stories of the company and one of the longest lived Jaguars

model and, at last, an open version – initially a cabriolet and later a proper convertible. Thus, from uncertain beginnings the XJ-S bounced back to become one of the success stories of the company and one of the longest-lived Jaguars of all – production lasted 21 years.

Those who had been expecting an E-Type replacement were disappointed not only by the sheer size of the XJ-S when it was launched at the Frankfurt show in 1975, but also by the fact that Jaguar had no plans to build an open version. In anticipation of forthcoming federal laws on roll-over safety, Browns Lane elected to produce the car as a tin-top only and pitch it towards mature buyers looking for the ultimate in silent, swift luxury motoring.

Moreover, with the average age of Jaguar customers rising, Browns Lane did not see much future in a close-coupled two-seater cast in the mould of the original E-type. Modish notions of a mid-engined design along the

Jaguar XJ-S V12
1975–81

ENGINE:
All-alloy 60-degree V12	
Bore x stroke	90 x 70mm
Capacity	5,343cc
Valves	single ohc
Compression ratio	8.7:1
Fuel system	Lucas/Bosch injection
Power	285bhp (DIN) at 5,500rpm
Torque	294lb ft (DIN) at 3,500rpm

TRANSMISSION:
Four-speed manual or three-speed automatic
Final drive	3.07 or 3.31:1

SUSPENSION:
Front: independent semi-trailing, double wishbones, coil springs, telescopic dampers and anti-roll bar.
Rear: independent lower wishbone/upper driveshaft link with radius arms and twin coil springs, anti-roll bar
Steering	Adwest rack-and-pinion with power assistance

BRAKES:
Discs, vented front

WHEELS:
Alloy, with Dunlop SP Sport E70 VR 15 tyres

BODYWORK:
Unitary all-steel construction

LENGTH:	15ft 11in (4.85m)
WIDTH:	4ft 10in (1.47m)
HEIGHT:	4ft 1½in (1.26m)
WEIGHT:	33.4cwt (1,698kg)
MAX SPEED:	153mph (246kph)
0–60mph (97kph)	6.7 seconds
PRICE NEW (1975)	£8,900 inc tax

Jaguar XJ-S HE
1981–91

As XJ-S V12 except:
Power	295bhp at 5,000rpm
Compression ratio	12.5:1
Final drive	2.88:1
WEIGHT:	35cwt (1,780kg)
MAX SPEED:	140mph (225kph)
0–60mph (97kph)	7.7 seconds
PRICE NEW (1981):	£18,950 (coupé HE)

Jaguar XJ-S 3.6
1983–91

ENGINE:
All-alloy straight-six	
Bore x stroke	91 x 92mm
Capacity	3,590cc
Valves	dohc, four valves per cylinder
Compression ratio	9.6:1
Power	255bhp at 5300rpm
Torque	240lb ft at 4,000rpm

TRANSMISSION:
five-speed manual, four-speed auto
Final drive	3.54:1
MAX SPEED	141mph (227kph)
0–60mph (97kph)	7.4 seconds
PRICE NEW (1984)	£19,248 (coupé)

Jaguar XJS 6.0
1993–96

As XJ-S HE except:
Capacity	5,994cc
Compression ratio	11:1
Power	302bhp at 5,350rpm
Torque	355lb ft at 2,850 rpm

TRANSMISSION:
four-speed automatic
MAX SPEED:	161mph (259kph)
0–60mph (97kph)	8 seconds
PRICE NEW (1993):	£55,300 (convertible)

Jaguar XJS 4.0
1991–96

As XJ-S 3.6 except:
Bore x stroke	91 x 102mm
Capacity	3,980cc
Power	223bhp at 4,750rpm

(244bhp with AJ16 engine from June 1994)
MAX SPEED:	147mph (237kph)
0–60mph (97kph)	6.9 seconds
PRICE NEW (1993):	£35,400 (coupé)

PRODUCTION FIGURES:
5.3 coupé (manual)	352
5.3 coupé (auto)	60,857
5.3 XJR-S	448
5.3 cabriolet	3,863
5.3 convertible	16,871
3.6 coupé	8,860
3.6 cabriolet	1,146
4.0 coupé	5,392
4.0 convertible	10,991
6.0 coupé	772
6.0 convertible	149
6.0 XJR-S	389

lines of the stillborn XJ13 racer were rejected as too impractical. What Jaguar needed was a luxury 2+2 to take on the BMW and Mercedes coupés but based squarely on its existing platform.

Styling of the new car was entrusted to Malcolm Sayer – architect of the C, D and E-Types – with input on the details from Sir William himself. Long and low but much less rounded and graceful than its predecessors, the XJ-S represented a radical break from Jaguar styling tradition with its oblong elliptical headlights and chunky rear lenses. There was a notable absence of chrome, too, the bumpers now being moulded in deformable plastic and carried on American silicon-filled Menasco struts to meet 5mph impact regulations.

More shocking were the rear quarters. Sayer, inspired perhaps by Pininfarina's Dino 206GT, blended flying buttresses into the tail and rear wings, turning in as they met the cut-off tail in the name of improved aerodynamic spillage. They did not do much for rearward vision through the curious vertical rear screen, but they did help to stiffen the shell, which was 100lb (45kg) lighter than that of the XJ saloon.

Although based on the XJ saloon platform, major changes were made. The wheelbase was shortened by moving the rear suspension and bulkhead forward, which gave the car more sporting proportions but a good deal less rear legroom – the rear seats were really only for children if a long journey was in prospect. A rear anti-roll bar and stiffer rack mountings for the power steering gave the XJ-S a sharper feel on the road than the saloons – more weight if no more feel to the steering – but strict attention to sound deadening meant that it was equally quiet and refined with the same world-beating ride. Under the bonnet, the latest fuel-injected version of the V12 engine was in residence, but as well

as the usual Borg-Warner automatic, XJ-S buyers could order a four-speed manual car, using the same gearbox found in the V12 E-Type.

Eschewing wood veneer, Jaguar went for a fashionable all-black dash with stylised cowled instruments and Citroën-inspired drum-type minor instruments, neither of which met with the approval of traditionalists. The slim sports seats had better lateral support than those found in the saloons, while the standard equipment list featured everything expected on a car pitched as the ultimate in high-performance Gran Turismo motoring: electric windows, central locking, an upmarket radio-cassette, and even air-conditioning as standard.

If the styling won few friends, at least nobody could level any serious criticisms at the way the new flagship performed. As a ground-coverer it was sensationally swift, silent and

Eschewing traditional veneers and instrumentation, the original XJ-S cabin used matt black and anodised alloy to then fashionable effect. The minor gauges rotated, Citroën-style, between the main speedo and rev counter. The standard XJ floorpan was shortened by 6 inches, so rear-seat legroom in the XJ-S was pretty tight.

utterly effortless, with a silken rush of
acceleration from a power unit that
had more in common with a turbine
than a conventional piston engine in
the manner and smoothness of its
delivery. Neither transmission option,
however, really equalled the
excellence of the engine. The manual
'box – rarely fitted, in fact – felt sticky
and suffered from a heavy clutch,
while the automatic, an elderly
design, made the car feel slow off the
mark and lacked kick-down response.
A change to GM's 400 automatic
gearbox solved this in 1977. The last
manual XJ-S V12s were built in 1979.

In America, emission equipment
sapped some of the V12's power and
the reaction to the styling was even
more mixed than it had been in
Europe. The car gained a poor
reputation for reliability in the States
where, in any case, big greedy cars
were rapidly falling out of favour.

Sales worldwide slumped from a peak
of 3,890 in 1977 to just 1,057 in 1980,
and Jaguar were seriously considering
dropping the model when salvation
came in the form of Michael May's
'Fireball' combustion chamber. As
applied to the V12 Jaguar engine, this
split-level arrangement gave a low-
turbulence concentrated charge
around the spark plugs with rapid
burning of lean mixtures under a high
compression ratio of 12.5:1.

With increased efficiency came extra
power, which enabled Jaguar to raise
the rear axle ratio, giving potential for
up to 20mpg on a run. Jaguar
addressed criticisms of the interior by
trimming the car in a more traditional
fashion with proper wood veneer on
the dash and door cappings and
using leather where previously there
had been plastic. They also badged
this revitalised XJ-S 'HE' for High
Efficiency, and the cars could be
spotted by their new 'starfish' alloys
and tapering twin coach-lines.

As quality improved under John
Egan's rule at Browns Lane, sales of

the XJ-S increased dramatically, with
an annual production of 5,814 cars in
1984. Building on this success Jaguar
set out to broaden the appeal of the
model. First, in October 1983, came
the XJ-S 3.6 with the new AJ6 straight-
six engine, set to replace the XK in
Jaguar's new XJ saloons that were still
three years away from introduction.
In the lower-volume coupé – which
was otherwise very lightly modified –
this was a good way of finding out

In 1981 the XJ-S HE was announced
with the new 'High Efficiency' engine
that allowed 20mpg or more. The
interior gained wood on the
dashboard and doors and an HE can
be identified by its 'starfish' alloys.

A full convertible XJ-S was announced in 1988, with the V12 engine and an electric mohair top in an extensively re-engineered shell. It was a great success and a waiting list quickly developed.

about the durability of the new engine in the field.

All-alloy in construction with twin cams and four valves per cylinder, this 225bhp engine, combined with a Getrag five-speed gearbox, gave the Lucas/Bosch-injected 3.6 a much more sporty flavour than the 5.3, and indeed road test figures showed that it was very little slower. The top speed was 141mph (227kph) with 0–60mph (97kph) being obtained in 7.4 seconds. Economy was also up, but the downside was a slight roughness in the delivery of this new engine, something that would have to

be sorted out before it found its way into the new saloon. Automatic 3.6 models did not arrive until 1987, incidentally, with the new four-speed ZF 'box as found in the 'XJ40' saloons. Later, in 1987, Jaguar would draw a more definite line between the V12s and 'sixes' by offering the latter with a sports handling package, with stiffer springs and dampers and reduced steering assistance, to give it more appeal to younger drivers.

At the same time as the 3.6 coupé was announced, a 3.6 cabriolet joined the range. This was not a full convertible, but used a centre bracing hoop, as Jaguar could not afford to strengthen the shell sufficiently. Park Sheet Metal converted the standard coupé shell by fitting a new rear deck – which took up all the rear seat space – beefing up the floorpan and transmission tunnel, and installing a centre cross-bar, which incorporated two steel roll-over bars extending down to the sills, with a further one in the cant rail over the door aperture. Aston Martin Tickford tailored the Targa-style hood, with its two detachable interlocking panels and an integral fabric rear section folding neatly away on the rear deck below a padded cover. With the top up, the cabriolet driver enjoyed almost saloon car levels of refinement.

A V12 version joined the range in 1985, but in 1988 both were replaced by a full open cabriolet, inspired by the US Hess & Eisenhardt conversions available on special order through American dealers since 1986, and by the Lynx version on offer in the UK since the late 1970s. For the factory car, Jaguar looked to the German firm of Karmann to design the hood, press tooling and assembly jigs, and a great deal of effort was put into reducing the scuttle shake that was the inevitable consequence of removing the coupé's roof. In total, the convertible, like its predecessor a strict two-seater, featured 108 new panels and 48 modified ones in the name of greater

In 1991 came the most radical rethink of the XJ-S, with new rear wings, windows and full-width rear lights in an attempt to bring the shape more up to date. The convertible version, by now out-selling the coupé three-to-one, gained 2+2 seating at last, while the V12s were now 6 litres with 318bhp. The six-cylinder models used the impressive new AJ16 4 litre engine, which would prove the more popular option in the twilight years of the model.

shell refinement and strength, combined with steel tubes in the sills and A-posts to enhance further the torsional rigidity. The electrically operated, precision-fitted top featured glass rear and side quarter windows and could be lowered in 12 seconds. Despite an increase in weight of approximately 2cwt (100kg), performance suffered very little and the convertible had all the refinements found on the latest coupé, including air-conditioning and heated seats with electric lumbar support. Anti-lock braking was now common across the XJ-S range.

It undercut the Mercedes SL considerably and was an immediate hit, accounting for two-thirds of XJ-S V12 sales worldwide. In Britain there was a black market in the cars in the late 1980s, so high was the demand for this ultimate in luxury convertibles.

The 6 litre XJR-S appeared in 1989, putting the XJ-S on a par with some of the world's most expensive supercars in the performance stakes. Developed by Tom Walkinshaw's TWR, it was fabulously fast yet still refined.

The most radical rethink of the XJ-S came in May 1991 when the bodyshell – now built by Venture Pressings, part-owned by Jaguar and GKN Sankey – was extensively restyled. There were new rectangular rear lights and revised side windows that deceived the casual observer into thinking that the glass area had been increased, and at the front the quarter lights were eliminated. The front grille was now black with an embellisher along the top and the sills were flared front and rear. Of the panels, 180 were changed or modified, and fit and finish were much improved, with £4 million having been spent at the Castle Bromwich plant on modern tools.

Out went the old 3.6 litre straight-six, in came a new longer-stroke 4 litre version with 223bhp and more torque. The ZF auto was beefed up to take the increased torque while the manual was a new Getrag design with a three-plane gate, far less clumsy than the old 'box with its dog-leg first.

Revisions to the V12's injection system upped the power output to 280bhp, countering the loss of performance that had occurred with the introduction of catalysts the year before. Inside the new car, conventional analogue minor instruments finally ousted the barrel-type dials and were set into a new burr walnut panel. It was at this stage, with the restyled models, that the hyphen was dropped from the model designation, the car now being known as the 'XJS' rather than the 'XJ-S'.

With the introduction of a 4 litre convertible in May 1992, Jaguar added a cruciform bracing member between the forward jacking points and the radiator on all the open models, thereby increasing torsional rigidity and reducing shudder. The 1993 model year convertibles, announced in September 1992, had even more attention paid to structural rigidity with the addition of underfloor struts at the rear.

More exciting news arrived in May 1993 when the capacity of the V12 was boosted to 6 litres, and a new four-speed automatic transmission was introduced. This longer-stroke V12 gave 302bhp and Jaguar claimed a top speed of 161mph (259kph). A new torque converter on the electronically managed GM 'box made the 6 litre feel livelier off the mark and featured sport and normal modes, the former allowing the car to start off in first and make snappier part-throttle kick-downs. Sports suspension was standard on the coupés and optional on the convertibles regardless of engine, and to improve the handbrake the rear brakes were moved outboard.

The introduction of the 6 litre model marked the end of the line for the JaguarSport TWR XJS. Formed in May 1988 and owned 50/50 by Tom Walkinshaw and Jaguar, JaguarSport engineered specialist high-performance versions of the XJS and the new XJ40 on behalf of Jaguar, orders being taken through specially selected dealers. Spoilered and skirted, what these cars lacked in good taste they made up for in chassis finesse by combining the ride quality of the original with much greater agility. Strangely, the original XJR-S cars were no more potent than the stock V12s of the day, but a 6 litre version offered from 1989 with 318bhp showed real benefits. The final XJR-S model – based on the facelifted '91 XJS – was by far the best with much more subtle styling add-ons and a 338bhp engine.

Anyway, back to 1993. Extensive re-engineering had at last brought 2+2 rear seating to the open model, under pressure from American dealers.

The Cabriolet versions of the XJ-S gave Jaguar a perfect retort to the open Mercedes SL models that had dominated the luxury drophead market for so many years. The Cabriolet came first in 1983 with a roll hoop and lift-out Targa panels. This is the V12 undergoing final inspection on the production line at Browns Lane in 1985.

Racing the XJ-S

After his success with the E-Type in 1975, Bob Tullius decided to contest the 1976 Trans-Am races held in America and Canada using the recently introduced XJ-S. These cars were to be surprisingly standard in some respects, but to gain more power the fuel injection was thrown away in favour of six Weber twin-chokes, boosting output to 525bhp. In search of greater braking capability water cooling was tried without success, but Group 44 still won the Category One title in 1977 against stiff Porsche and Corvette opposition. In 1978, with a lighter shell and 560bhp thanks to reworked camshafts and heads, the Group 44 XJ-S won seven races to the Corvette's three, despite the fact that the rules had now been tipped in favour of the latter.

Impressed by the success of Tullius, the now more independent Jaguar supported the Group 44 XJ-S in 1981 in the Trans-Am series. Under

new rules the car was much more fundamentally changed, with its engine – now dry-sumped and delivering 570bhp – moved back 8 inches (203mm) in a tubular frame to improve the handling. Suspension was also heavily modified and a lightweight steel and aluminum shell was really only a silhouette to retain the basic XJ-S appearance. The car was quick but not reliable enough, and gave best by a narrow margin to a Corvette.

In Britain the XJ-S was not seriously considered as a racing machine until 1982 when Tom Walkinshaw of TWR decided to campaign the model in the European Touring Car Championship. Despite its weight, Walkinshaw's study of the regulations – which placed heavier restrictions on engine and body modifications – confirmed that the Jaguar had potential in that it was homologated for wide tyres (205/70 VR) and had independent rear

Group 44 campaigned a highly modified 475bhp XJ-S in the Trans-Am series in 1981, which it came close to winning.

suspension. The American team had dispensed with the V12's fuel injection, but with new restrictions on manifolding under ETC rules it was now a positive advantage. Power was restricted to 400bhp to keep the fuel consumption in check, but the TWR cars were still good for 170mph (274kph). Although Jaguar could only offer moral support by the end of the 1982 season, Walkinshaw had achieved four outright wins – including a 1–2 in the Tourist Trophy, which Jaguar had not won since Stirling Moss's C-Type victory in 1951 – and a third and fourth overall placing in the Championship. This was just one fewer win than the all-pervading 6 Series BMWs whose dominance in the ETC Walkinshaw had at last challenged. The Jaguars came

second in 1983, narrowly defeated by BMW.

In 1984, running three cars, TWR (now officially supported by Jaguar) won five of their first six races – Monza, Donington, Pergusa, Brno and Zeltweg – and followed that up with wins at Salzburg and the Belgian Spa 24-hour classic. At last BMW had been defeated; Jaguar were ETC Champions and Tom Walkinshaw – later to become heavily involved in the conception and marketing of factory road-going TWR Jaguars – could turn his attention to international sports car racing and the XJRs, which were destined to win the Sports Car Championship and Le Mans for Jaguar in the late 1980s.

TWR raced the XJ-S for Jaguar and gained 20 outright wins in the European Touring Car Championship between 1982 and 1986.

The Lynx XJ-S Eventer

Lynx Motors International Ltd of Sussex built their reputation on their superb D-Type replicas, but they also conceived one of the best-looking of all Jaguar conversions – the XJ-S Eventer. This was perhaps the ultimate in high-performance estate cars and in many respects a much nicer and more practical machine than the notoriously cramped factory original. By slicing off the controversial buttresses and fashioning their own longer estate roof-line, they created a 150mph (241kph) estate with a 6-foot (1.83m) load area (with the rear seats folded), much better vision than the coupé, more headroom, and – best of all – a much more elegant profile. It had a lighter, more modern look than the parent car, with slim elegant rear quarters that were said to promote better aerodynamics.

Although the fuel capacity was slightly reduced, the conversion added very little weight to the XJ-S so the Eventer went and handled just like the coupé. It did add a good deal to the price, however – £7,000 in the early 1980s when it was introduced and, latterly, nearly £30,000. Even so, it has proved popular – 63 have been built and production continues on used cars – and it seems likely that Lynx will follow it up with a small number of XK8 Eventers.

Lynx of Hastings built the first true convertible XJ-S in 1978 and followed it up with the handsome Eventer in the early 1980s.

A new sub-assembly was welded on to the existing underframe to form a rear seat pan, and this had the dual benefit of further strengthening the shell. To make extra room, the pump for the hood was moved to a space above the battery box. A post-1993 XJS can be identified by its colour-coded bumpers.

The last major change to the XJS was the introduction of the AJ16 six-cylinder engine for the 4 litre models in 1994. These greatly refined engines incorporated new porting and cam profiles, sequential injection, a higher compression ratio and new pistons. The resulting 244bhp shaved the 0–60mph (97kph) time down to 6.9 seconds and wound the top speed out to 147mph (237kph). In fact, so swift and silent were these last-of-the-line 'sixes' that the flagship V12 was becoming rather sidelined as fewer buyers saw the need to spend so much extra on a car that was only marginally faster and quieter; by 1995 the V12 was built to special order only.

Jaguar marked the 20th year of XJS production with a special Celebration limited edition 4 litre model featuring flush (rather than dished) 'Aerosport' alloy wheels, a black front grille and chrome door mirrors. In the background the factory was gearing up for the introduction of the XK8, the replacement for the XJS, announced in the spring of 1996. Jaguar's most controversial car was dead, but its spirit, and to some extent substance, lived on in the XK8s, which retain many of its underpinnings.

Unlike the original XJ-S, critics liked this new V8 coupé immediately, but it is a fair bet that the XK8 will not stay around as long as its predecessor.

Buying Hints

1. Because of its long production life, the XJ-S is not just one car but a whole range, and one of the most temptingly inexpensive exotics of all. Purists will love the 1970s feel of the original, which – apart from the 6 litre TWR model – is the fastest-accelerating V12 model, although it lacks the sporting flavour of later models in terms of steering and body control. As the emphasis tipped from ultimate comfort to crisper response through the 1980s, the ride quality of later models suffered, so a good compromise XJ-S might be one of the HEs, which manages to feel more taut without much loss of ride comfort.

2. All the 'sixes', particularly the manuals, feel crisper, but the 4 litres are easily the best, particularly the late models, which almost attained V12 levels of smoothness with 20mpg potential. As for the open cars, the cabriolets are versatile but not as elegant as the full convertibles, although early examples of the latter suffered surprisingly badly from scuttle shake.

3. Rust protection improved over the years, so it is a case of the later the better with the XJ-S, which all the same did not suffer quite as badly as its saloon siblings. Check the jacking points, radius arm mountings, inner and outer sills, boot floor and inner wings. Bootlids suffer on the lower skin, doors along the bottoms and around the door mirrors, and valances front and rear.

4. The V12 engine is strong, but overheating can be fatal as the heads weld themselves to the block and warp. Water pumps need to be watched, and be aware of leaks from the rear main bearing oil seal.

As on any car, the fuel injection can give trouble on the V12s – it should run on all cylinders immediately from cold – and these engines should not use much oil.

5. The six-cylinder engines are strong and capable of high mileages. Look for oil leaks and smoke, and evidence of overheating.

6. Check the power steering for play, leaks or a noisy pump. Air-conditioning usually suffers from lack of use and can usually be revived when recharged with gas.

7. Of the transmissions, the GM 400 used on the V12s from the mid-1970s is the strongest. On all the autos look for rough, snatchy changes and dirty fluid, and be aware that spares for the earlier Borg-Warners are now difficult to obtain. Manuals are strong but rare; the Getrag used in the 3.6 models is difficult to repair effectively, although it is durable on the whole.

8. The front springs sag with age and use, which can sometimes lead to tyres fouling the arches. At the rear there are four expensive springs and dampers to replace, together with the often neglected inboard disc brakes. Look for leaking dampers, rusty radius arms and softening and separating of the rubber bushes that isolate and locate the subframes.

9. The brakes should be powerful and pull the car up square. Servo problems and seized callipers will show themselves in a dead-feeling pedal. If the front discs are cracked or distorted, the pedal will 'pulse'. On ABS-equipped cars the warning light on the dash should go out after a few seconds.

The XK8 *series*

Although it took its curvy styling details from the E-Type, the XK8, launched at Geneva in 1996, was really a replacement for the then 21-year-old XJS. More obviously a sports car, it nonetheless largely fulfilled the same role as the XJS.

The XK8 was a long time coming. Pininfarina's XJ Spider showcar of the late 1970s had first raised the question of how a new sporting Jaguar in the mould of the E-Type might look. Then the XJ41 of the mid-to-late 1980s – dubbed the F-Type and something of an open secret in the motoring press at the time – seemed for a while as if it might go ahead, but was rejected by new owners Ford as too heavy.

As a sybaritic coupé for rich 40-to-50-somethings the XK8 was a car with its sights firmly set on the Mercedes SL and BMW 850 coupés – a swift, silent, soft-riding express for drivers who might like the look of a modern E-Type interpretation but would not be able to come to terms with its raw aggression and lack of space. (The E-Type buyer of the '90s, with his heart set on a British car, would probably end up with a new TVR.) Certainly the XK8's styling was rated as much more attractive than the ageing German opposition, and at launch the XK8 undercut the then current SL Mercedes handsomely on price – the cheapest 280SL was £15,000 more than the Jaguar. However, the launch since then of a new SL meant that Jaguar could not afford to rest on their laurels.

Curvaceous and elegant but not too self-consciously retro, its oval air

Inspired by the E-Type, the curvy XK8 had rave reviews for its speed, refinement and handling, although it was more of an XJ-S than an E-Type successor.

DB7: a Jag in drag?

The introduction of the XK8 raised some uncomfortable questions for Aston Martin (also owned by Ford) and its DB7 coupé, conceived by AM boss Walter Hayes as the volume-built car Aston needed for survival and still only three years old.

Here was a very slightly slower, equally well-made Jaguar that undercut the Aston by £35,000. Both cars used a modified XJS platform and the Aston even used the old AJ6 3.2 litre engine block, yet on the whole the DB7 did not ride or handle as well as the Jaguar. As to which was the better-looking, the jury could not decide, but there was no denying a certain family resemblance. If anything the DB7 was a slightly tauter, more muscular design.

A Jag in drag? Aston did not think so, but then that was only to be expected. The facts were that the DB7 was developed by Tom Walkinshaw of TWR and built at the Bloxham factory in Oxfordshire on the lines that delivered the Jaguar XJ220. It seemed probable that it was developed indirectly from the remains of the XJ41 'F-Type' project that was canned by Ford when they took over at Jaguar. Volume was a relative term of course; Aston built only 625 DB7s a year compared to the 12,000 or so XK8s that came out of the Jaguar factory.

intake, glassed-in lights and bonnet bulge clearly recalled the E-Type, but there were elements of the XJ220 supercar in the long overhangs and big wheel arches. Styling chief Lawson's job was made more difficult by the fact that the XK8 was to be based loosely on the floorpan of the XJS, with revised double wishbone front suspension and the double transverse link arrangement of the XJ-300 saloon at the back. These elements were complemented by state-of-the art traction control and, at extra cost, computerised active damping. There was also a choice of 17-inch or 18-inch wheels, the latter with 245/45 front and 255/45 rear Pirelli P-zero tyres.

Few could fault the handling of the XK8. Here was a car that handled with inch-perfect precision. Grip was prodigious

There were no straight-sixes or V12s in the XK8 line-up. As the name suggests, the XK had a V8 – Jaguar's first, and built at the Ford plant in Wales – seamlessly combined with a bespoke five-speed automatic transmission with no manual option.

Light in weight and commendably stiff in construction, this 4 litre 290bhp unit had quad cams, 32 valves and highly efficient sequential injection, combining supreme refinement with real push. Touching 151mph (243kph) at 4,800rpm in its high fifth, it took the XK8, a substantially lighter car than its predecessor, to 60mph (97kph) in 6.6 seconds and to 100mph (161kph) in 16.7 seconds – figures that were well on the pace for its class. Just as

Jaguar XK8 1996–

ENGINE:

All-alloy 90-degree V8	
Bore x stroke	86 x 86mm
Capacity	3,996cc
Valves	double ohc, 32 valves
Compression ratio	10.75:1
Fuel system	injection with electronic management
Power	289.7bhp (DIN) at 6,100rpm
Torque	290lb ft (DIN) at 4,250rpm

TRANSMISSION:

Five-speed auto	
Final drive	3.06:1

SUSPENSION:

Front: independent double wishbones, coil springs, telescopic dampers
Rear: independent double wishbone/ upper driveshaft link with radius arms and coil springs, anti-roll bar

Steering	rack-and-pinion with power assistance

BRAKES:
Vented discs, ABS

WHEELS:
Alloy, with 245/70 ZR 17 tyres

BODYWORK:
Unitary all-steel construction

LENGTH:	15ft 6¾in (4.74m)
WIDTH:	6ft 0in (1.83m)
HEIGHT:	4ft 2½in (1.28m)
WEIGHT:	32.5cwt (1,652kg)

MAX SPEED:	151mph (243kph)
0–60mph (97kph)	6.6 seconds

MPG:	19

PRICE NEW (1996): £47,950 (coupé)

Jaguar XKR 1998–

As XK8 except:

ENGINE:	Supercharged V8
Power	370bhp at 6,150rpm
Torque	387lb ft at 6,150rpm

MAX SPEED:	155mph (249kph)
0–60mph (97kph)	5.2 seconds

PRICE NEW (1998): £60,005

Buying Hints

1. XK8s in need of a service have been known to flood. You may be able to start the car, but it may stall and then prove difficult to re-start. This problem is unique to the 4-litre cars.

2. On the XK8 convertible, look at the hood. If the previous owner has not been using the tonneau cover when the hood was folded, it may be stained and bleached and there is no effective way of treating this.

3. Later XK8s can suffer from juddering brakes – an annoyance more than a serious concern.

4. Look at all the tyres, including the spare, as these cars, such is their weight and performance, eat through expensive tyres fairly quickly.

5. A 'clonky' differential may be evident in higher mileage examples, but transmissions seem to be bullet-proof.

XK8 with the E-Type in 2+2 form. The family likeness was clear, although the newer car was rather larger.

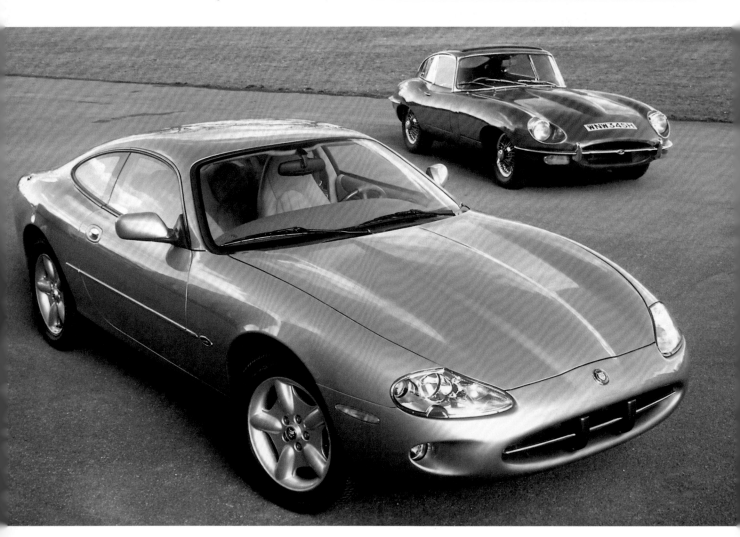

magnificent as the engine was the new five-speed automatic, which combined seamless full-throttle upshifts with crisp kick-down response.

Moreover, few could fault the handling of the XK8. Here was a car that handled with inch-perfect precision, its crisp variable-ratio rack-and-pinion steering bestowed a pleasing feel without nervousness, two generations removed, it seems, from the sometimes rubbery and over-servoed feel of the XJS and its siblings. Grip was prodigious, of course, the traction control subtle rather than sudden, and the XK8 had great brakes, massive ventilated discs combined with the Teves three-channel anti-lock system. In fact, in its class there was nothing to beat

the XK8 dynamically, especially as the ride remained superbly composed, if not quite as cosseting as that of the XJS.

Inside, the car had all that the tired executive could want: multi-adjustable seats and steering, air-conditioning, air bags, together with a wood veneer dash bristling with dials and redolent of the old-style XJ6 saloons, although the proliferation of Ford switchgear was perhaps a little too evident. However, in the tradition of Jaguar coupés, rear legroom was lacking in the XK8.

Jaguar had promised a convertible XK8 and it arrived a month after the coupé, just in time for the New York show. It was a nicely timed début, as the New York Museum of Modern Art was just

The coupé and convertible. The open version had a powered top that sat, when folded, under a padded cover of traditional style.

The F-Type

Jaguar announced early in 2001 that it would be building its F-Type two-seater sports car one day. Aimed squarely at the Porsche Boxster market, Jaguar said it was to be a pure and compact car of 'radical' design in the vanguard of a new more progressive generation of Jaguars. There was talk initially of using an X-Type floorpan with a transverse engine and four-wheel drive but this was rejected in favour of a more specialised solution using an aluminium structure.

The shape would be an evolution of the 2000 Detroit show car – itself a development of the XK180 show car, inspired by the D-Type, and revealed in 1998 – but with a more cutting edge, modernist design from the pen of Ian Callum. The base model would have a V6 engine and rear-wheel drive, later models a supercharged V6 with four-wheel-drive.

about to put an E-Type on display, only the third car ever in the collection.

The XK8 convertible, which Jaguar at launch expected to account for 70 per cent of US XK8 sales, had a fully padded power hood, engineered by Karmann, with electric catches, so raising or lowering the top was literally a one-finger operation. There was no metal cover for the hood when it was stowed, but a padded cover, which Jaguar claimed gave 'a classic British sports car appearance' and took up less space in the boot.

Another variation on the XK8 theme was the XKR, announced at Geneva in 1998. The fastest accelerating Jaguar road car ever built, it used the 370bhp supercharged V8 first seen in the XJR saloon. There were subtle external modifications to give the shape added aggression, including a wire mesh grille, louvred panels on the bonnet and a small lip spoiler to improve high-speed stability. This was a ballistically quick machine that left the majority of the opposition looking rather irrelevant at the price.

The car received some mild up-dating in the autumn of 2000. Outwardly it gained flush-fitting fog lamps, jewelled tail lamps with a chrome surround, and a deeper rear bumper the better to obscure the fuel tank. Inside there were new seats and an improved air bag system that took into account the weight of the passenger and, via sensors in the headlining and door pillars, where he/ she was sitting. The seats themselves were of a new design, with separate rather than integral head restraints.

Now that the excitement surrounding the XK8 had faded, it was easier to take stock of a car that in many ways was a very safe design compared to its sports car predecessors, yet had managed to put Jaguar right back among the best in the world in the luxury sports car market. It was a fine achievement.

As revealed at Detroit in 2000 – the stunning F-Type, a new two-seater sports car for launch some time in the future.

The R-Coupé

Shown at the Frankfurt show in September 2001, the R-Coupé was built to show the direction that Jaguar styling might go rather than to represent a potential production model. It was, more than anything else, a showcase for future ideas for there were no plans for Jaguar to produce such a car in the foreseeable future. The shape, by Julian Thomson, was built to embody the stance and proportions of the classic Lyons-designed cars of the '50s and '60s without being an attempt at a retro car with endless nudges and winks from the back catalogue of Jaguar styling.

It was a four-seater coupé, cast in the mould of the old XJC of the '70s, and seemed to put as much emphasis on the richness of its interior as it did the outer styling, which was uncharacteristically subtle and restrained. Inside, wood veneer swept elegantly around the cabin and leather covered the floor, not just the seats. Paddle-shift gearchanging was proposed, while the headlamp beams followed the direction of the steering rather like the Citroën DS. Some of the interior details were silver plated.

The R-Coupé was the first design to emerge from Jaguar's Advanced Styling department led by Ian Callum.

The four-seater R-Coupé, first displayed at the Frankfurt show in 2001, was a showcase for Jaguar's styling expertise rather than being a potential new model.

The supercharged V8 engine was offered in the XK8 from May 1998, with uprated CATS suspension, 18-inch alloy wheels, sports leather pack, cruise control, headlamp washers and a CD auto-changer. Its mesh grille singled it out from the normally aspirated version.

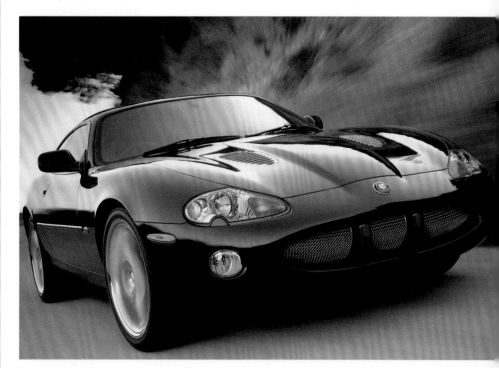

The XK *series*

Project X150, the successor to the XK8, was named simply XK. This range of V8-engined GT cars was launched at the Frankfurt show in 2005 to rave reviews, not only for the elegant Ian Callum-styled bodywork but also for accomplished dynamics which were the result of some clever engineering.

Faster, lighter (just a door on its own weighed 13lb (6kg) less than its equivalent on the XK8) and roomier than the outgoing model, at the heart of the car was a brilliantly rigid body structure that, even in convertible form, was stiffer than the old XK8 coupé, with deep rectangular section sills. The all-aluminium structure, previewed on the Advanced Lightweight Coupé concept car, used aerospace techniques and was variously riveted, epoxy bonded and bolted together. There was only one conventional welded joint in the body.

Over this structure Callum had fashioned a svelte and athletic GT car body that was a lot less flabby in its overhangs than the XK8, had a 160mm longer wheelbase and bore more than a passing resemblance to his Aston Martin Vanquish design. It was the first Jaguar to use the signature 'power vents' on the wings that would become familiar on the late model XJ saloons and the XF. At the front Bi-Xenon headlamps flanked an oval E-Type-style grille.

The XK was previewed in the form of the Advanced Lightweight Coupé concept car.

The XK convertible was designed from scratch as an open-topped car.

Jaguar made the point that the convertible – launched slightly later at the Detroit show in early 2006 – was designed *before* the coupé and had thus been created from scratch as an open-topped car. Thus it managed to not look like an aesthetic afterthought and was only a marginal 70lb (32kg) heavier than its coupé sibling at 3,600lb (1,636kg). Although folding metal hardtops were very much in vogue, Jaguar elected to fit a conventional hood that allowed the retention of the rear seats and a nice slim rear deck. Electro-hydraulics could raise and lower the nicely finished triple-layer convertible roof in 18 seconds and, should the car's sensors detect an imminent 'inversion', roll hoops popped up automatically.

Not that there was much chance of getting the XK out of shape, what with its plethora of advanced systems. These included stability and traction control, active differential and adaptive dynamic damping –

these electronically managed oversteer, understeer, steering wheel angle and brake force and all other aspects of the car's attitude when underway.

Brakes were big vented discs with four channel ABS and electronic brake force distribution plus an electronic handbrake. Should the worst happen and your XK hit something hard then intelligent head and thorax airbags, plus headrests that moved forward under impact to counter whiplash, allowed you a good chance of walking away.

The familiar Bridgend-built 4.2-litre (4,196cc) quad camshaft V8 engines, with stiff lightweight block architecture, were used in supercharged and non-supercharged form with an improved injection system. The naturally aspirated car, with its variable valve timing, gave 294bhp at 6,000rpm and a nice flat torque curve that delivered 85 per cent of its torque between 2,000 and

6,000rpm. Such was the weight-saving delivered by Jaguar's lightweight chassis technology that the naturally aspirated 2006 XK could get within a quarter of a second of the old supercharged XK in a quarter-mile dash and still deliver mid-twenties mpg.

The supercharged engine, used in the XKR – offered from October 2006 – boasted 390bhp thanks to its Eaton blower. Outwardly the XKR models were recognisable by their louvred bonnets, mesh grille, quad tail pipes and 20-inch wheels. Aimed at the BMW M6 and Mercedes SL500 market, the XKR made many European exotics look overpriced. Its additional 96bhp gave 0–60 in 4.9 seconds and an electronically limited 155mph, although it would probably have topped 180mph unfettered. Supercharger whine was muted compared to the previous model but exhaust bypass valves gave XKR a thunderous yet curiously cultured exhaust note.

On both versions, the superb ZF 6HP 26 gearbox, was the world's first six-speed automatic when it was introduced in 2000 and perhaps the best torque converter auto-box available, had paddle shifts on the steering wheel to accommodate those who wanted manual control.

Inside, the XK was handsome and modern even if some of the plastic finishes didn't quite look worthy of the car's price and ambitions. The standard specification included the 7-inch touch screen (to use the sat-nav, telephone and climate control), rain-sensitive wipers and cruise control, although the adaptive type with radar (it automatically pre-engaged the brakes if you got too close to the car ahead) was extra. Buyers could add upwards of £6,000 to the car's price choosing options such as a Smart Key, heated steering wheel, tyre pressure monitoring and active lighting.

Despite the low, snug driving position, the XK was easy to see out

Not a strip of walnut in sight! The tastefully modern interior of the XK.

Special editions: XK60 & XKR-S

A special edition of the XK was offered in 2008 called the XK60, marking 60 years since the introduction of the XK120 in 1948. At no extra cost it offered 20-inch alloys, an alloy gear-selector knob and deeper spoiler and rear valance. The 174mph XKR-S was a little more interesting, a 416bhp car with its speed limiter removed thus allowing a further 19mph. Revised suspension, a higher geared steering rack and bigger 'R' Performance brakes were part of the package with bigger discs and six piston callipers. They were the biggest brakes fitted to any Jaguar.

The cars were all painted Ultimate Black and rode special lightweight Vortex 20-inch alloy wheels. Styling features included aerodynamic splitters, side sill extensions and rear spoiler and diffuser. The interior had piano-black veneer, special twin-needle stitching and contrast stitching on the plus XK-R-branded head restraints and door sill kick plates. Jaguar planned to build 200 of these cars for Europe only with 50 earmarked for the UK.

The special edition XKR-S – available in any colour you like, as long as it's black!

Driving the XK

The XK is not a bare-knuckled sports car but a muscular and luxurious Grand Tourer with a steely wallop that few would find disappointing. Many believe it is the best driving GT car in its class regardless of price, mixing exciting driver appeal with refinement in a way that rivals have found hard to match. The engine and gearbox are hard to fault, wafting the XK up to 140mph-plus cruising speeds with effortless thrust. The performance is totally accessible and can be delivered with an authoritative hum or a throaty warble depending on your mood. The fabulous ZF gearbox anticipates your every whim, it seems, and flatters the ego when it blips the throttle automatically on a down change. Paddle shifting on so many cars in this class is such a tiresome business that even enthusiastic drivers tend to give up on it and treat the robotised automatics as normal automatics. The Jaguar's perfectly smooth and quick-shifting torque converter gearbox makes a nonsense of some of the fussy Italian units and its 'paddle' system is so friendly that most drivers feel at ease with it straight away and continue to use it. Few would ever be left hankering for a clutch pedal and a gear lever. The car's myriad electronics systems that constantly recalibrate and reassess the whims of the driver versus speed, road condition and vehicle attitude interface seamlessly and unobtrusively so that on a twisty road the XK and XKR feel neutral and athletic, flowing over all surfaces without a trace of harshness. If the naturally aspirated car's 300bhp is not enough, the XKR adds another heroic dimension to the performance with steering, suspension and brakes tweaked to suit but with no real deterioration in refinement.

The classic simplicity of the XK convertible interior.

of, not something that could be said of many modern cars. Although claiming increased head, shoulder and front legroom, both open and closed versions were still cramped in the rear for adults and had a modest 300 litres of luggage space – designed to carry two golf bags – which, on the coupé, was accessed through a hatchback. However, judged as a luxurious two-seat grand touring car the XK was a success, a very fast and hugely capable mile eater with neutral handling. Not an aggressive driver's car in the Porsche 911 mould, but a refined and nicely-built sports car that anyone could enjoy at any speed. Even pedestrians could savour the XK's carefully-tuned rich V8 woofle and should one of them be unfortunate enough to be run down by an XK or XKR then Jaguar's new 'pyrotechnic pedestrian deployable bonnet' would raise itself several inches above the engine's potentially lethal 'hard points'.

There was a light touch to the way this car rode on its double wishbone suspension that gave it an advantage

not only over the German opposition but also over the vastly more expensive Aston Martin DB9. Even stiffer springs and thicker anti-roll bars on the supercharged model had no noticeable effect on its suppleness. One of the great achievements of the XK was that Jaguar had managed to build a convertible version that rode and handled every bit as well as the closed coupé, on identical suspension settings with almost no shudder over bumps. On all versions, the DSC – Dynamic Stability Control – used signals from the anti-lock braking and traction control to make rapid adjustments to control wheelspin and, thus, oversteer (or understeer).

XK and XKR prices spanned £60,000 to £78,000 with a £6,000 premium on the convertible body. A popular choice in its class, judged less clinical than its German rivals and more than a match for some true exotica, the XK range was joined by a Portfolio model in 2007 with its special paint and interior finishes (engine-spun aluminium veneer, soft grain leather with double stitching), plus heated and fan-cooled memory seats and a high-end sound system. Beefier six-piston brake callipers worked on larger 16-inch discs.

At the 2009 Detroit show, Jaguar announced the first significant enhancements to the XK, XK Portfolio and XKR. These refreshed cars featured a new slightly wider front bumper, new door mirrors with integrated LED indicators and chrome detail around the windows. The redesigned tail lights were LED-type now.

However, the main news was the introduction of a new version of the Jaguar V8, a 5.0-litre direct injection unit that shared almost nothing with its predecessor. The aim had been more power and better emissions with comparable fuel economy. The direct injection is at the heart of the improved

V8, delivering fuel at 150bar directly into the cylinder with charge cooling effects that allowed the compression ratio to be raised from 9.0:1 to 11.5:1. Combined with improved variable camshaft timing, the outcome is, says Jaguar, a more responsive engine. Matched to this was ZF's second generation six-speed automatic, the 6HP 28, for which it claimed 50 per cent faster shifts. It was controlled by paddle shifts as before but instead of a conventional selector the JaguarDrive selector was used, the drum that rises from the centre control when the pulsing starter button is pressed, a feature first used on the XF.

As this is written there are no independent figures available, but Jaguar claims a 29 per cent power increase for the naturally aspirated XK (379bhp) and 23 per cent for the supercharged XKR (502bhp) which featured a more efficient and now almost silent Eaton supercharger buried deep in the 'vee' of the shorter, stiffer alloy block. Jaguar gave

blistering 0–60 figures of 5.2 seconds for the XK and 4.9 seconds for the XKR which, as before, was mainly recognisable by its handsome 20-inch alloy wheels, bonnet louvres and, inside, dark aluminium veneers. Standard on the XKR, the most powerful Jaguar since the XJ220, was the so-called Active Differential which adapted to driver demands and available grip to find traction and so had more finesse than a traction control system which applied brakes when traction was lost.

The world is not short of luxury GT coupés with huge speed, muscular styling and massively impressive capability. In the XK, Jaguar has succeeded in producing a car that can square up to the most exotic names in the world that match, and often then beat them, on every score. It is undoubtedly beautiful and has years of development in it – and perhaps even a few surprises. In 2010 there will probably be a diesel version. Who'd have thought it...

The muscular lines of the 2006 XKR convertible.

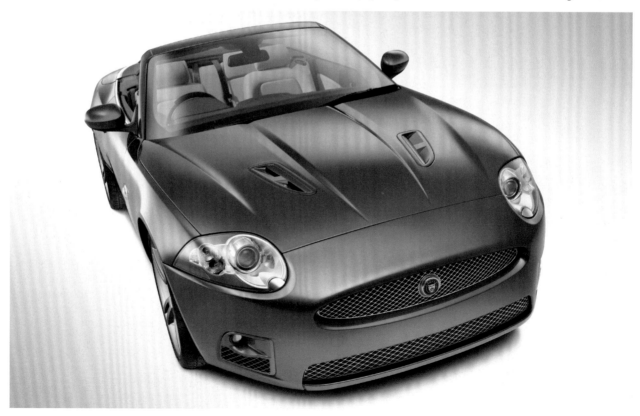

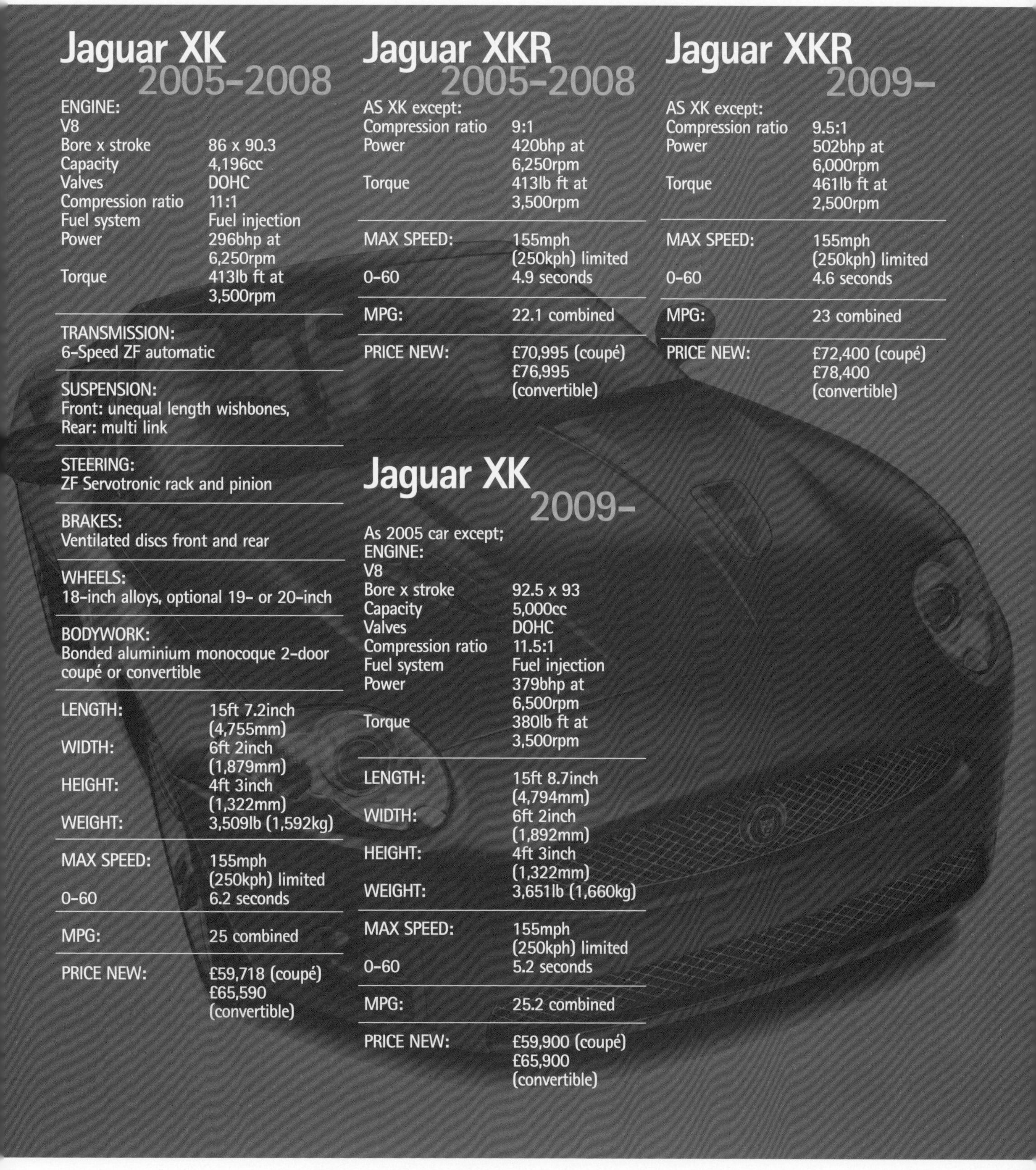

Jaguar XK
2005-2008

ENGINE:
V8
Bore x stroke — 86 x 90.3
Capacity — 4,196cc
Valves — DOHC
Compression ratio — 11:1
Fuel system — Fuel injection
Power — 296bhp at 6,250rpm
Torque — 413lb ft at 3,500rpm

TRANSMISSION:
6-Speed ZF automatic

SUSPENSION:
Front: unequal length wishbones,
Rear: multi link

STEERING:
ZF Servotronic rack and pinion

BRAKES:
Ventilated discs front and rear

WHEELS:
18-inch alloys, optional 19- or 20-inch

BODYWORK:
Bonded aluminium monocoque 2-door coupé or convertible

LENGTH:	15ft 7.2inch (4,755mm)
WIDTH:	6ft 2inch (1,879mm)
HEIGHT:	4ft 3inch (1,322mm)
WEIGHT:	3,509lb (1,592kg)
MAX SPEED:	155mph (250kph) limited
0-60	6.2 seconds
MPG:	25 combined
PRICE NEW:	£59,718 (coupé) £65,590 (convertible)

Jaguar XKR
2005-2008

AS XK except:
Compression ratio	9:1
Power	420bhp at 6,250rpm
Torque	413lb ft at 3,500rpm
MAX SPEED:	155mph (250kph) limited
0-60	4.9 seconds
MPG:	22.1 combined
PRICE NEW:	£70,995 (coupé) £76,995 (convertible)

Jaguar XKR
2009-

AS XK except:
Compression ratio	9.5:1
Power	502bhp at 6,000rpm
Torque	461lb ft at 2,500rpm
MAX SPEED:	155mph (250kph) limited
0-60	4.6 seconds
MPG:	23 combined
PRICE NEW:	£72,400 (coupé) £78,400 (convertible)

Jaguar XK
2009-

As 2005 car except;
ENGINE:
V8
Bore x stroke — 92.5 x 93
Capacity — 5,000cc
Valves — DOHC
Compression ratio — 11.5:1
Fuel system — Fuel injection
Power — 379bhp at 6,500rpm
Torque — 380lb ft at 3,500rpm

LENGTH:	15ft 8.7inch (4,794mm)
WIDTH:	6ft 2inch (1,892mm)
HEIGHT:	4ft 3inch (1,322mm)
WEIGHT:	3,651lb (1,660kg)
MAX SPEED:	155mph (250kph) limited
0-60	5.2 seconds
MPG:	25.2 combined
PRICE NEW:	£59,900 (coupé) £65,900 (convertible)

Acknowledgements and Bibliography

Most of the colour pictures are courtesy Haymarket/LAT, but some recent pictures were supplied by Jaguar. All the mono pictures come from the author's collection, except where stated. Jacket pictures courtesy Neill Bruce.

For background information I am indebted to the following authors for their books on the subject:

Jaguar Saloon Cars (Haynes), Paul Skilleter

Jaguar MkI & MkII, The Complete Companion (Bayview), Nigel Thorley

Jaguar XJS Collectors' Guide (MRP), Paul Skilleter

Jaguar Saloon Cars (MRP), Chris Harvey

The Jaguar XK (Oxford Illustrated Press), Chris Harvey

E-Type, End of an Era (Oxford Illustrated Press), Chris Harvey

The Jaguar XKs (MRP), Paul Skilleter

Jaguar, The Complete Works (Bayview), Nigel Thorley

The Jaguar Scrapbook (Haynes), Philip Porter

Jaguar (Sidgwick & Jackson), Philip Porter

Original Jaguar MkI and MkII (Bayview), Nigel Thorley

Jaguar Sports Racing Cars (Bayview), Philip Porter

Jaguar XK8, The Authorised Biography (Bayview), Philip Porter

Jaguar MK II Saloons Superprofile (Haynes), Paul Skilleter

Jaguar (Quiller Press), Lord Montagu of Beaulieu

Mon Ami Mate (Transport Bookman Publications), Chris Nixon

My sincere thanks to everyone who has been involved in the writing, checking and production of this book. All errors in commission or omission are mine alone.

Index

Adams, Ronald 19
Alcan 103
Alexander Engineering 56
Alf Romeo 119
Allard J2 137
Alpine Rally 136-137
Alvis 16, 7, 36
    Grey Lady 46
Appleyard, Ian 19, 136, 145
Appleyard, Pat 136
Armstrong-Siddeley 16, 36
    234/236 46
Ashworth, J. 19
Aston Martin 123
    DB2 137
    DB4 48, 156
    DB7 115, 123, 185
    DB7 V-12 Vantage 123
    DB9 195
    Vanquish 123, 190
Aston Martin Lagonda 86
Aston Martin Tickford 177
Audi 110, 104, 124
    A4 110, 116, 121
    A8 100, 104–105
Austin-Healey 56, 155
Austin
    Seven 7
    Westminster 19

Baillie, Sir Gawaine 42, 56
Baily Claude 134
Bamford, Anthony 131
Barter, Nick 110
Behra, José 56
Bell, Derek 79
Bentley S1 22
Berry, Bob 19
Bertone 68
Bertone Aston Martin DB MkIII 155
Bigger, Frank 19
Biondetti, Clemente 136, 138
Bira, Prince 136
Birmingham Motor Show 112
Black, John 13
Blond, Peter 42
Bloomfield Road premises 7
Bloxham factory 185
BMW 79, 86, 95, 104, 110, 112,
    118–119, 121, 124, 126, 175
    MINI 104
    M5 96, 103, 110, 130
    M6 192
    328 132–133
    507 145
    850 184
    3 Series 116, 121
    5 Series 110, 121, 124
    6 Series 165
Bolster, John 59
Brabham, Jack 56
Brands Hatch 42, 56
Bridgend plant 191
Brinkman, Eric 42
Bristol 36
British Leyland 89, 98
Brno 79, 181
Broad, Ralph 79
Browning, Jonathan 119
Browns Lane factory, 16, 41, 54,
    146–147, 175
    factory fire 149

Bueb, Ivor 42
Bugatti Type 57 SC Atlantic 140
Buying Hints:
    E-Type Ser. I and II 165
    E-Type Ser. III V12 171
    MkI 47
    MkII and 240/340 61
    MkV 15
    MkVII, MkVIII and MkIX 23
    MkX and 420G 35
    S-Type and 420 71
    XJ6 Ser. I and II 83
    XJ6 Ser. III 91
    XJ40 99
    XJ-S 183
    XK8 186
    XK120 141
    X-300 103

Callum, Ian 121, 123, 125, 188–190
Castle Bromwich factory 86–87,
    112, 124, 178
Chapman, Colin 60
Charles Faroux team award 42
Chevrolet
    Corvette 145, 169, 180
    Impala 56
Citroën DS 189
Claes, Johnny 137
Clark, Jim 56
Classic Saloon racing 19
Cocker Street premises 7
Collins, Peter 45
Coombs, John 19, 42, 45, 56, 163
Costen, Bernard 56
Coupe des Alpes 136
Crook, Tony 19
Crystal Palace 56
Cuff, John 42–43, 56
Cunningham, Briggs 42, 163

Daewoo 113
Daily Express International Trophy
    136
Daily Express Production Saloons 19
Daimler 16, 19
Daimler models:
    Century 101
    Conquest 46
    Double-Six 88, 100–101
    DS420 30, 97, 103
    Insignia 97
    Majestic 97–98
    Majestic Major
        Limousine 30, 33, 55
    Sovereign 30, 70–71, 86,
        93–94, 101
    SP250 54
    Super V8 100, 108
    V8 33, 54–55, 61
    3.6-litre 96
Data:
    Daimler Sovereign 63
        Sovereign Ser. I 73
        V8 49
    Jaguar E-Type Ser I and II 157
        E-Type Ser. III 167
        MkI 37
        MkII 49
        MkV 11
        MkVIIM 17
        MkVIII 17
        MkVIX 17
        MkX 25
        S-Type 63
        S-Type (X200) 111

X-Type 117
XF 129
XJ (X-350) 109
XJ Super 8 108
XJ6 Ser. I 73
XJ6 Ser. II 73
XJ6 Ser. III 85
XJ8 101
XJ12 Ser. I 73
XJ12 Ser. II 73
XJ40 (XJ6/XJ12) 93
XJR 101
XJ-S/XJS 173
XK 197
XKR 185, 197
XK8 185
XK120 133
XK140 143
XK150 151
240 49
340 49
420 63
Detroit Motor Show 125, 188, 191
Dewis, Norman 137
Dixon, Roy 56
Dodson, Charlie 136
Donington 181
Dundrod 138

Eagle Specialist Vehicles 103
Earls Court Motor Show 7, 10,
    25, 32, 48, 74, 132, 141–142,
    147, 154
Écurie Ecosse team 146
Edwardes, Sir Michael 89
Egan, Sir John 30, 87, 89, 98, 175
Engines
    Audi V8 102
    BMW V8 102
    Cadillac V8 134
    Daimler V8 54–55
    Ford V6 115
    Jaguar
        AJ6 93–95, 101 176, 185
        AJ16 101–102, 183
        AJ V8 127
        AJD V6 diesel 127
        V6 105, 114–115, 118–119, 121
        V6 diesel 106, 108, 121
        V8 105–106, 108, 114–115,
            130, 191, 196
        V12 74–76, 91, 99, 166,
            170, 174
        XFR V8 126
        XK 6, 8, 11, 23, 44, 52, 56,
            59, 74, 133, 157, 161, 166
        XK 'S' 153, 160
    Mercedes V8 102
    Peugeot/PSA 127
    Standard 13
England, 'Lofty' 60
Equipe Endeavour team 163
European Touring Car
    Championship 79, 180–181
Exner, Virgil 155

Fairman, 138
Fangio, Juan Manuel 45
Ferrari 45, 48, 76, 123, 138, 155,
    163
    250GT 123
Ferrari, Enzo 6
Fiat 8V 155
Fitch, John 138
Fitzpatrick, John 79
Foleshill factory, Coventry 7

Ford 89, 98, 100–101, 110, 116,
    123, 126, 129, 131, 168–169
    Anglia 42
    Cortina 67
    Escort 119
    Fiesta 123
    Galaxie 56
    Granada Scorpio 95
    Mondeo 115, 119, 123
    Mustang 56
    Probe 123
    Thunderbird 145
    RS Cosworth 123
    RS 200 123
Ford USA 112–113, 115
Frankfurt Motor Show 124, 173,
    189–190
Frère, Paul 42
Frua, Pietro 68, 155

Gandini, Marcello 68
General Motors 145
Geneva Motor Show 68, 107, 123,
    149, 156, 184
Ghia of Turin 123, 155
Ghia Aigle 155
Ginther, Richie 137
GKN Sankey 178
Goodwood 56, 145, 163
Grade, Lew 158
Group 44 169, 180
Guido 19
Gurney, Dan 56

Haines, Nick 136
Halewood plant 116, 119
Hamilton, Duncan 19, 42, 61, 136,
    138
Hansgen, Walt 42, 137
Hassan, Walter 134, 168
Hawthorn, Mike 19, 42, 45, 61
Hayes, Walter 181
Healey Elliott saloon 19
Henlys 7
Hess & Eisenhardt 177
Heynes, William 6, 11, 40, 64, 132,
    134
Hill, Graham 56, 60, 163
Hill, Phil 137
Hinton, Graig 33
HM Queen Elizabeth II 30
HM The Queen Mother 30, 103
Hobbs, David 79
Holbrook Lane factory,
    Coventry 13
Howarth, George 42
Hudson, 1948 24
Huffaker, Joe 169
Hull, Douglas 155
Hulme, Denny 56
Humber Snipe 20
Humble, George 56

Ireland, Circuit of 43
Ital Design 96, 98
    Kensington 96
Italian 1,000-mile classic 136

Jabbeke 134, 136–137
Jaguar Cars 8
Jaguar Engineering 98
Jaguar models:
    Advanced Lightweight
        Coupé 190
    Broadspeed Racers 79
    C-Type (XK120 C) 138, 146,

150, 174
C-XF concept car 124–125
D-Type 146–149, 156, 174, 188
D-Type Replicas 182
E-Type 24, 64, 72, 112, 146,
    154, 174, 180, 184, 186–187,
    190
E-Type Ser. I and II 156–165
E-Type Ser. III V12 164,
    166–171
F-Type 188
FT 68
Italian S-Types 68
MkI 36–47, 52
MkII 6, 26, 36, 48–61, 62, 82,
    110, 112,116
MkV 10–15, 50, 135
MkVII 10, 15, 16–23, 38, 41,
    134, 137, 140, 143, 155
MkVIIM 17
MkVIII 16–23, 36
MkIX 16–23, 50, 52, 154
MkX 6, 16, 24–35, 62, 70, 74,
    112, 160
R-Coupé 189
S-Type 32, 58, 62–71, 82, 110
S-Type (X200) 106, 110–124,
    126, 128; MkI 112; MkII 113;
    MkIII 113; MkIV 113
S-Type R 115–116
X-Type 115–117, 188
X-Type Diesel 121
X-Type Estate 121–122
XF 121, 124–131, 190
XFR 127–128
XJ 3.2 Executive 101
XJ6 6, 34, 62, 70, 123, 134,
    168, 170
XJ6 Gold 97
XJ6 Ser. I and II 72–83
XJ6 Ser. III 84–91, 100
XJ8 100, 102–103
XJ12 69, 69, 76–81, 86, 168
XJ12 HE 87
XJ13 170, 174
XJ40 72, 84, 88, 92–100, 104, 179
XJ41 (F-Type) 184
XJ220 125, 185, 196
XJ300 185
XJC 74, 81, 189
XJR 95, 97, 99, 101–102, 108, 188
XJR-S 178–179
XJ-S/XJS 74, 83, 154, 164, 169,
    171–184
XJS Celebration 183
XJ-S HE 175
XJ Spider 184
XJ TDVi 105
XJ (X-350) 104–109
XK (X150) 190–197
XK Portfolio 195–196
XKE 154
XKR 127–128, 185, 192, 194–196
XKR-S 193
XKSS 146–149
XK8 102, 113, 183–188, 190
XK60 193
XK100 134
XK120 10, 15, 41, 132–142,
    153, 193
XK140 17, 39, 141–149, 152
XK150 46, 50, 149–155
XK150S 153, 157, 160
XK180 188
X-300 98, 100–104

X351 108
240/340 48–61, 110
420 62–71
420G 16, 24–35
Jaguar Rover Triumph Inc. 90
JaguarSport 96, 179
JCB 131
JD Power Customer Satisfaction
    Index 88, 103, 126
Johnson, Leslie 136
Johnson, Sherwood 137
Jopp, Peter 56

Karmann 177
Kelsey, Charles 56
Knight, Bob 26, 41, 43, 64, 75, 98

Ladbroke Motor Group 90
Lamborghini 76
Lancaster aircraft 8, 112
Lancia
    Aurelia 19
    Flaminia 32
Land Rover 131
    Discovery 127
    Freelander 119
    Range Rover Sport 127
Lawson, Geoff 100, 112–113, 123,
    185
Le Mans 8, 45, 134, 136, 143, 150,
    163, 181
Lea Francis 7
Lexus 102–103
Leyland Cars 79, 112
Lincoln LS 112, 114
Lotus Cortina 56
Lynx Motors International Ltd
    177, 182
    XJ-S Eventer 182
Lyons, Sir William 6, 8–9, 32, 38,
    44, 48, 83, 89, 94, 98, 136, 156,
    171, 174, 189

Mallory Park 56
Marathon de la Route 137
Margulies, Dan 56
Martin Brothers of Ealing 155
Martin, Michael 42
Maserati 48, 155
    Mexico 68
    Quattroporte 32
Maudslay, R. W. 13
May, Michael 86, 175
Mayfair Hotel 7
McLaren, Bruce 56, 163
Mercedes 19, 74, 86, 95, 101,
    104, 124, 126, 174
    300SE 24
    AMG 130
    C-Class 121
    E-Class 124
    SL 45, 48, 145, 178, 184
    SL500 192
    S-Class 87, 97, 105
Michelotti, Giovanni 149
Mille Miglia 132–133, 136
Mon Ami Mate, book 45
Mont Agel hillclimb 56
Monte Carlo Rally 14, 19, 42, 56
Montlhéry 137
Monza 56, 79
Morecambe rally 136
Morley, Don & Earle 42
Morris 7
Morris Minor Traveller 155

Mosquito aircraft 8
Moss, Stirling 19, 136, 138, 181
MoT test 36, 38
Mueller, Lee 169
Mundy, Harry 168

New York Motor Show 187
New York Museum of Modern
    Art 187
Nixon, Chris 45
Nockold, Roy, 61
Novelli 19
NSU Ro80 75
Nürburgring 79

O'Connor-Rorke, H. J. 43
Oulton Park 56, 163

Palm Beach, Florida 168
Park Sheet Metal 177
Parkes, Bobby 42, 56
Parkes, Mike 56, 163
Parkinson, Don 137
Pergusa 181
Pininfarina 84, 98, 174, 184
Porsche 123
    Boxster 188
    356 123
    911 169, 180, 195
Pre '57 Historic Saloon racing 42
Pressed Steel Co. 11, 16, 25, 38,
    134, 156

Quester, Dieter 79

RAC Rally 14, 42, 56, 136, 145
Raiders of the Lost Ark, film 33
Randle, Jim 95
Regent Hotel, Hong Kong 30
Renault Floride 155
Richard, René 56
Riley Pathfinder 46
Road Atlanta 169
Rolls-Royce 72, 75, 96
    Corniche 33
    Phantom VI 30
    Silver Cloud II 24
Rolt, Tony 19, 138
Rootes 134
Rouse, 79
Rover
    3-litre 20
    75
    800 95
Royal College of Art 123
Rubery Owen 13

Saab 56
Sachs, Peter 56
Saint, The TV series 158
Salmon, Mike 56
Salvadori, Roy 42, 56, 163
Salzburg 79, 181
Sayer, Malcolm 138, 146, 156,
    172, 174
Schenken, Tim 79
Scott-Brown, Archie 42
Scott, Dennis 19
Sears, Jack 56
Seattle 169
Second World War 9
Shelsley Walsh hillclimb 136
Silva, Ramos Da 42
Silverstone 19, 42, 45, 56,
    79, 136

Snetterton 56
Sopwith, Tommy 42, 56
Spa 24-hour Classic 181
Spitfire aircraft 8, 112
Sports Car Championship 181
Sports Car Club of
    America 147, 169
Standard 7
Stewart, Jimmy 19, 138
Stirling aircraft 8
Stokes, Lord 74
Surtees, John 56
Swallow models
    Airline saloon 7
    SS Jaguar 8–9
    SS1 7, 8, 13
    SSII 7, 13
    SS90 8
    SS100 6, 8
Swallow Side Car Co. 7
Swift 7

Talbot 136
Talbot Lago 138
Targa Florio 136
Tarquini, Dr G. 68
Tata 131
    Nano 131
Thomson, Julian 189
Titterington, Desmond 19
Tivey, Colin 120
Tour de France 19, 42, 56
Touring 132–133
Tourist Trophy,
    Silverstone 45, 79, 136, 181
Triumph TR 155
Tulip Rally 42, 136
Tullius, Bob 169, 180
Turner, Edward 33, 54
TVR 180, 184
TWR 123, 178, 185
    body kits 101

US Federal crash
    regulations 171

Vanden Plas Kingsbury
    factory 30, 78
Vanden Plas models:
    Double-Six 78, 86
    Princess 30
    XJ40 99
    4-litre R 32
Venture Pressings 178
Villoresi, 'Gigi' 138

Walker, Peter 136
Walker, Rob 45
Walkinshaw, Tom 96, 178–179,
    185
Walmsley, William 6
Walton, Philip 42, 56
Watkins Glen 169
Weslake, Harry 8, 13, 134, 153
Wharton, Ken 19
Whitehead, Graham 43, 90, 138
Whitehead, Peter 43
Whitley headquarters 124
Wilcox Limousines 103
Wisdom, Tommy 136

Zagato 155
Zandvoort 79
Zeltweg 181
Zolder 79